Florida Butterfly Caterpillars and Their Host Plants

Florida A&M University, Tallahassee
Florida Atlantic University, Boca Raton
Florida Gulf Coast University, Ft. Myers
Florida International University, Miami
Florida State University, Tallahassee
University of Central Florida, Orlando
University of Florida, Gainesville
University of North Florida, Jacksonville
University of South Florida, Tampa
University of West Florida, Pensacola

University Press of Florida
Gainesville · Tallahassee · Tampa · Boca Raton
Pensacola · Orlando · Miami · Jacksonville · Ft. Myers

Florida Butterfly Caterpillars

AND THEIR HOST PLANTS

Marc C. Minno, Jerry F. Butler, and Donald W. Hall

Copyright 2005 by Marc C. Minno, Jerry F. Butler, and Donald W. Hall
Printed in Hong Kong on acid-free paper

10 09 08 07 06 05   6 5 4 3 2 1

Library of Congress Cataloging-in-Publication Data
Minno, Marc C.
Florida butterfly caterpillars and their host plants / Marc C. Minno, Jerry F. Butler,
and Donald W. Hall.
p. cm.
Includes bibliographical references and index (p.).
ISBN 0-8130-2789-6 (alk. paper)
1. Caterpillars—Florida—Identification. 2. Caterpillars—Host plants—Florida—
Identification. 3. Butterflies—Host plants—Florida—Identification.
I. Butler, Jerry F. (Jerry Frank). II. Hall, Donald W. III. Title.
QL551.F6M552 2005
595.78'9139'09759—dc22   2004058380

p. i. Florida Purplewing larva.
p. ii. (above) Dingy Purplewing; (below) Pupa of the Dingy Purplewing.
p. iii. (above) Caterpillar of the Dingy Purplewing; (below) Dingy Purplewing nest.
p. vii. (above) Dingy Purplewing; (below) Spicebush Swallowtail larva.
p. viii. (above) Silver-spotted Skipper larva; (below) Sugarberry.

The University Press of Florida is the scholarly publishing agency for the State
University System of Florida, comprising Florida A&M University, Florida Atlantic
University, Florida Gulf Coast University, Florida International University, Florida
State University, University of Central Florida, University of Florida, University
of North Florida, University of South Florida, and University of West Florida.

University Press of Florida
15 Northwest 15th Street
Gainesville, FL 32611-2079
http://www.upf.com

To my loving mother, Claudia J. Minno, and father, Paul T. Minno, who have passed from this world of wonder and beauty.

Marc C. Minno

Affectionately dedicated to my wife, Marilyn, who has enabled my love of nature's beauty.

Jerry F. Butler

To my parents, William and Bessie Hall, who sacrificed to support my education and encouraged my love for insects, and to Diane, my wife and best friend.

Donald W. Hall

Contents

Foreword ix
Acknowledgments xi

Introduction 1

Anatomy 3
Biology and Ecology 8
Caterpillar Behavior and Defense 12
Identifying Caterpillars 23
Metamorphosis and Life Cycles 25
Finding and Rearing Caterpillars 46
Butterfly Gardening 50
Butterfly Habitats 50
Host Plants 65

Florida Butterfly Caterpillars 67

Swallowtails (family Papilionidae) 67
Whites, Orangetips, and Sulphurs (family Pieridae) 74
Whites (subfamily Pierinae) 74
Orangetips (subfamily Anthocharinae) 76
Sulphurs (subfamily Coliadinae) 77
Harvesters, Hairstreaks, and Blues (family Lycaenidae) 84
Harvesters (subfamily Miletinae) 84
Hairstreaks (subfamily Theclinae) 85
Blues (subfamily Polyommatinae) 96
Metalmarks (family Riodinidae) 100
Brushfoots and Relatives (family Nymphalidae) 101
Snouts (subfamily Libytheinae) 101
Heliconians (subfamily Heliconiinae) 102
Brushfoots (subfamily Nymphalinae) 104

Admirals (subfamily Limenitidinae) 112
Leafwings (subfamily Charaxinae) 115
Emperors (subfamily Apaturinae) 116
Satyrs and Wood-Nymphs (subfamily Satyrinae) 117
Milkweed Butterflies (subfamily Danainae) 121
Skippers (family Hesperiidae) 123
Spread-winged Skippers (subfamily Pyrginae) 123
Grass-Skippers (subfamily Hesperiinae) 136
Giant-Skippers (subfamily Megathyminae) 159

Plates 161

Host Plants of Florida Butterflies 219

Gymnosperms (Cone-bearing Plants) 219
Monocotyledons (Plants with One Seed Leaf) 221
Dicotyledons (Plants with Two Seed Leaves) 237

Checklist of Butterflies That Breed in Florida 313

References 319
Index 321

Foreword

Butterflies are the epitome of freedom in nature. The adults fly from flower to flower, filling the skies at times with migrating masses, at other times flitting across a dry lawn on a cold winter day and reminding us of the beautiful spring to come.

Much less attention has been paid to butterfly caterpillars, the lowly, terrestrially bound, larval stage of the beautiful adult. Yet caterpillars in their own right have great fascination in their endless diversity of colors and shapes, unique behaviors, and of course their close relationships with plants that we all love and enjoy. When they eat our garden flowers or vegetables, we often respond by reaching for a spray gun. But without the caterpillar stage, the beautiful butterflies that we enjoy in Florida would soon be gone, never to reappear. Butterfly gardeners are responding to this fact, forgoing the use of chemical pesticides and paying more and more attention to planting larval food plants in addition to nectar sources for the freely flying adults.

Now Marc Minno, Jerry Butler, and Donald Hall have provided a wonderful new field guide to the caterpillars of Florida butterflies and their host plants. Abundantly illustrated in color, the authoritative text goes into all the detail you need to know about these caterpillars and where they live, how to identify them, and which plants they eat. Thus this book will be a rich source of reference material for students, teachers, naturalists, butterfly gardeners, butterfly farmers, and indeed naturalists of all sorts, from the earliest beginner to the most professional among us.

Summarized in this expertly written book is a bountiful basket of information that not only describes Florida caterpillars and compares them with those of similar species, but also gives the wider distribution of the species across the United States, the known host plants, and the natural history, including the number of seasonal broods and other valuable information. No one who opens this book will fail to see how it will soon become an indispensable reference for enjoying this facet of Florida's exciting natural history.

Thomas C. Emmel, director, McGuire Center for Lepidoptera Research
University of Florida, Gainesville

Acknowledgments

We wish to thank Lyn Atherton, John Calhoun, Jaret Daniels, Mark Deyrup, Alana Edwards, David Fine, Mary Ann Friedman, Roger Hammer, Robert Kelley, John Kutis, and Jeffrey Slotten for their help in finding caterpillars and providing information about Florida butterflies and their host plants. Joe Maguire kindly gave us a permit to look for rare butterflies in Miami-Dade County Parks. We also wish to thank Maria Minno for her help in the field and for carefully reading and editing the manuscript. Margo Duncan expertly created the caterpillar and life cycle drawings. We greatly appreciate the help of Steve Brown, Matt O'Malley, and the St. Johns River Water Management District for kindly providing the Florida topography and vegetation maps. Joseph D. Culin, Jr., and an anonymous reviewer carefully read the manuscript and provided many helpful suggestions for improving the text.

All photographs are by Marc C. Minno, Jerry F. Butler, or Donald W. Hall, except for the following: Sourwood (Mary Ann Friedman); Hogpeanut flowers (Tony Presley); Cofaqui Giant-Skipper larva (Deborah Lott); 'Seminole' Texan Crescent (Dale Habeck); Lyside Sulphur (Jim Brock); Mimosa Yellow (Keith Wolfe); King's Hairstreak, Striped Hairstreak, and Nickerbean Blue (Jeffrey R. Slotten); Hoary Edge, Pepper and Salt Skipper, Zabulon Skipper, Falcate Orangetip, Pine Elfin, 'Summer' Spring Azure, 'Edwards' Spring Azure, and Pine Elfin (Tom Allen). We heartily thank these naturalists for permission to use their beautiful slides in the book.

Lastly, we thank the staff of the University Press of Florida, especially Kenneth J. Scott, Lynn Werts, Larry Leshan, Gillian Hillis, and David Graham, for their patience and help in bringing this book to fruition.

Introduction

Insects are among the most abundant and diverse animals on earth. The variety is staggering. As with birds, the ranges of sizes, colors, and behaviors of insects hold a special fascination.

Insects are six-legged animals that have jointed appendages. There are thirty major groups or orders of insects, with about 80 percent of the species consisting of beetles (Coleoptera), moths and butterflies (Lepidoptera), wasps, bees, ants (Hymenoptera), and flies (Diptera). Lepidoptera are distinguished as scale-winged insects with long strawlike sucking mouthparts. The colors of the wings are largely derived from tiny flattened hairs called scales. Their closest living relatives are the caddisflies, which have aquatic larvae, short hairs covering the wings, and chewing mouthparts.

Of the insects, butterflies are not only familiar, but they also hold a certain magic for us. Children and adults delight in just watching butterflies as they sip nectar from flowers or frolic about the garden. Those of us who have found and reared caterpillars, the young of butterflies and moths, express wonder in the miracle of metamorphosis, as the wormlike larvae transform into beautiful winged adults. Some of us have even devoted our lives to studying butterflies as a result of discoveries made in childhood. One of us on a spring day, as a little boy, happened to see a female Black Swallowtail laying an egg on a sprig of Queen Anne's Lace on the school playground. The boy picked the flower with the egg attached and, when the caterpillar emerged, raised it through stages to the green and yellow pupa. Many days later he observed the adult burst forth, expand and dry its wings, and fly away, never to be forgotten.

Throughout the world there are more than 15,000 different species of butterflies. The caterpillars of about 170 species of butterflies can be found in Florida. In addition, a number of species have been found in the state only as adults, sometimes as single individuals straying far from their normal breeding range.

Florida has an interesting butterfly fauna consisting of temperate species from eastern North America, tropical species from the Caribbean region, and unique races that are found nowhere else. Eleven species of exotic butterflies from tropical America are thought to have become established in the state over the last hundred years. With so much shipping and travel between Florida and Latin America, other butterflies will likely be accidentally introduced, or will find their own way via roadsides or transport by storms. Florida is a good place to look for caterpillars because of their diversity, and because the climate is so mild that one can find butterflies all year long.

Moths are much more numerous than butterflies (nearly 200,000 species are known worldwide), and are active mostly at night. Adult moths have feathery or simple antennae, and typically hold the wings rooflike over the body or outstretched at rest. By contrast, butterflies have clubbed antennae (knobbed tips) and usually hold the wings together over the body at rest. Each family or subfamily of moths and butterflies has a characteristic caterpillar with unique features by which it can be identified. There are 45 different families and around 4,000 species of moths in Florida, but only six families of butterflies. Generally, each species of plant has at least one kind of moth or butterfly caterpillar that eats it, but chances are that if you happen to find a caterpillar, it will belong to a moth. The way to find butterfly caterpillars is to locate and search the plants on which they feed.

In a world of voracious predators, diseases, and unpredictable weather and food supplies, it is hard to imagine how caterpillars live and survive. Emerging from an egg the size of a pinhead, a tiny caterpillar must find food and escape from predators for several weeks, until it passes into the pupal stage. Only a few of the dozens or hundreds of eggs laid by a female butterfly are likely to become adults.

Caterpillars play important ecological roles in the cycling of nutrients. By eating plants and being eaten, they are links in food webs. Further, feeding by caterpillars on young leaves and flowers naturally prunes their hosts, limiting plant growth and reproduction, thereby influencing the butterfly's future habitat and success. Certain butterfly caterpillars are sometimes pests of crops, and may damage entire fields of cabbages, beans, or alfalfa. Caterpillars are important food items for birds, lizards, bugs, ants, flies, wasps, and other organisms. Even the droppings of some caterpillars are collected by ants. In their underground nests, the ants use the droppings as a mulch for growing a special fungus that they eat.

You may find a caterpillar munching away at a beloved plant in the garden and wonder, should I kill it? We suggest that you watch it, instead, or raise the caterpillar to find out more about its natural history. Although it may appear that much is known about butterflies and their caterpillars, there is a vast wealth of discovery to be made. As an example, it has taken us years of study to acquire the images of caterpillars that you see in this book but, to our knowledge, no one has ever photographed the larva of the Amethyst Hairstreak. Much, much more remains to be learned about the biology and behavior of caterpillars, the host plants they eat, and the places they live.

In this book we present images of nearly 170 butterfly caterpillars and many pictures of plants that they eat. We hope that you will be stimulated to seek out and observe caterpillars. Below, you will find discussion on how caterpillars are arranged externally and internally, how and where they live, how to identify them, and which plants they eat. At the end is a checklist of resident Florida butterflies, to help you keep track of the different species.

Anatomy

The outer covering or exoskeleton of insects is very different from our skin. Their integument consists of a living layer of cells (the epidermis) that secretes a nonliving protective layer called the cuticle. The cuticle is made up of proteins and chitin, a kind of nitrogenous polysaccharide, and is soft and flexible when first secreted, but quickly changes into a tough covering. Some areas of the cuticle become hardened through a tanning process called sclerotization, while others may remain flexible or rubbery to allow movement. In addition, the hardened plates (sclerites) are divided by enfoldings of the cuticle that allow flexibility or become lines of weakness during molting. The cuticle is further covered by a waxy coating that is secreted through pores by the special cells in the epidermis. The wax helps to waterproof the body and to conserve water internally. Thus, the exoskeleton is made up of hardened plates with flexible joints and seams. The cuticle of caterpillars is composed mostly of flexible material, with hardened areas limited to the head, thoracic legs, and occasionally special plates or ornaments.

Caterpillars have long tubular bodies that, like those of adult butterflies, are divided into three regions: the head, thorax, and abdomen (fig. 1). The head is the sensory and feeding section of the body. The thorax is used mostly for locomotion, and in some species for defense. Major functions of the abdomen are digestion, excretion of waste products, locomotion, circulation, and absorption and storage of nutrients. The thorax and abdomen are divided into segments. The segment boundaries are usually discernible as indentations, but may be somewhat obscured by secondary segmentation, as in the skippers.

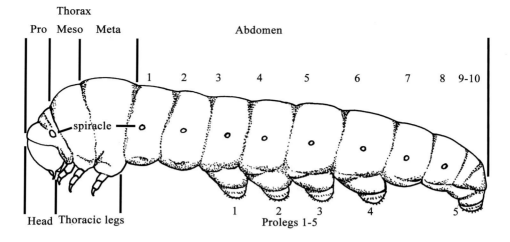

Figure 1. External features of a caterpillar.

The head of a caterpillar is a hard capsule composed mostly of the large epicranium, the triangular frons, and the adfrontal sclerites (figs. 2, 3). There are six simple eyes or stemma arranged in a semicircle, and a short antenna on each side of the mouth. The head is usually conspicuous in most caterpillars, except for the harvester, hairstreaks, and blues, in which the head is retracted into the thorax. The heads of brush-footed butterflies and their relatives usually have a pair of horns on top and some also have spines along the sides. The back of the head of skipper larvae is usually more narrowed than in other butterfly caterpillars and they are often referred to as having a narrow "neck."

The mouthparts of caterpillars consist of a pair of jaws that are bounded by an upper flap (labrum) and a lower structure (labium). The jaws swing from side to side and often bear a semicircle of teeth. The labrum usually has a notch or indentation that helps guide the edge of the leaf for the jaws to cut. The blocky labium has two pairs of sensory structures that are similar to the antennae, but smaller, and a spinneret or opening of the silk glands.

Caterpillars are clothed by hairlike structures called setae. Each seta represents a single epidermal cell that extends through and far beyond the cuticle. Setae serve to protect the caterpillar, act as sensors, or sometimes secrete substances. The setae of the first stage caterpillars of butterflies and moths are extremely useful for classification. The study of their setal patterns is called chaetotaxy. Primary setae occur in specific positions on the head and body. Their length and position are unique for each family or group of butterflies and moths. The primary setae may persist as the only setae in many moth families, but in butterflies the patterns usually become obscured by the presence of numerous secondary setae in subsequent stages. Skippers and some hairstreaks also have tiny sclerites called lenticles that occur singly or in small groups in the same positions as the primary setae. The function of lenticles is not clear, but they may be secretory structures. The forked hairs on the Sleepy Orange larva produce droplets of liquid that may help repel predators. Other types of ornamentation on butterfly caterpillars include fleshy filaments (pipevine swallowtails and milkweed butterflies), hardened cones (sulphurs), sticklike tubercles (admirals), branching spines called scoli (brushfoots), prothoracic shields (hairstreaks and skippers), and patches of microspines (Long-tailed Skipper).

The thorax is made up of three segments called the prothorax, mesothorax, and metathorax. Each has a pair of small, segmented legs that will even-

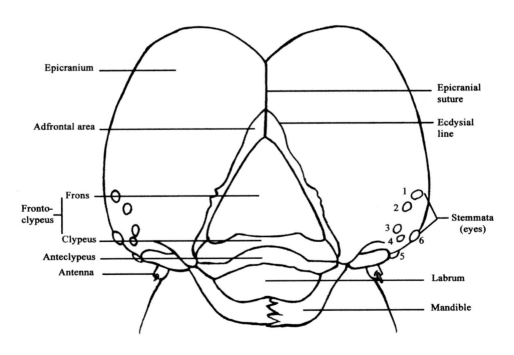

Figure 2. Frontal view of the head of a caterpillar.

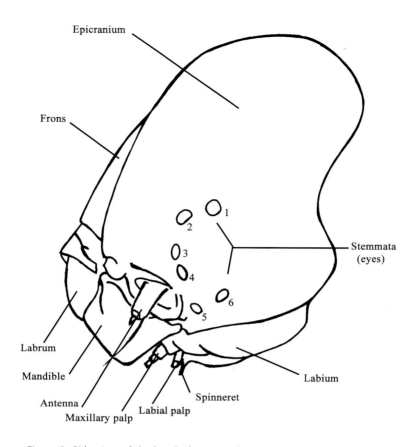

Figure 3. Side view of the head of a caterpillar.

tually become the adult legs. The legs are used not only for walking, but also for holding leaves while eating. The thorax is enlarged in some groups, such as the swallowtails, and may have defensive glands, eyespots, or a sclerite on top of the first thoracic segment called the prothoracic shield. The prothorax is the only thoracic segment having a pair of spiracles on the sides. The oval-shaped spiracles are the openings to the tubular respiratory or tracheal system.

The abdomen is the largest part of the caterpillar. It consists of ten similar segments. The abdominal legs or prolegs are quite different from those of the thorax. They are fleshy, shaped somewhat like elephant legs, and bear bands of tiny hooks or crochets on the bottom. Butterfly caterpillars have four pairs of prolegs on abdominal segments 3–6, and another pair on the combined segments 9 and 10. There are pairs of spiracles on all of the abdominal segments, except for the last two. The last pair of spiracles is usually larger than the others, because these supply oxygen to the entire posterior part of the caterpillar. The abdomen may have special glands, and the upperside of the last segment may be protected by a sclerotized patch called the suranal plate. Skippers and some brushfoots have a small hand-shaped sclerite near the anus that flicks away the droppings, often with considerable force.

The internal organ systems of caterpillars (fig. 4) are very different from our own. It's not necessary to dissect a specimen in order to see many of the internal structures if you can find a large caterpillar of the Brazilian Skipper. This species has a transparent cuticle that readily allows viewing of the internal organs.

The nervous system is made up of a tiny brain in the lower part of the head and nerve cord that runs down the belly of the caterpillar. Most body segments have a ganglion or small cluster of nerve cells that helps control locomotion and other activities.

The aorta or heart is a long tube with pairs of valves that create chambers along its length. Each chamber has a pair of holes (ostia) that allow the blood or hemolymph to flow in. Pulsations of the heart move the blood forward to the head. The dark line down the back of the caterpillar is the heart. It can be seen beating, especially in mature caterpillars that are nearly ready to pupate. The blood is a clear, greenish or yellowish fluid and flows through cavities in

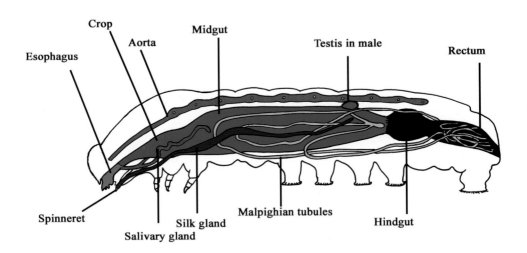

Figure 4. Major internal features of a caterpillar.

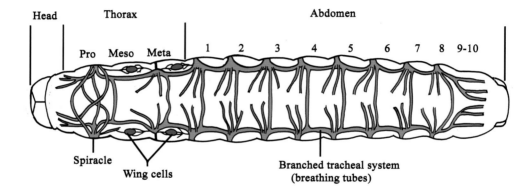

Figure 5. The respiratory or tracheal system of a caterpillar.

the body rather than in closed vessels. Since the respiratory system consists of finely branching tubes that reach throughout the body, the blood does not need to contain hemoglobin to carry oxygen (fig. 5).

Much of the internal volume of caterpillars is taken up by the gut, especially the midgut. Food is passed from the mouth, down the esophagus, to the muscular crop, where it is ground into smaller pieces and then moved to the midgut. The cells lining the midgut produce a membrane of protein and chitin that envelopes the food particles. The membrane helps to protect the gut, while allowing nutrients to pass through. Much of the digestion of the food takes place in the midgut. The Malpighian tubules are long slender tubes that, like kidneys, remove nitrogenous wastes from the body. The wastes are dumped into the hindgut. The hindgut is important in water balance and removes much of the water from the gut materials. Finally, the fecal material is moved to the rectum and ejected through the anus as a dry pellet or frass. Nutrients that have been absorbed into the body are stored in large fat bodies. Located at specific sites in the body are small groups of cells that will proliferate to form the adult during the pupal stage.

Biology and Ecology

Caterpillars spend most of their time either feeding or digesting, and grow larger very rapidly. The cuticle that surrounds their bodies allows limited growth, but at some point this nonliving layer becomes a barrier and must be shed. Before shedding, the larva usually finds a secluded spot and spins a mat of silk on the substrate. The tiny hooks (crochets) on the bottoms of the prolegs are entangled in the silk, anchoring the old cuticle.

Over a period of about a day, the innermost layers of the cuticle are digested away and reformed into a new larger and baggier skin. The new head will be slightly larger than the old one. As the process proceeds, the new head is withdrawn from the old capsule and can be seen as a pale-colored bulge in the neck area. Just before shedding, the larva swallows air to increase internal pressure and its body size. With a few muscular contractions, the cuticle splits around the back of the head, and the caterpillar quickly walks forward, often carrying the old head capsule around its mouth. When free from the old cuticle the head capsule is dislodged by a few swings of the new head. The first and last sections of the gut as well as the beginnings of the airways (trachea) are lined with cuticle, and are also shed with the skin. If you are able to observe a caterpillar molting, watch for the whitish tracheal linings to be pulled out of the spiracles. The caterpillar now sits very still for a few hours while the new cuticle hardens.

The last molt of the larval period from caterpillar to pupa differs from the regular molts in that the old head capsule remains attached to the shed cuticle. The old head splits open along the suture lines and the skin splits along the back of the thorax to reveal the new, soft, and not yet completely formed chrysalis. Then the larval cuticle is wiggled off as a single piece.

With all those pairs of legs so characteristic of caterpillars, walking takes a bit of body coordination. A resting caterpillar usually begins walking by reaching forward with the thoracic legs. The motion is carried forward as a wave, one segment at a time, along the abdomen. As it walks forward, the caterpillar swings the head from side to side, laying down a trail of silk for

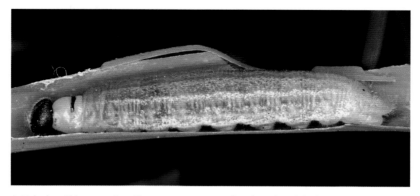

A Zabulon Skipper caterpillar preparing to molt. The whitish bulge in the neck area is the head of the larva.

the prolegs to grip and also seeing where to go with the minute eyes on each side of the mouth.

Silk is produced in the tubular silk glands inside the body (fig. 4). The spinneret is the short opening of the silk glands on the underside of the mouth. Silk is not ejected through the spinneret. Rather, the caterpillar simply touches a bit of silk to the substrate, and pulls. Silk consists of liquid proteins that solidify on contact with air, forming a thread. The silk also shrinks as it hardens, so some caterpillars, such as the Tiger Swallowtail and Spicebush Swallowtail, form shelters by spinning a mat of silk over the top of a leaf. As the silk dries, the leaf curls into a U shape. Caterpillar silk has a different consistency than that made by spiders, which also sometimes make shelters or take over those of caterpillars. The silk made by caterpillars tends to be more threadlike and stronger.

Caterpillars usually eat the margins of leaves, rather than chewing holes through the surface of the blade. After the body is positioned along the edge of the leaf, the thoracic legs are often used to grasp the leaf margin. Then the head is extended and drawn toward the body as the jaws quickly snip tiny bites of leaf that are swallowed. The process is repeated until the larva is satiated. Mature caterpillars will eat away large sections of a leaf at a single sitting.

One of the greatest challenges facing caterpillars in temperate areas is surviving through the winter, or in the case of tropical species, the dry season. The different groups of butterflies have devised a number of ways to overwinter or hibernate. Table 1 compares overwintering stages by butterfly group. Many tropical species in Florida have continuous generations or overwinter as adults. The very first butterflies flying in the spring overwintered as either adults, mature larvae, or pupae. Having spent several months in diapause or a resting state, overwintering pupae respond to lengthening daylight and increasing temperatures by completing metamorphosis and emerging as adults. In northern Florida, swallowtails and whites that have diapaused as pupae begin to emerge as adults as early as mid to late January in some years.

Some of our hairstreaks overwinter as eggs. After the eggs are laid, the embryos soon develop into caterpillars that wait nearly a year before emerging from the eggs to begin feeding. Many other butterflies pass the winter as partly grown larvae in specially constructed nests. Young Viceroy caterpillars begin making overwintering shelters or hibernacula in fall. The hibernaculum is constructed from a single small leaf. The larva eats most of the leaf except for the midrib and lower section of the blade, which is tied together with silk to form a small tube. The caterpillar also anchors the leaf petiole to

A Viceroy hibernaculum or overwintering shelter.

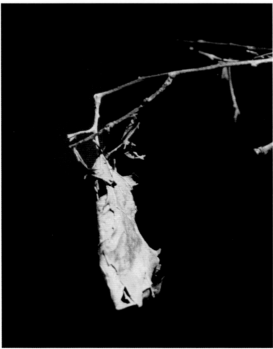

Tawny Emperors over-winter in a leaf shelter attached to the twigs of the host plant.

Sleepy Duskywing caterpillars change color from green to brown as they stop feeding in the fall and prepare to overwinter.

the stem with silk to prevent the hibernaculum from falling to the ground. The gregarious young larvae of the Tawny Emperor tie two leaves together and also attach the petioles to the twigs with silk. Duskywing skippers overwinter as mature larvae in cocoons made from the last larval shelter. In the early spring, the caterpillars pupate without any further feeding, and then a few weeks later, emerge as adults.

There is often a color change in overwintering larvae, from green to brown, as they cease feeding in the fall and prepare for winter. The physiology of the caterpillar changes as well. Butterflies protect themselves from freezing during the winter by producing glycerol, lowering the water content of the body, and converting water into a gel-like form.

Caterpillar Behavior and Defense

Caterpillars tend to be most active at night (nocturnal), although you will find some eating in the daytime as well. It may be rewarding to search patches of particular host plants with a flashlight during the evening. You

Table 1. Overwintering stages of Florida butterflies.

Family	Egg	Larva	Pupa	Adult	None
Swallowtails			X		
Whites			X		X
Orangetip			X		
Sulphurs		X		X	X
Harvester			X		
Hairstreaks	X		X		X
Blues			X		X
Metalmark		X		X	
Brushfoots		X		X	X
Snout				X	
Heliconians		X			X
Admirals		X			X
Leafwings				X	X
Emperors		X			
Satyrs and Wood-Nymphs		X			
Milkweed Butterflies				X	X
Spread-winged Skippers		X	X		X
Grass-Skippers		X			X
Giant Skippers		X			

will likely find many more Common Buckeye larvae on Canada Toadflax stalks at night, as well as White Peacock caterpillars on Herb-of-Grace.

Nighttime activity helps conceal caterpillars from predators and also protects them from sunlight. Since caterpillars eat green leaves, which contain chlorophyll, some chlorophyll is absorbed into the body and this is what gives caterpillars their green color. A fun experiment is to feed Cloudless Sulphur or Orange-barred Sulphur caterpillars either green leaves or yellow flowers of their senna host plants. The caterpillars fed leaves will be green, while those given only flowers will become bright yellow.

One problem caterpillars have with chlorophyll, however, is that it is a very reactive molecule that can damage cells if fully exposed to bright light. Most caterpillars tend to avoid strong sunlight, probably in part to help protect them from chlorophyll damage. When not feeding, caterpillars usually

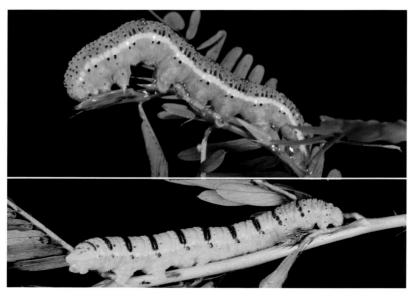

Cloudless Sulphur caterpillars that feed on senna flowers become bright yellow.

hide under leaves, on the lower stems of their host plants, near the ground, or in leaf shelters. Caterpillars of swallowtails sometimes raise the front end of the body and orient the head toward the sun, apparently to minimize exposure.

All of the skipper caterpillars make leaf shelters in which to hide. As noted, the shelters help caterpillars hide from predators and reduce their exposure to sunlight. Skippers make their shelters by cutting channels in a leaf and folding over the resulting flap, or by tying the edges of two leaves together with silk. The interior of the shelter is also lined with silk. Except for skippers, the only other Florida butterfly caterpillars that hide in leaf shelters are a few swallowtails, brushfoots, the emperors, and the Goatweed Leafwing.

Since adult female butterflies tend to only lay one or a few eggs per host plant, their caterpillars lead mostly solitary lives. Larvae of the Zebra Swallowtail, some hairstreaks and blues, and others are even cannibalistic toward their younger siblings. This trait becomes apparent if you are raising more than one caterpillar together in the same container, especially if the supply of fresh leaves runs low.

Still, a few of our butterflies are gregarious in the younger larval stages. Adult females of the Polydamas Swallowtail, Texan Crescent, Pearl Crescent,

From left to right,
top row: the larval shelters
of the Spicebush Swallowtail,
American Lady, Red Admiral
middle: Eastern Comma,
Dingy Purplewing
bottom: Goatweed Leafwing,
Silver-spotted Skipper, and
Long-tailed Skipper

From left to right,
top row: the larval
shelters of the Sleepy
Duskywing, White
Checkered-Skipper,
Brazilian Skipper
middle: Palmetto Skipper,
Clouded Skipper,
Southern Broken-Dash
bottom: Yucca Giant-
Skipper, and Cofaqui
Giant-Skipper

Phaon Crescent, Silvery Checkerspot, Dingy Purplewing, and Tawny Emperor lay clusters of eggs on the leaves of their host plants. When the eggs hatch, the larvae stay and feed together. All of these species, except for the Polydamas Swallowtail, live in a silken nest when not feeding. This communal lifestyle may help the individual caterpillars fend off predators or chew into tough leaves. Polydamas Swallowtails and Dingy Purplewings are distasteful to birds because of chemicals in their bodies. The sight of groups of caterpillars may help birds learn that they are distasteful. Upon tasting one caterpillar, a predator will learn to leave the others alone. As the caterpillars of these gregarious species become mature, they tend to wander off from the group and become more solitary.

The first line of defense of caterpillars is their coloration, and this is one of their most interesting features. Most have colors and patterns that blend with their background (cryptic coloration). Thus the caterpillars of sulphurs are typically green, like the leaves they eat, whereas many skippers that live in shelters or near the ground are brown.

A few of our swallowtail caterpillars have color patterns that frighten predators. Some have an enlarged thorax adorned with eyespots that confer the appearance of a small snake. Many broad-winged skipper caterpillars have large yellow patches around the eyes that probably serve a frightening purpose. A bird or lizard peering into the shelter may be scared away after a quick glance at the false face of a Silver-spotted or Long-tailed Skipper. Some swallowtails and skippers also have false face patterns on their posterior ends.

Animals with red, yellow, or white-on-black patterns are using warning or aposematic colors to let potential predators know that they contain poisons. Brightly colored butterfly caterpillars such as the Atala, Monarch, or Pipevine Swallowtail are usually protected by strong chemicals that they acquire from their host plants. All of these species eat plants that contain compounds poisonous to most other herbivores. The butterflies, however, are able to sequester the poisons for their own defense. Birds that eat Monarch or Pipevine Swallowtail caterpillars become very ill and vomit up their stomach contents. Through this sampling process, birds learn to avoid eating any caterpillars that resemble those that made them sick.

Other caterpillars with stripes, such as the Black Swallowtail, or patches of contrasting colors, like the Giant Swallowtail, may not have poisons for protection, but are using disruptive coloration to deter a predator's search image. As the stripes on zebras help to conceal these otherwise distinctive animals among the grasses and shrubs of the African plains, so do contrasting colors help break up the body outline of caterpillars. In areas of dappled

The young caterpillars of the Polydamas Swallowtail live and feed together on the leaves of pipevines.

Tawny Emperor caterpillars live together in a nest of leaves tied together with silk.

light, predators have a more difficult time finding caterpillars with disruptive patterns.

Butterfly larvae also have ways to actively protect themselves from predators. Silver-spotted Skipper caterpillars display open jaws and try to look very fierce if disturbed. If further provoked, they spit a bitter-tasting green fluid from the mouth. In addition to this species, many other broad-winged skippers and brushfoots produce the green fluid. Skipper and brushfoot caterpillars also have a special gland on the underside of the prothorax that is

The false face pattern on the rear end of a Black Swallowtail caterpillar.

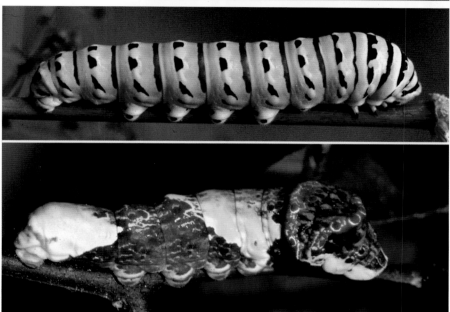

The disruptive coloration of the Black Swallowtail (*top*) and Giant Swallowtail (*bottom*) helps the caterpillars to blend in with their background.

thought to produce defensive chemicals. Similar glands in Prominent Moths (family Notodontidae), such as the Variable Oakleaf Caterpillar, spray a pungent mixture of formic acid and ketones at attackers. Although people do not seem to be able to detect the chemicals produced by the prothoracic gland of butterfly caterpillars, ants, flies, wasps, or other predaceous insects may be repelled.

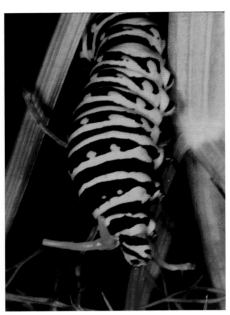

A Zebra Swallowtail caterpillar displaying its osmeterium.

The Black Swallowtail osmeterium.

Swallowtails have a very smelly defensive gland called the osmeterium. This eversible gland normally lies hidden behind the head. When perturbed, the forked, brightly colored osmeterium shoots out, perhaps frightening predators, or fending them off with strong scent and foul taste. The smell is hard to describe, but has an aromatic quality mixed with butyric acid, which also gives rotten butter its pungent smell. Most swallowtails have a yellow osmeterium, but the gland is bright red in the Giant Swallowtail and white in the Schaus' and Bahamian swallowtails.

Ants are among the most persistent and aggressive predators of small caterpillars. Ants constantly search stems and leaves for food to bring back to their nests. Some plants such as passionflowers, sennas, and cherries have special nectar glands on their leaves, usually near the base of the blade. Ants are attracted to the nectar, and also carry off any eggs or young caterpillars they find. Adult females of the Gulf Fritillary lay their eggs on passionflowers, often at the tips of tendrils where ants are unlikely to find them. Silver-spotted Skipper females sometimes lay their eggs on plants adjacent to the true host. The tiny caterpillars must find their own way to the host plant after emerging from the eggs.

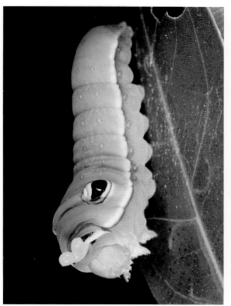
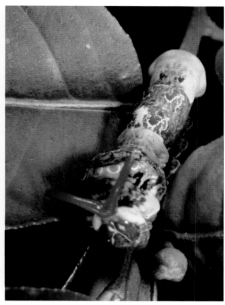

The Palamedes Swallowtail osmeterium.

The Giant Swallowtail has a distinctive crimson osmeterium.

Young caterpillars of the Red-spotted Purple, Florida Purplewing, and Goatweed Leafwing eat away the tip of a host leaf, except for the midrib. Then they attach their droppings with silk to form a long thin spar jutting from the end of the midrib. When not feeding, the larvae rest near the tip of the frass spar, making it difficult for ants to find them. The young larvae of the Goatweed Leafwing make themselves less palatable to predators by adorning their bodies with their own droppings. Young caterpillars of the Eastern Tiger Swallowtail pick up their frass with their jaws and throw it to the ground, apparently to avoid leaving accumulations of feces that may attract parasites or predators.

In the same way that passionflower vines recruit ants to act as their bodyguards, some hairstreak and blue caterpillars, such as the Spring Azures, have special glands that actually attract ants. These larvae are generally slow moving, and tend to stay put feeding on flower buds for long periods of time. Glands called perforated cupolas seem to produce scents (pheromones) that cause aphid-tending ants to stroke the larva. In some species, the mature caterpillars also reward ants with honeydew secretions produced by Newcomer's gland, located on top and toward the posterior of abdominal

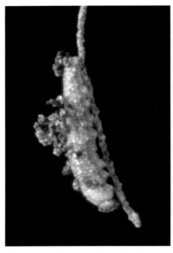
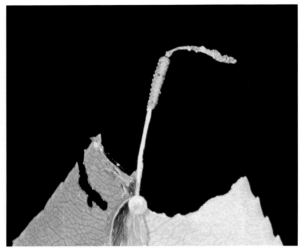

The young larva of the Goatweed Leafwing covers itself with frass and rests at the tip of a frass spar to help deter predators.

The young Red-spotted Purple larva rests at the tip of a Black Cherry leaf. Notice the egg shell from which the larva emerged.

The young caterpillar of the Florida Purplewing eludes predators by resting at the tip of a line of frass pellets held together with silk.

segment 7. The ants become intent on caring for the resting caterpillars, just as they tend and care for aphids, and help defend them from parasitic wasps. If the caterpillar moves, however, the ants may attack. A pair of eversible glands called tentacles located on short stalks on top of abdominal segment 8 seem to produce pheromones that repel the ants. The tentacles consist of clusters of short hairs (hair pencils) that normally lie hidden within the stalk. When everted, the hairs spread out, helping to disseminate the ant-repelling scent. The caterpillar is thus able to manipulate the ants depending on its need for protection versus its own need to move about.

Identifying Caterpillars

Many Florida butterfly caterpillars, such as the Pipevine Swallowtail or Atala, have unique shapes or color patterns that distinguish them from all other species in the state. Some closely related species, however, are often very similar, such as the Spicebush and Palamedes swallowtails, and can be distinguished only upon careful examination. Many of the hairstreak and blue caterpillars are very similar, and are best identified by their host plants. For some caterpillars, it's necessary to raise the individuals you find in the wild to the adult stage to be sure of the species.

Usually, each family or subfamily of butterflies has certain larval characteristics that are useful for identification. The following key and descriptions should help in determining to which group an unknown Florida butterfly caterpillar belongs. One of the best ways to identify caterpillars is to compare and become familiar with the photos of the various species and to learn about their host plants.

Key to the Mature Larvae of Florida Butterflies

1a. Caterpillar slug-shaped, the head usually retracted into the prothorax .... (2)
1b. Typical caterpillar shape, the head clearly visible .... (4)
2a. Body covered with long setae (hairs) .... Little Metalmark
2b. Body with short hairs .... (3)
3a. Eating aphids .... Harvester
3b. Eating flower buds or young leaves .... Hairstreaks and Blues
4a. Forked tails present on posterior end .... (5)
4b. Posterior end rounded or pointed, but not forked .... (6)

5a. A pair of simple spines on top of the head; eating grasses and sedges .... Wood-Nymphs and Satyrs

5b. Head with short branching spines on top; eating hackberries . Emperors

6a. Head large, rounded or triangular, prothoracic shield usually present, and lenticles present .... Skippers (7)

6b. Not as above .... (9)

7a. Eating dicots, many with red, orange, or yellow colors .... Spread-winged Skippers

7b. Eating monocots .... (8)

8a. Mostly eating the leaves of grasses and sedges .... Grass-Skippers

8b. Boring into the stems and roots of yuccas .... Giant-Skippers

9a. Osmeterium (eversible, forked, smelly and brightly colored gland located behind the head) evident when provoked .... Swallowtails

9b. Osmeterium absent .... (10)

10a. Body with spines or sticklike scoli .... (11)

10b. Body without spines or scoli .... (13)

11a. Spines long and slender; eating passionflowers .... Heliconians

11b. Spines relatively short and thick; eating other plants .... (12)

12a. Spines on body branched and of uniform size and shape ... Brushfoots

12b. Spines on body simple or of various sizes and shapes .... Admirals

13a. Head with a pebbly texture .... Leafwings

13b. Head smooth .... (14)

14a. Body with 2 or 3 pairs of long fleshy filaments, head with black stripes .... Milkweed Butterflies

14b. Body without fleshy filaments, head usually green .... (15)

15a. Head and body with few hairs, thorax with one pair of small black spots .... American Snout

15b. Head and body with numerous hairs, body with or without numerous small black spots or spikes .... (16)

16a. Posterior often with a pair of bumps or short tails, body with numerous small blue or black spots .... (17)

16b. Posterior rounded, body without small blue or black spots .... Sulphurs

17a. Body with a wide white stripe on the side .... Orangetips

17b. Body without white markings .... Whites

Although this is the most complete guide to Florida butterfly caterpillars and host plants available, there are a number of other good references covering adult identification and biology. Books that we find very useful include *Florida's Fabulous Butterflies* by Thomas Emmel, *Florida Butterflies* by Eugene Gerberg and Ross Arnett, Jr., *Butterflies Through Binoculars: Florida* by

Jeffrey Glassberg, Marc Minno, and John Calhoun, *Butterflies of the Florida Keys* by Marc Minno and Thomas Emmel, *Butterflies and Moths: A Guide to the More Common American Species* by Robert Mitchell and Herbert Zim, *Florida's Butterflies and Other Insects* by Peter Stiling, and *Peterson First Guide to Caterpillars of North America* by Amy Bartlett Wright.

Metamorphosis and Life Cycles

Butterflies have a complete metamorphosis consisting of four distinct stages (fig. 6). The cycle begins after a male and female mate. The female then flies in search of plants of the proper kind and quality on which to lay eggs. Females searching for host plants have a slow, fluttering type of flight. Most species lay only one egg at a time, but some, such as the Eastern Comma and Long-tailed Skipper, often lay eggs in short strings or small clusters, while the Tawny Emperor and Pearl Crescent lay many dozens of eggs in a single group.

Butterfly eggs typically hatch in three to five days. Species such as the Giant-skippers take several weeks to hatch, while some hairstreaks spend most of the year as eggs. The eggs often change color as development proceeds. The eggs of some species such as the Hackberry Emperor and Delaware Skipper develop a reddish ring after a few days. Just before the caterpillar is ready to emerge, the head may be visible near the top of the egg. When ready, the caterpillar chews its way out of the egg. Some species consume the shell as the first meal.

The growth of caterpillars is limited by the nonliving cuticle covering the body. To grow larger, a caterpillar must shed the old cuticle through the process of molting and form a new, larger cuticle. Most butterfly caterpillars have five larval stages or instars. Some, like the Harvester, may have fewer. Species overwintering as caterpillars may have extra molts if reared indoors under poor conditions. At each molt, the size, color, and shape of the caterpillar may change, sometimes dramatically. Body size within each instar may double. The best way to determine a caterpillar's stage is to examine and compare the size of the head. Because the head is a hard capsule that does not change in size except at molting, it remains an accurate guide. If you are raising butterflies indoors, the shed head capsules can be collected from the bottom of the rearing container and glued in a line on a note card as a reference. The head increases in width at each molt by a factor of 1.2 to 1.4.

Giant-skipper and many grass-skipper caterpillars develop special wax glands on the underside of the body during the last part of the larval period.

The pupae of some broad-winged skippers such as the Long-tailed Skipper are heavily covered with wax.

Typically the wax glands form two bands on the underside of segments 7 and 8. Depending on the species, the glands may be distributed either longitudinally along the body axis or across the body. The wax is shed as small flakes that the caterpillar uses to coat the inside of its cocoon. The Palmetto Skipper and related species plug the entrance to the cocoon with wax flakes. Broad-winged Skipper pupae may also be heavily waxed, but the wax is secreted through pores in the cuticle after the larval skin is shed.

When fully mature, the last stage caterpillar clears the gut of waste and usually crawls away from the host plant to find a site to pupate. Some species such as the Spicebush, Tiger, and Palamedes swallowtails change color from green to brown before entering their wandering phase. After perhaps a few hours, the caterpillar selects a site for pupation and spins a mat of silk threads over the area. Some prepare a silk girdle around the thorax and/or a silk pad to anchor the last pair of legs. After about a day, the larval cuticle splits down the back of the thorax and is wiggled down to the posterior end. Two abdominal segments pinch together and clasp the cuticle while the tip of the abdomen of the pupa is withdrawn from the larval skin and then reattached to the silk pad with small hooks. The pupa wriggles around until the larval skin drops away, and then settles down to harden into the final chrysalis form.

Moth caterpillars either spin a silken cocoon about themselves, or burrow into the ground before they pupate. Skippers fashion a simple cocoon by closing off the larval shelter or by tying a few leaves together with silk prior to pupating. Other butterflies do not make cocoons, but attach the pupa directly to the substrate with silk. The specialized pupae of butterflies are called chrysalids (chrysalis, singular), a term derived from a Greek word for

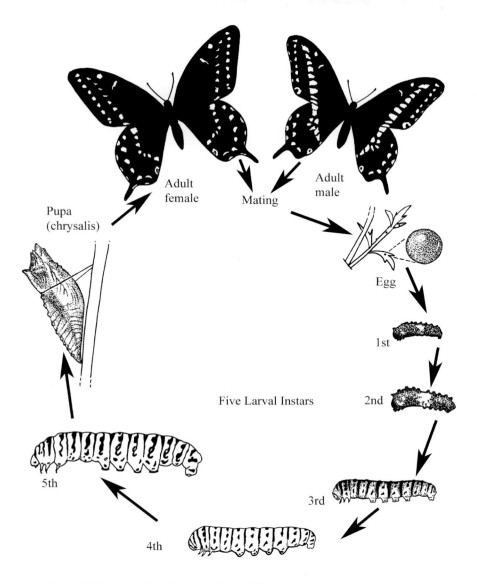

Figure 6. Diagram of the Black Swallowtail life cycle.

gold. The pupae of many brushfoots are adorned with gold or silver markings.

In the following section, we illustrate the egg, larva, pupa, and adult of one species for each of the eighteen families or subfamilies of butterflies found in Florida. This picture guide will help in identifying specimens, and will also show similarities and distinctions among the groups.

The Spicebush Swallowtail life cycle (family Papilionidae).

The Checkered White
life cycle (family Pieridae,
subfamily Pierinae).

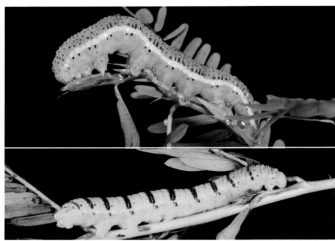

The Cloudless Sulphur life cycle (family Pieridae, subfamily Coliadinae).

The Harvester life cycle
(family Lycaenidae,
subfamily Miletinae).

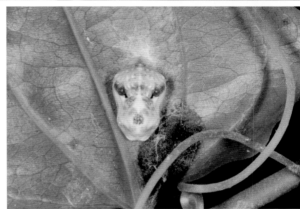

The Red-banded
Hairstreak life cycle
(family Lycaenidae,
subfamily Theclinae).

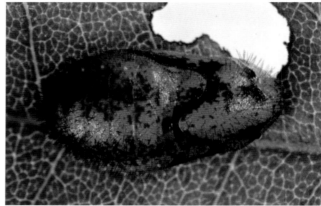

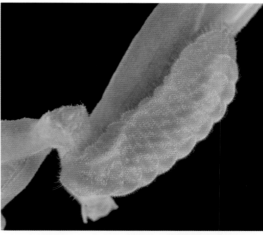

The Cassius Blue life cycle
(family Lycaenidae,
subfamily Polyommatinae).

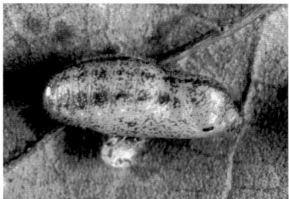

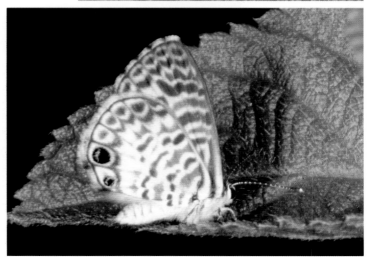

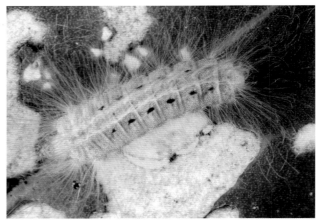

The Little Metalmark
life cycle
(family Riodinidae).

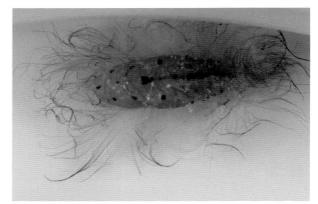

The Pearl Crescent life cycle
(family Nymphalidae,
subfamily Nymphalinae).

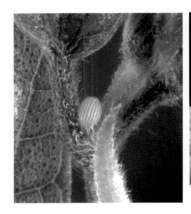

The American Snout life cycle
(family Nymphalidae,
subfamily Libytheinae).

The Gulf Fritillary life cycle
(family Nymphalidae,
subfamily Heliconiinae).

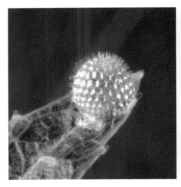

The Red-spotted Purple life
cycle (family Nymphalidae,
subfamily Limenitidinae)

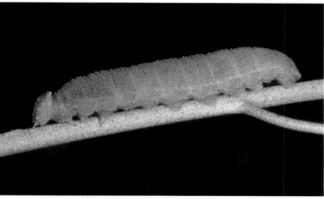

The Goatweed Leafwing life cycle (family Nymphalidae, subfamily Charaxinae).

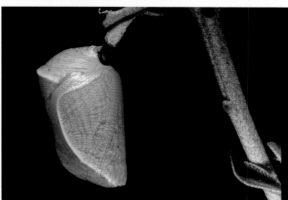

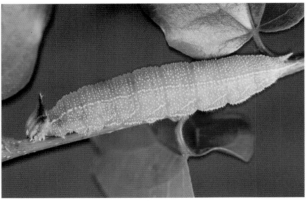

The Hackberry Emperor
life cycle
(family Nymphalidae,
subfamily Apaturinae).

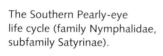

The Southern Pearly-eye
life cycle (family Nymphalidae,
subfamily Satyrinae).

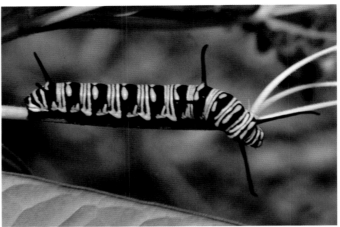

The Queen life cycle
(family Nymphalidae,
subfamily Danainae).

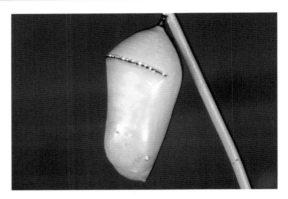

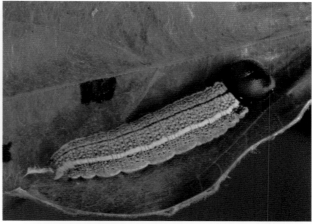

The Long-tailed Skipper
life cycle
(family Hesperiidae,
subfamily Pyrginae).

The Brazilian Skipper
life cycle
(family Hesperiidae,
subfamily Hesperiinae).

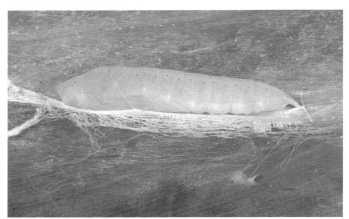

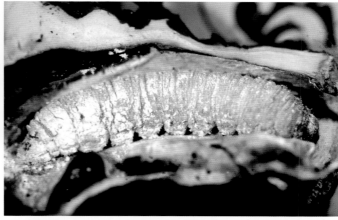

The Cofaqui Giant-Skipper
life cycle
(family Hesperiidae,
subfamily Megathyminae).

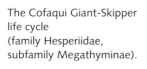

Finding and Rearing Caterpillars

For a land of slight topography, Florida has an amazing number of natural communities. Soil nutrients and permeability, water levels, climate, interactions between species, and extreme events such as freezes or droughts determine which plants are able to survive and reproduce in any particular area. Florida has some of the most abundant and diverse wetlands in North America as well as special upland habitats such as Sand Pine scrubs, dry prairies, and the Everglades marshes. In just a short drive inland from the coast you may encounter mangrove forest, salt marsh, hammock, scrub, flatwoods, freshwater marsh, swamp, and perhaps other habitats. Each region of Florida has interesting habitats to explore, such as the tropical hardwood forests and pine rocklands of extreme southern Florida, the marshes and dwarf cypress stands of the Everglades, the prairies and scrubs of central Florida, the swamps, sandhills, and pine flatwoods of northern Florida, and the pitcher plant savannas and hardwood forests of the Panhandle. Each natural community supports plants, butterflies, and other animals that live only or mostly in that particular habitat.

Hunting for caterpillars takes a bit of patience and some skill in observing nature. Since butterflies are very host specific and seasonal, it's necessary to know something about the places they live, the plants they eat, and the timing of their larval stages, in order to track down the caterpillars. For example, if one is interested in finding caterpillars of the Checkered White, the first place to start is a field or roadside with lots of Virginia Pepperweed. This is the only known host plant for this butterfly in Florida. Caterpillars of the Checkered White occur during spring, summer, and fall, so looking in winter would not be productive.

Once the proper habitat and host plant have been found, and the season is correct, the caterpillar hunt can begin. Often the plants selected by the females are not the largest or most robust. They frequently select small or isolated plants near larger patches, which may help them evade predators that are also hunting for them on the best plants. Most caterpillars eat the young leaves or flowers at the tips of shoots, but may rest or hide under the lower leaves or near the ground. Sure signs of caterpillar activity are chewed leaves, silken trails, and nests. If the caterpillar cannot be located, it may have been eaten by a predator, or perhaps it finished feeding and crawled away to find a pupation site.

Caterpillars can also be gathered from shrubs and trees by laying a white sheet on the ground and shaking the overhanging branches vigorously or striking them sharply with a stick. This will dislodge caterpillars, beetles, spiders, and other critters onto the sheet where they can easily be seen. Some researchers use beating trays in one hand and a stick in the other to collect insects. A garbage can lid or short-sided cardboard box can be used as a beating tray. A large plastic bin covered by a piece of coarse wire mesh works well for collecting larvae from tall grasses and herbs. By placing the mouth of the bin next to the vegetation and beating the plants against the wire, one will dislodge caterpillars into the bin. Nets may also be used to sweep vegetation, but soft-bodied caterpillars may be damaged unless the net is emptied frequently.

The caterpillars of hairstreaks and blues are slow moving and blend in extremely well with the flower buds and leaves of their host plants. Sometimes, the only way to find these caterpillars is to clip the flowers and young leaves from potential hosts and place them in a layer in a rearing container. Caterpillars can be found by looking for droppings in the bottom of the container. Often hairstreak and blue larvae can be easily raised indoors on the seeds of fresh beans or peas from the market. Another clue to finding hairstreak and blue caterpillars, such as the Spring Azures, is to look for clusters of ants on the flower buds. The ants may be gathering nectar from the flowers or tending aphids, but also may be attending caterpillars, as previously noted in Caterpillar Behavior and Defense.

You may find eggs of some species on the tender young growth at the tips of shoots, or observe a female that is searching for host plants. Female butterflies are very choosy when selecting plants on which to lay eggs. They may briefly hover over and inspect certain plants or land on the leaves to taste them with special receptors on their feet. When a shoot is selected, the female will land, curl its abdomen to touch the tip to the leaf, deposit an egg, and then quickly fly away to look for other shoots. The females will usually not be disturbed if you stand quietly nearby. After the female has flown away, closely inspect the shoot to find the egg.

Eggs and caterpillars can be brought indoors and reared in a safe location. It's best to keep the caterpillars out of the sun, and to have a lot of air circulation to prevent disease. Small potted plants work well for rearing caterpillars, but are not always practical. Sprigs of host plants can also be placed in containers of water to keep them fresh. The top of the water container should be sealed with plastic wrap or paper towels, because the caterpillars will sometimes crawl down the shoot into the water and drown. Small aquariums, cages with fine screening, or bags of fine netting are ideal for keeping the caterpillars from crawling away and becoming lost. Very small caterpillars are often hard to find even when raised in cages. For these, plastic film containers, clear plastic deli tubs or small wide-mouthed jars will help you to observe and track the caterpillars' progress. Host leaves or shoots can be kept fresh in small containers by placing the cut ends in small vials of water. Fine netting securely fastened over the top will allow air circulation, and a layer of paper towels or tissue in the bottom of the container will help absorb moisture and collect droppings. If any mold shows up, it's definitely time to clean the culture. Be aware that pesticides sprayed in the home to control roaches or fleas may also affect caterpillars.

Caterpillars need a lot of young, tender leaves in order to complete their development. Mature leaves may be too tough or too toxic for very small caterpillars, but may be tolerated by older larvae. If you are raising a dozen or more caterpillars, it may be difficult to supply them with enough food. It's usually best to use the same species of host plant through the entire larval stage, because the kinds and levels of toxic chemicals plants use to defend themselves from herbivores vary from species to species. The caterpillars also adapt to the specific plant they are eating, and usually won't grow as fast or as large if hosts are switched from time to time. Sometimes, however, the original host may not be available and one must use alternative plants. Switching caterpillars to another plant in the same genus may not cause any harm. Thus, many of the large sulphurs will usually accept any of the *Senna* species, and oak feeders will eat the leaves of many kinds of oaks.

Transfer very young caterpillars with care. Pieces of old leaf with eggs or young caterpillars can be clipped with sharp scissors and transferred to the new host with tweezers. Larger caterpillars can be carefully picked off the old plant material with the fingers, but they often hold on tight with the tiny hooks on the bottom of the legs. Caterpillars that are about to shed their skin are especially vulnerable to rough handling. When fully mature, the caterpillar will stop eating, clean out the gut by passing a watery frass pellet, and begin wandering to find a pupation site. A stick placed in the rearing container will often give the caterpillar a convenient place to pupate.

Butterfly eggs, caterpillars, or chrysalids collected from the wild may be harboring parasitoids and diseases. You may be disappointed to have your caterpillars die suddenly and surprised to find a wasp or fly in the rearing container. In nature, these organisms help to keep butterfly and moth populations in a delicate balance.

Parasites are organisms that harm a host, but usually do not kill it. Certain mites and biting midges (Ceratopogonidae) are examples of parasites that attack butterfly immatures. Parasitoids are animals that feed on and eventually kill a single host organism, and these are of greater concern to butterfly farmers. There are numerous types of parasitoids that attack eggs, larvae, and pupae of butterflies and moths.

Several families of minute wasps, especially the families Mymaridae and Trichogrammatidae, attack butterfly and moth eggs. The adults of these wasps range in size from 0.25 to 1 millimeter. These tiny wasps easily pass through most types of netting and frequently attack the eggs of butterflies laid in insectaries or screen enclosures; often eggs parasitized by the wasps turn black. Eventually a dozen or more tiny adult wasps may emerge from a single butterfly egg.

Many other kinds of wasps attack butterfly and moth caterpillars. The female wasps lay their eggs inside the caterpillar using a sharp ovipositor or egg guide. Upon hatching, the wasp larvae feed on the internal parts of the caterpillar. When mature, the wasp larvae burrow out of the caterpillar and spin white, yellow, or banded cocoons on or underneath the host. The cocoons may be oblong and fuzzy or flat and smooth, depending upon the group. The largest and most common wasps that attack butterfly and moth caterpillars are in the families Braconidae and Ichneumonidae, but other wasps in the Pteromalidae, Eulophidae, and Chalcididae may also be obtained from caterpillars collected from the wild. The larger parasitoid wasps usually lay only one egg per caterpillar, but smaller species may lay dozens of eggs. In some species, especially in the latter groups, the wasp larvae allow the caterpillar to form a chrysalis but eventually consume most of the contents. The wasps pupate inside the chrysalis shell. The adult wasps chew a small round hole in the side of the chrysalis to escape. The caterpillars you raise may appear normal until the wasps burrow out and spin cocoons or the wasp adults emerge from the chrysalis.

Flies in the family Tachinidae also attack butterfly caterpillars. The female fly lays flat white eggs on the skin of the caterpillar. The eggs hatch in a few days and the fly maggots burrow into the caterpillar. When mature, the maggots burrow out of the caterpillar or chrysalis and drop to the ground, where they pupate. The maggots often leave strands of a slimy texture from the exit holes. The strands quickly dry into diagnostic filaments. After leaving the host, the white or cream-colored maggots are quite active at first, but soon settle down to form pupae. Unlike other insects, flies pupate within their last larval skin. If raised in containers, you may find the oblong dark brown or reddish brown fly puparia (pupae) at the bottom. Signs of fly attack include the flat egg shells on the skin or small dark spots where the maggots burrowed out of the caterpillar, as well as the exit filaments on the chrysalis.

Predators frequently capture and eat immature butterflies and moths. Predators are animals that kill and feed on several to many hosts during their lifetime. The most common predators of caterpillars are ants (especially *Pseudomyrmex* spp. and fire ants), paper wasps (*Polistes* spp.), and other large wasps in the families Vespidae and Sphecidae, spiders, stink bugs and other predaceous bugs, arboreal crickets, lizards, and birds.

Butterfly Gardening

In Florida, butterflies visit gardens all year long. Butterfly gardens can be an elegant way to beautify the urban landscape while also providing high quality habitat for many species. Attracting butterflies to your garden is relatively easy if you plant flowers that butterflies prefer. Plants with small clusters of flowers, including Pentas, Lantana, Verbena, Porterweed, Heliotrope, Turkey Tangle Fogfruit, and Aster, are often favored by butterflies in Florida gardens. The flowers attract adult butterflies into your garden as they fly about looking for food. Adding plants that the caterpillars eat (host plants) will turn your yard into a butterfly farm. Some commonly used host plants in Florida gardens are Sweet Fennel, Scarlet Milkweed, Canna, Pipevine, Passionflower, Wild Lime, Hackberry, Senna, and Leadwort.

We recommend that you try planting native species in your garden. Natives are the plants that the butterflies have been associated with for thousands of years and reflect the beauty of natural Florida landscapes. Some exotic plants have escaped from gardens and become invasive pests in natural areas. A few invasive plants such as Brazilian Pepper (*Schinus terebinthifolius*), Valamuerto (*Senna pendula*), and Cogongrass (*Imperata cylindrica*) are eaten by butterfly caterpillars, but should never be planted in your garden.

There are several good guides to butterfly gardening available, including *Florida Butterfly Gardening* by Marc and Maria Minno, *Your Florida Guide to Butterfly Gardening* by Jaret Daniels, and *Gardening for Florida's Butterflies* by Pam Trass (see references at the end of this book). These guides will help you to design a butterfly garden. They also discuss nectar and host plants and illustrate common butterflies, caterpillars, and flowers.

Butterfly Habitats

More than 2,600 species of native plants occur in Florida, and many thousands of plant species from other parts of the world (exotics) are cultivated in the state. Although Florida lacks much in the way of topographic relief (the highest point is only about 370 feet above sea level), soil characteristics and natural communities are related to elevation (fig. 7). Slight differences

The elegant butterfly garden at the Marie Selby Botanic Garden in Sarasota.

in elevation may determine whether the area will support wetland or upland vegetation. The distribution of major vegetation types is shown in figure 8.

The various plant communities (habitats) form a patchwork across the landscape, changing where specific ecological conditions, such as soil permeability or water level, shift. For instance, one of the most common natural communities, pine flatwoods, is found on nearly level, poorly drained soils, but commonly embedded within the flatwoods are swamps where shallow depressions and drainage ways hold more permanent water.

Generally, the greatest number of butterfly species will be found in areas that have the greatest plant diversity and structure. Plant diversity will be

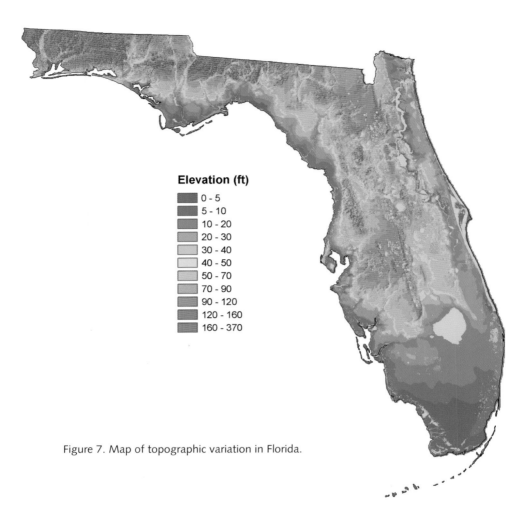

Elevation (ft)

- 0 - 5
- 5 - 10
- 10 - 20
- 20 - 30
- 30 - 40
- 40 - 50
- 50 - 70
- 70 - 90
- 90 - 120
- 120 - 160
- 160 - 370

Figure 7. Map of topographic variation in Florida.

highest at the edges of plant communities (ecotones) where one type blends in with another, and forests will typically have more species than grasslands. Communities with low diversity may have very special plants and butterflies if conditions are very harsh or unusual, as in scrubs, pine rocklands, salt marshes, seeps, and Atlantic White Cedar swamps. The richest natural communities for butterfly host plants and caterpillars include grassy sandhills, upland hardwood forests, and swamps, but weedy areas and gardens often have high diversity as well. In the following section we describe the major types of plant communities found in Florida.

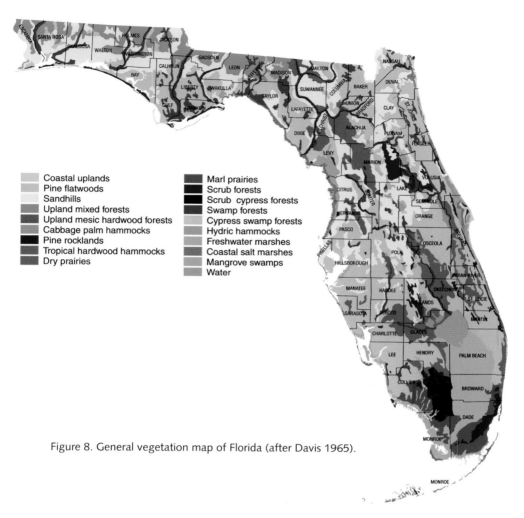

Coastal uplands
Pine flatwoods
Sandhills
Upland mixed forests
Upland mesic hardwood forests
Cabbage palm hammocks
Pine rocklands
Tropical hardwood hammocks
Dry prairies

Marl prairies
Scrub forests
Scrub cypress forests
Swamp forests
Cypress swamp forests
Hydric hammocks
Freshwater marshes
Coastal salt marshes
Mangrove swamps
Water

Figure 8. General vegetation map of Florida (after Davis 1965).

Dry Places

Coastal Uplands

Coastal uplands are the beaches, dunes, and maritime forests found along Florida's coasts. The soils are very sandy, and plants that grow in coastal uplands are tolerant of drought and salt spray. Coastal uplands are especially well developed where wave action from the sea is intense. The best examples can be found along the coastline and barrier islands of the Panhandle and along the Atlantic coast. Butterflies often migrate along Florida's coastlines in large numbers, but host plant diversity is relatively low.

Sandhill habitat at the Katherine B. Ordway Preserve in Putnam County east of Melrose.

Uplands along the Gulf Coast near Carrabelle, Franklin County.

Sandhills

Longleaf Pine savannas and sandhills were the dominant plant community of the southeastern United States before Europeans arrived in North America. Most of the trees were harvested for lumber from the mid-1800s into the mid-1900s. Today, only small fragments of this once extensive ecosystem survive. Many of the cutover sandhills grew back as Turkey Oak barrens, or were converted to Slash Pine plantations. As the name implies, sandhill forests in peninsular Florida occur on sandy, well-drained hills and ridges. In the Panhandle, sandhill vegetation also occurs on red sandy clay soils that are very acidic and poor in nutrients. Generally this forest type consists of widely spaced pines with a diverse Wiregrass and herb ground cover. Sandhill vegetation must be burned on a regular basis to maintain its grassy character. Plant and butterfly diversity in grassy Longleaf Pine forests is very high.

Sand Pine scrub near
the Fort Lauderdale
Executive Airport,
Broward County.

Scrub Forests

Scrub forests occur only on the most permeable sandy ridges along the coastline and on ancient beach dunes inland. They are typically dominated by Sand Pine with a dense tangle of shrubs, especially oaks, below. The scrubs in the central part of Florida have many rare plants and animals that are found nowhere else. Fire occurs rarely in scrubs, but will kill the sand pines and many of the shrubs. After a fire, however, some shrubs resprout, and the pines and other species release their seeds, rejuvenating the habitat.

Moist Places

Pine Flatwoods

The most abundant and widely distributed plant community in Florida is pine flatwoods. This forest type has a dense to open cover of pine trees with dense patches of Saw Palmetto and/or Gallberry interspersed with grassy areas, swamps, wet prairies, or savannas. Flatwoods typically occur on soils with a spodic horizon or hardpan that restricts water from percolating through. The spodic horizon is a dark colored, dense accumulation of organic material and minerals that have been translocated from the upper soil. During the summer rainy season in Florida, pine flatwoods soils become very wet and may have standing water, but then become droughty during the dry season. In southern Florida, South Florida Slash Pine is the dominant tree. In northern Florida, pine flatwoods may be composed of pure or mixed stands of Longleaf Pine, Slash Pine, Pond Pine, or Loblolly Pine. Flatwoods are maintained and rejuvenated by frequent fires.

Pine Savanna

Pine savannas are similar to flatwoods, but have lower densities of pine trees and more extensive areas of mixed grasses and wildflowers. Often carnivorous plants, such as pitcher plants and sundews, as well as terrestrial orchids are present. This once extensive ecosystem has been mostly changed to pine plantations, pastures, and other uses. Some of the best remaining savannas can be found in the Apalachicola National Forest.

Flatwoods habitat near Okefenokee Swamp in southeastern Georgia.

Longleaf Pine savanna at Apalachicola National Forest, Liberty County.

Mesic hardwood forest at the Apalachicola Bluffs and Ravines Preserve, Liberty County.

Cabbage Palm hammock at Highlands Hammock State Park, Highlands County.

Upland Mixed and Mesic Hardwood Forests

Upland hardwood forests occur on moist, well-drained, but relatively rich soils in the Panhandle and areas of northern and central Florida where limestone is close to the surface. These forests contain a great diversity of trees and shrubs. The mixed forests of the Panhandle contain hardwoods and Loblolly Pine or Spruce Pine as well as a wide variety of spring wildflowers. Many species of butterflies occur in upland hardwood forests, especially along trails, in clearings, or near the edges of the forest.

Cabbage Palm Hammocks

Relatively pure stands of Cabbage Palm are often associated with marshes near the coast or with prairies in central and southern Florida. Cabbage Palms have a high tolerance of fire and thrive near grassy areas where wildfire is frequent. Although an interesting community type, diversity of both plants and butterflies in Cabbage Palm hammocks is low.

Dry prairie habitat at Kissimmee Prairie Pre- serve State Park, Okeechobee County.

Pine rockland at the National Key Deer Ref- uge, Big Pine Key, Monroe County.

Dry Prairies

One of Florida's rarest habitats is the dry prairie community. This diverse type of grassland is similar to pine savanna, but fires occur too frequently for pines and other trees to survive. The prairie areas of central and southern Florida have a very high incidence of lightning strikes from thunderstorms that result in frequent wild fires. The upland prairies are often interspersed with wet prairies and shallow marshes, creating a mosaic of different habitats.

Pine Rocklands

Rocky areas of southeastern Florida and the Keys have a very special forest composed of South Florida Slash Pine, palms, and tropical shrubs. Much of this habitat has been destroyed by urban development, but remnants of pine rockland still occur in a few parks. Some of our rarest butterflies, such as Bartram's Hairstreak, Nickerbean Blue, Florida Leafwing, Florida Dusky-

Tropical hardwood hammock at the Bartlett Estate in Fort Lauderdale, Broward County.

wing, Meske's Skipper (Keys race), and Palatka Skipper (Keys race), occur in pine rocklands.

Tropical Hardwood Hammocks

Forests of tropical trees and shrubs are found in a narrow band along the coast from Tampa and Merritt Island southward and throughout the Keys. Diversity of woody plants is very high in these tropical forests, and many special butterflies occur only near this habitat. Tropical hammocks are typically a dense tangle of woody plants, making walking difficult. The richest tropical forests occur from Key Largo to the area around Biscayne Bay, where the Gulf Stream provides a mild climate. Only a few kinds of butterflies prefer the deep shade within the forest, but many kinds occur along trails and clearings.

Wet prairie habitat at Moccasin Island Marsh Restoration Area, Brevard County.

Bottomland hardwood swamp along the floodplain of the Apalachicola River, Liberty County.

Wetlands

Wet Prairies and Marl Prairies

Shallowly flooded areas and seeps may be dominated by grasses and herbs, especially in areas prone to frequent wildfires. Wet prairies occur most commonly in central and southern Florida, but smaller areas, especially seeps, can be found in the Panhandle and northern parts of the state. There were extensive wet prairies bordering the Everglades on marl (basic) soils, but much of these have been drained and converted to agriculture or urban landscapes in recent times. Butterfly abundance in wet prairies can be high, especially in late summer and fall.

Hardwood and Cypress Swamp Forests

Swamps or forested wetlands occur in low-lying areas bordering streams, rivers and lakes, and in depressional areas of the landscape. Water levels in swamps fluctuate with the season. During the spring, swamps may be dry,

Cypress swamp at Fort Drum Marsh Conservation Area, Indian River County.

Hydric hammock along the Ocklawaha at Caravelle Ranch Wildlife Management Area, Putnam County.

but with the summer rains, water levels may rise several feet above ground surface. Cypress used to be a dominant tree in many swamps in peninsular Florida, but nearly all of the large trees were cut decades ago for lumber, and smaller trees are shredded for mulch today. Cypress is still a common tree in many swamps and in the scrub cypress forests that lie west of the Everglades. The southern Florida scrub cypress forests are intricate mosaics of dwarf cypress trees, wet prairies, and shallow marshes. Isolated cypress swamps usually have the tallest trees toward the middle and small trees around the edges, and are called cypress domes. Many swamps also contain Red Maple, several species of ash, and tupelo, as well as other hardwood trees. Forested wetlands along rivers are sometimes called bottomland swamps, and linear cypress swamps are known as strands. Evergreen broadleaved trees such as Loblolly Bay, Sweetbay, and Swamp Bay are often called bays. These trees occur on hillside seeps or isolated wetlands where fire frequency is low. Bay swamps are sometimes called bayheads. Atlantic White Cedar is a locally common wetland tree found along blackwater streams in the Panhandle.

Freshwater marsh habitat with cypress swamps in the background at Blue Cypress Marsh Conservation Area.

Salt marsh with small Black Mangroves at Flagship Park, Flagler County.

Hydric Hammocks

Hydric hammocks commonly form the transition between wetlands and uplands, or occur on moist, low-lying land. These forests contain a variety of evergreen and deciduous hardwood trees, cabbage palms, shrubs, and ferns. Butterflies may also be abundant in sunny openings or around the edges of hydric hammocks.

Freshwater Marshes

The largest freshwater marshes in Florida occur in the Everglades and the headwaters region of the St. Johns River. There are many smaller freshwater marshes throughout the state as well. Water levels may fluctuate several feet between seasons and from year to year, depending upon rainfall. Plant and butterfly diversity in marshes is generally low. Roadside ditches often have plants characteristic of marshes as well as weedy wetland species.

Mangrove swamp at Hutchinson Island, St. Lucie County.

Coastal Salt Marshes

There are two main types of salt marshes in Florida. Grassy salt marshes occur in estuary zones that are inundated by the tides. In places that are flooded only occasionally by brackish water, evaporation causes the soils to become excessively salty (hypersaline). Under these harsh conditions, only a few species of succulent plants such as glassworts and Saltwort thrive. Patches of barren ground and small mangroves may also be present. Butterfly diversity in salt marshes is low, but some species occur only in this habitat.

Mangrove Swamps

Of the four mangrove species found in Florida, two are used as host plants by butterflies. The Red Mangrove is eaten by the caterpillars of the beautiful Mangrove Skipper, and the Mangrove Buckeye feeds on Black Mangrove.

A pitcher plant seep at Blackwater River State Forest, Okaloosa County.

The various mangroves may grow in mixed forests or in monocultures. Red Mangroves, with their arching prop roots, thrive where the ocean meets the land. More to the landward side grow Black Mangrove, White Mangrove, and finally Buttonwood. Black Mangrove is the most cold-tolerant species, being found as far north as Cedar Key and St. Augustine. The other mangrove species occur from Tampa Bay and Merritt Island southward.

Pitcher Plant Seeps

A very special natural community occurs at the edges of flatwoods and sandhills where water seeps to the surface of the ground. Sometimes the seepage slope is along the side of a hill, but it may also occur over a nearly imperceptible gradient of just a few inches in the flatwoods. Seepage slopes have a diverse flora that often includes terrestrial orchids, carnivorous plants, St. John's-wort, Toothachegrass, and many interesting wildflowers.

Host Plants

Plants defend themselves from herbivores in a variety of ways. Some use mechanical structures such as spines or hairs to deter animal feeding. Grasses have high silica content and are difficult to digest. Grazing animals must chew and rechew the grasses they eat and have separate stomachs for fermentation by microorganisms before digestion. Plants also make chemicals specifically to keep caterpillars and other animals from eating them. The main classes of these chemicals (secondary compounds) are nitrogen compounds, terpenoids, and phenolics that are bitter tasting, toxic, or interfere with digestion.

Some of the most common secondary plant compounds that contain nitrogen are alkaloids. Tens of thousands of alkaloids have been identified in plants. Many such as nicotine, cocaine, caffeine, morphine, and codeine are powerful drugs to humans. Others such as strychnine and coniine (from Poison Hemlock) are extremely toxic.

Additional toxic nitrogenous compounds include certain amino acids found in legumes, cyanogenic glycosides that are common in plants in the rose family, and the glucosinolates of mustards. Cyanogenic glycosides are composed of cyanide and sugar subgroups. When eaten, digestive enzymes split off the sugar subunit and release the toxic cyanide. Glucosinolates are similar, but contain sulfur as well as cyanide.

Terpenoids are varied in structure, but are based on five carbon isoprene molecules. They include the aromatic oils of citrus, laurels, mints, pines, and eucalyptus, steroids that mimic sex hormones, latex compounds, saponins that rupture blood cells and cause irregularities in heartbeat, and cardenolides (the heart poisons found in milkweeds).

Unlike toxic compounds, tannins are a type of phenolic chemical that bind to proteins, starch, and minerals. They are what give tea its rich color and make acorns astringent to the taste. By binding with proteins and starch, they reduce the availability of nutrients and neutralize digestive enzymes. Tannins from the bark of oaks, hemlock, and other trees have been used for centuries to tan or transform animal skins into leather. Some skipper caterpillars that feed on oak leaves take months to reach maturity, probably because of the low amount of available nutrients.

Butterflies flourished during the rise of mammals and flowering plants, after the dinosaurs died out. Their caterpillars feed on plants that would be toxic to us, but over millions of years of association they have developed enzymes to detoxify the poisons in their food. Some, such as the Monarch, are able to sequester the cardenolides from the milkweeds they eat as caterpillars, and use them for their own defense. However, since plant chemistry varies greatly among the thousands of species, the butterflies become linked to just a few species of plants that the caterpillars can eat.

For a butterfly to survive its first few days, the female must be able to choose a plant that the caterpillar can eat, and the plant must be of the correct quality. If she lays her eggs on the wrong plant, or the leaves are too tough or too toxic, the caterpillars will starve or die from the poisons. Often, the secondary compounds in the plant are one of the cues females use to make the right choice. Thus, the aromatic scent of trees and shrubs in the laurel family are a sign that female Spicebush or Palamedes swallowtails use to locate host plants. If the plant also has young tender leaves, she may lay an egg or two.

Sometimes, though, the potential plant has the correct chemistry, but is too toxic for the larvae. For example, the Long-tailed Skipper will occasionally lay eggs on Showy Rattlebox, which is in the pea family, but the caterpillars cannot survive on this plant. The same is true for our passionflower butterflies, which can eat our native passionflowers, but cannot tolerate many of the exotic species that are often planted in gardens.

At other times the female butterfly makes mistakes and lays eggs on plants that are not even closely related to the true host. The Long-tailed Skipper sometimes lays eggs on the leaves of Turnip, Cabbage, and Woolly Dutchman's-Pipe. Larvae of the Long-tailed Skipper also sometimes build their shelters on plants adjacent to the actual host. Thus you may find the caterpillar in a shelter on Spanish Needles or blackberry leaves, but it is feeding on some nearby legume.

Florida Butterfly Caterpillars

Swallowtails (family Papilionidae)

Swallowtails are among the largest butterflies in Florida. Their caterpillars are also large and thick bodied. Swallowtail larvae have a brightly colored, forked defensive gland, the osmeterium, behind the head, which is normally hidden from view. The young caterpillars are colored like bird or lizard droppings. The thorax of older larvae is often enlarged and bears eyespots. Some species have fleshy tubercles or rows of small blue spots on the abdomen. They feed on plants in the Birthwort, Custard-Apple, Carrot, Citrus, Laurel, Magnolia, Olive, and Rose families.

Battus philenor
Pipevine Swallowtail

Photo, p. 163

Description: To 2.1" in length. Head and body dark brown to black with short orange tubercles on the back and longer, black filaments on the sides. The osmeterium is bright yellow.
Similar Species: The Polydamas Swallowtail also uses Dutchman's-Pipe.
Habitat: Uplands. Sandhills, dry pinelands, and hammocks.
U.S. Distribution: Florida westward to Arizona and northward into Kansas, Missouri, Illinois, Indiana, Ohio, and New York. Also found in California.
Natural History: This common swallowtail occurs in northern and central Florida. At least three generations are produced each year. Females lay orange colored eggs one or a few at a time on the young shoots of the host plants. The common host throughout most of Florida is Virginia Snakeroot. A single individual of this small herb is insufficient to feed a caterpillar to maturity, and soon the larvae must search along the ground for more plants, often many feet away, to eat. The two very long front filaments are used as feelers as the caterpillar moves about. The pupae overwinter.
Caterpillar Season: February through early November.
Host Plants: An herb, Virginia Snakeroot (*Aristolochia serpentaria*, p. 253), and vines in the Birthwort family (Aristolochiaceae) including Woolly Dutchman's-Pipe (*Aristolochia tomentosa*, p. 252) and occasionally the exotic Elegant Dutchman's-Pipe (*Aristolochia littoralis*, p. 252).

Battus polydamas

Polydamas Swallowtail

Photo, p. 163

Description: To 2.1" in length. Head black; top of prothorax orange; body dark purplish brown with short dark stripes and fleshy tubercles. Tubercles orange, tipped with black, much shorter than those of Pipevine Swallowtail, and mostly absent from the sides. The osmeterium is bright yellow.

Similar Species: The Pipevine Swallowtail also uses Dutchman's-Pipe.

Habitat: Uplands. Mostly in urban areas and gardens having the host plants.

U.S. Distribution: Peninsular Florida and southern Texas.

Natural History: This swallowtail is often locally abundant throughout peninsular Florida near patches of the host plants, but is infrequently seen away from the vines. Three or more generations are produced per year. The orange colored eggs are laid in small clusters on the young shoots of the host. The caterpillars feed in groups (p. 18), especially when small, and devour the youngest leaves and flowers first, and then the older foliage. Often the vines become defoliated by the caterpillars.

Caterpillar Season: Throughout the year in southern Florida.

Host Plants: Vines in the Birthwort family (Aristolochiaceae) including Woolly Dutchman's-Pipe (*Aristolochia tomentosa*, p. 252), Marsh's Dutchman's-Pipe (*Aristolochia pentandra*), and the exotic species Giant Dutchman's-Pipe (*Aristolochia gigantea*, p. 251), Largeflower Dutchman's-Pipe (*Aristolochia grandiflora*, p. 251), Elegant Dutchman's-Pipe (*Aristolochia littoralis*, p. 252), and Gaping Dutchman's-Pipe (*Aristolochia ringens*, p. 253).

Eurytides marcellus

Zebra Swallowtail

Photo, p. 163

Description: To 1.8" in length. Various color forms including light green with tiny black spots, green with pale blue and yellow stripes, and brown with white and yellow stripes; body thickest at the thorax and strongly tapering toward the posterior end; top of prothorax with black and yellow stripes; a transverse blue, black, and yellow stripe between the thorax and abdomen above that is usually hidden from view. The osmeterium is yellow (p. 20). First-stage caterpillars are black. Intermediate stages are dark brown with transverse black, yellow, and white bands.

Similar Species: None.

Habitat: Uplands. Scrubs, sandhills, and flatwoods.

U.S. Distribution: Florida westward to eastern Texas and northward into southern Iowa, Wisconsin, Michigan, Pennsylvania, and New Jersey.

Natural History: This common swallowtail is found throughout Florida, but is very local in the southern part of the state. Two to three generations are produced per year. Females lay the pale green eggs singly on young leaves of the host plants. The caterpillars eat new growth and flowers. They often hide on the undersides of the leaves, in the flowers, or in the leaf litter at the base of the plant when not eating. When disturbed, the caterpillar enlarges the body, prominently displaying the blue, black, and yellow stripe on the back, and shoots out the foul-smelling osmeterium. The pupae overwinter.

Caterpillar Season: February through early November.

Host Plants: Shrubs in the Custard-Apple family (Annonaceae) including Slim-leaf Pawpaw (*Asimina angustifolia*, p. 241), Woolly Pawpaw (*Asimina incana*, p. 241), Bigflower Pawpaw (*Asimina obovata*, p. 242), Smallflower Pawpaw (*Asimina parviflora*), Dwarf Pawpaw (*Asimina pygmaea*, p. 242), Netted Pawpaw (*Asimina reticulata*, p. 243), Fourpetal Pawpaw (*Asimina tetramera*), Common Pawpaw (*Asimina triloba*), Pretty False Pawpaw (*Deeringothamnus pulchellus*), and Rugel's False Pawpaw (*Deeringothamnus rugelii*).

Heraclides cresphontes (formerly *Papilio cresphontes*)
Giant Swallowtail

Photo, p. 165

Description: To 2.5" in length. Head dark brown; body brown with white patches on the posterior end, middle, and thorax, mixed brown and white patches on top of the middle, and scattered small blue spots; thorax enlarged and having two dark pits that resemble eyes when viewed from the front; posterior end with a false face pattern. The osmeterium is bright red. Young caterpillars are brown with a white and yellowish patch in the middle and a shiny skin.

Similar Species: The Schaus' Swallowtail and Bahamian Swallowtail also use Sea Torchwood and Wild Lime.

Habitat: Uplands. Sandhills, hammocks, citrus groves, and urban areas.

U.S. Distribution: Florida westward to southern California and northward into eastern Colorado, Nebraska, Iowa, southern Wisconsin, Michigan, New York, and Massachusetts.

Natural History: This common swallowtail occurs throughout Florida. At least three generations are produced per year. The orange colored eggs are laid singly on very young leaves of the host plants. The caterpillars eat the new growth first. Small larvae often rest on the upper surfaces of leaves where they resemble bird droppings. The larger caterpillars tend to rest on the branches or trunk of the host plant. Giant Swallowtail caterpillars are sometimes called Orange Dogs and may defoliate shoots or small citrus trees. The pupae overwinter.

Caterpillar Season: February through early November.

Host Plants: Herbs, shrubs, trees in the Citrus family (Rutaceae) including Sea Torchwood (*Amyris elemifera*, p. 302), Common Hoptree (*Ptelea trifoliata*, p. 303), Hercules-club (*Zanthoxylum clava-herculis*, p. 304), Wild Lime (*Zanthoxylum fagara*, p. 305), and the exotic Key Lime (*Citrus aurantifolia*), Lemon (*Citrus limon*), Tangerine (*Citrus reticulata*, p. 303), Sweet Orange (*Citrus sinensis*),

Grapefruit (*Citrus x paradisi*), Sour Orange (*Citrus aurantium*), Trifoliate Orange (*Poncirus trifoliata*), Box Thorn (*Severinia buxifolia*), and Rue (*Ruta graveolens*, p. 304).

Heraclides aristodemus (formerly *Papilio aristodemus*)
Schaus' Swallowtail

Photo, p. 165

Description: To 2.0" in length. Head dark brown; body dark brown above, mottled with golden brown, with white patches on the posterior end and along the sides, and rows of blue spots. The osmeterium is white.

Similar Species: The Giant Swallowtail and Bahamian Swallowtail also use Sea Torchwood and Wild Lime.

Habitat: Uplands. Tropical hardwood hammocks.

U.S. Distribution: Upper Florida Keys.

Natural History: This very rare swallowtail has only one generation per year. The pale green eggs are laid singly on the very young leaves of the host plants. The caterpillars eat the young growth and may move to other shoots to complete their development. When not feeding, they tend to rest on the branches. Young caterpillars are black with a white posterior and resemble lizard droppings. The Schaus' Swallowtail is an endangered species protected by state and federal law. The pupae overwinter.

Caterpillar Season: Mid-May to late June.

Host Plants: Trees in the Citrus family (Rutaceae) including Sea Torchwood (*Amyris elemifera*, p. 302) and Balsam Torchwood (*Amyris balsamifera*); also eats Wild Lime (*Zanthoxylum fagara*, p. 305) in captivity.

Heraclides andraemon (formerly *Papilio andraemon*)
Bahamian Swallowtail

Photo, p. 165

Description: To 1.8" in length. Head dark brown; body brown with a short whitish patch in the middle and a white posterior; thorax enlarged, prothorax white on top with small earlike points. The osmeterium is white. Young caterpillars are black with a white posterior and resemble lizard droppings.

Similar Species: The Giant Swallowtail and Schaus' Swallowtail also use Sea Torchwood and Wild Lime.

Habitat: Uplands. Tropical hardwood hammocks.

U.S. Distribution: Upper Florida Keys.

Natural History: This very rare swallowtail has up to three generations per year. Females lay the pale green eggs singly on the young leaves of the host plants. The caterpillars eat the new growth first. Larger larvae often rest on the lower branches when not feeding. The pupae overwinter.

Caterpillar Season: Mid-May through early November.

Host Plants: Trees in the Citrus family (Rutaceae) including Sea Torchwood (*Amyris elemifera*, p. 302), Wild Lime (*Zanthoxylum fagara*, p. 305), and sometimes the exotic Key Lime (*Citrus aurantifolia*).

Papilio polyxenes
Black Swallowtail

Photo, p. 165

Description: To 1.8" in length. Head pale green with black stripes; body green with black bands interspersed with yellow spots. The width of the black bands varies and, occasionally, individuals may be nearly all black with yellow spots. There is an interesting false face pattern on the posterior end (p. 19). The osmeterium is orange (p. 20). Young larvae are black with a white middle and look like bird droppings (p. 27).

Similar Species: None.

Habitat: Uplands and wetlands. Wet prairies, flatwoods, pine savannas, roadsides, weedy disturbed sites, and gardens.

U.S. Distribution: Florida westward to eastern Arizona and northward into Colorado, North Dakota, Michigan, New York, and Maine.

Natural History: This common swallowtail occurs throughout Florida. At least three generations are produced per year. The greenish white eggs are laid singly on the leaves and flowers of the hosts. The caterpillars eat leaves, but prefer flowers and immature seeds. Small plants may be defoliated by the voracious larvae. The pupae overwinter.

Caterpillar Season: February through early November.

Host Plants: Herbs in the Carrot family (Apiaceae) including Spotted Water Hemlock (*Cicuta maculata*, p. 243), Water Cowbane (*Oxypolis filiformis*, p. 244), Mock Bishopsweed (*Ptilimnium capillaceum*, p. 245), Roughfruit Scaleseed (*Spermolepis divaricata*, p. 245), Wedgeleaf Eryngo (*Eryngium cuneifolium*), and the exotic Queen Anne's Lace (*Daucus carota*), Sweet Fennel (*Foeniculum vulgare*, p. 245), and Parsley (*Petroselinum crispum*). Spotted Water Hemlock and other wild members of this group are extremely poisonous to humans if consumed.

Pterourus glaucus (formerly *Papilio glaucus*)
Eastern Tiger Swallowtail

Photo, p. 163

Description: To 2.5" in length. Head pale brown; body green with rows of blue spots, and a yellow and black transverse stripe between the first and second abdominal segments that is usually hidden from view; thorax enlarged and bearing a pair of small eyespots. The osmeterium is orange. Young caterpillars are dark brown with a white middle and resemble bird droppings.

Similar Species: None.

Habitat: Uplands and wetlands. Hammocks, flatwoods, and swamps.

U.S. Distribution: Florida westward to western Texas and northward into South Dakota, Minnesota, Wisconsin, Michigan, New York, and Maine.

Natural History: This familiar swallowtail occurs commonly in northern and central Florida, but is very local in the southern part of the state. At least three generations are produced per year. Females lay dark green eggs singly on uppersides of mature leaves near the tip. The caterpillar eats leaves and rests in a silk-lined curled leaf. When disturbed, the body is enlarged, displaying the black and yellow transverse stripe on the back. The eyespots and osmeterium give the caterpillar the appearance of a small green snake. When ready to pupate, the caterpillar turns from green to brown and wanders away from the host plant. The pupae overwinter.

Caterpillar Season: February through early November.

Host Plants: Trees including Tuliptree (*Liriodendron tulipifera*, p. 291) and Sweetbay (*Magnolia virginiana*, p. 292) in the Magnolia family (Magnoliaceae), White Ash (*Fraxinus americana*), Carolina Ash (*Fraxinus caroliniana*), and Green Ash (*Fraxinus pennsylvanica*, p. 296) in the Olive family (Oleaceae), and Black Cherry (*Prunus serotina*, p. 301) in the Rose family (Rosaceae). All of these hosts may be used in northern Florida, but only Sweetbay is eaten in the central and southern parts of the state.

Pterourus palamedes (formerly *Papilio palamedes*)

Palamedes Swallowtail

Photo, p. 163

Description: To 2.4" in length. Head pale brown; body green above, pinkish brown below, a narrow yellow line on the sides, and rows of blue spots; a pair of orange spots on the first abdominal segment, each with a blue spot adjacent to the leading edge; thorax enlarged and bearing a pair of large eyespots, prothorax yellow and black on top. The osmeterium is bright yellow (p. 21). Young larvae are brown with a white middle and have a pair of eyespots on the thorax. They differ from the Spicebush Swallowtail in having an all-white posterior end.

Similar Species: The Spicebush Swallowtail also uses bay trees.

Habitat: Uplands and wetlands. Hammocks, flatwoods, and swamps.

U.S. Distribution: Florida westward to eastern Texas and northward along the Atlantic coast to southeastern Virginia.

Natural History: This common swallowtail occurs throughout the state, except for the Florida Keys. At least three generations are produced each year. The pale green eggs are laid singly on the young leaves of the hosts. The caterpillars eat the new growth first, and do not make nests. Larger larvae rest on the twigs and branches of the host. Upon reaching maturity, the caterpillars change color from green to pale yellow and usually wander away from the host plant to pupate. The pupae overwinter.

Caterpillar Season: February through early November.

Host Plants: Trees in the Laurel family (Lauraceae) including Red Bay (*Persea borbonia* var. *borbonia*, p. 290), Silk Bay (*Persea borbonia* var. *humilis*), and Swamp Bay (*Persea palustris*).

Pterourus troilus (formerly *Papilio troilus*)

Spicebush Swallowtail

Photo, p. 163

Description: To 2.2" in length. Head pale brown; body green above, pinkish brown below with a broad yellow line on the sides and rows of unequal-sized blue spots; a pair of orange spots on the first abdominal segment, each with a blue spot within; thorax enlarged and bearing a pair of large eyespots, prothorax yellow and black on top. The osmeterium is bright yellow. The young caterpillars closely resemble those of the Palamedes Swallowtail, but have a dark patch on the posterior end.

Similar Species: The Palamedes Swallowtail also uses bay trees.

Habitat: Uplands and wetlands. Hammocks, flatwoods, and swamps.

U.S. Distribution: Florida westward to eastern Texas and northward into Iowa, Wisconsin, Michigan, New York, and southern Maine.

Natural History: This swallowtail occurs commonly in northern and central Florida, but is more local in southern parts of the state. At least three generations are produced per year. Females lay pale green eggs singly on the young leaves. The caterpillar eats the new growth first and hides in a nest when not feeding. The young caterpillar makes a nest near the tip of a leaf by eating a channel from the edge of the blade to the midrib, folding over the flap, and tying it down with silk (p. 15). Older caterpillars live in curled, mature leaves. The larva applies silk across the surface of a leaf to make the nest. As the silk dries, it contracts, causing the leaf to curl. When disturbed, the caterpillars enlarge the body and display the osmeterium. They resemble the heads of green snakes or tree frogs. The pupae overwinter. The life stages of the Spicebush Swallowtail are shown on p. 28.

Caterpillar Season: February through early November.

Host Plants: Trees in the Laurel family including Northern Spicebush (*Lindera benzoin*), Pondspice (*Litsea aestivalis*), Red Bay (*Persea borbonia* var. *borbonia*, p. 290), Silk Bay (*Persea borbonia* var. *humilis*), Swamp Bay (*Persea palustris*), Sassafras (*Sassafras albidum*, p. 291), and the exotic Camphortree (*Cinnamomum camphora*).

Whites, Orangetips, and Sulphurs (family Pieridae)

Whites, Orangetips, and Sulphurs have slender caterpillars with numerous short hairs. The caterpillars of Whites are variable, being either uniformly green, or gray with yellowish stripes and small shiny black spots. The Falcate Orangetip has a characteristic broad white stripe on the sides. The caterpillars of these groups eat mostly plants in the Mustard family, but a few also eat species in the Saltwort and Spurge families. Sulphur larvae are usually green with a narrow yellowish or white stripe along the sides, and sometimes have very short black or blue spines on the body. Sulphurs eat plants mostly in the Pea family, but some species also use plants in the Aster, Caltrop, and Carpetweed families.

Whites (subfamily Pierinae)

Appias drusilla
Florida White

Photo, p. 169

Description: To 1.5" in length. Head and body bluish green with scattered blue dots and small yellow tubercles; posterior end with a pair of short tails.
Similar Species: None.
Habitat: Uplands. Tropical hardwood hammocks.
U.S. Distribution: Southern Florida and southern Texas.
Natural History: This species is sometimes locally common in southern Miami-Dade County and the Florida Keys, but is generally uncommon elsewhere in the state. At least three generations are produced each year. The slender, whitish eggs are laid singly on the new growth of the host plants. The caterpillars eat the young leaves first. They feed mostly at night and rest on leaf petioles during the daytime. When provoked, they spit a bitter-tasting greenish fluid.
Caterpillar Season: Throughout the year.
Host Plants: A shrub in the Mustard family (Brassicaceae), Bayleaf Capertree (*Capparis flexuosa*, p. 259), and trees in the Spurge family (Euphorbiaceae), Whitewood (*Drypetes diversifolia*), and Guiana Plum (*Drypetes lateriflora*, p. 264).

Pontia protodice
Checkered White

Photo, p. 167

Description: To 1.1" in length. Head gray with yellow patches; body gray with yellow stripes, rows of small black spots, and short hairs; posterior end with short tails.
Similar Species: The Great Southern White also uses Virginia Pepperweed.
Habitat: Uplands. Roadsides, citrus groves, weed lots, and other disturbed sites.

U.S. Distribution: All states except Maine, Vermont, New Hampshire, Alaska, Hawaii; scarce in Oregon and Washington.

Natural History: This species is often common in northern and central Florida, but is more local in southern parts of the state. Three or more generations are produced per year. The slender, orange colored eggs are laid singly, usually on the flowers. The caterpillars eat leaves, but prefer flowers and immature fruit. The pupae overwinter. The life stages of the Checkered White are shown on p. 29.

Caterpillar Season: February through early November.

Host Plants: Herbs in the Mustard family (Brassicaceae), mostly Virginia Pepperweed (*Lepidium virginicum*, p. 260), but probably also eats the exotic Shepherd's Purse (*Capsella bursa-pastoris*).

Pieris rapae

Cabbage White

Photo, p. 167

Description: To 1.2" in length. Head and body green with numerous tiny blue dots, a pale yellow line down the back, and a broken yellow line on the sides. The body is covered with fine white hairs.

Similar Species: None.

Habitat: Uplands. Agricultural fields, gardens, weed lots, and other disturbed sites.

U.S. Distribution: All states except Hawaii.

Natural History: The Cabbage White was accidentally introduced into North America from Europe during the late 1800s and is a pest of cultivated mustards. This species is locally common in northern and central Florida. Three or more generations are produced each year. The slender, pale yellow eggs are laid singly on the leaves and flower buds of the hosts. The caterpillars hide under the leaves, and may bore into the heads of cabbage. The pupae overwinter.

Caterpillar Season: February through November.

Host Plants: Herbs in the Mustard family (Brassicaceae) including the exotic India Mustard (*Brassica juncea*), Abyssinian Mustard (*Brassica nigra*, p. 258), Cabbage (*Brassica oleracea*), Turnip (*Brassica rapa*), Wild Radish (*Raphanus raphanistrum*), Garden Radish (*Raphanus sativus*), and occasionally the native Virginia Pepperweed (*Lepidium virginicum*, p. 260).

Ascia monuste

Great Southern White

Photo, p. 167

Description: To 1.5" in length. Head yellowish brown with small back spots and short hairs; body gray with yellow stripes, rows of shiny black plates, small black spots, and short hairs; posterior end with short tails.

Habitat: Uplands and wetlands. Found inland in citrus groves and weedy areas, but typically in salt marshes and open coastal uplands.

Similar Species: The Checkered White also uses Virginia Pepperweed.

U.S. Distribution: Peninsular Florida and southern Texas. Occasionally found in coastal Georgia and South Carolina.

Natural History: This white occurs abundantly in coastal areas, sometimes dispersing northward by the millions. It also occurs inland, but is more local. At least three generations are produced per year. The slender, pale yellow eggs are laid singly or in small groups. The young caterpillars may feed together, but become more solitary as they mature.

Caterpillar Season: Throughout the year in southern Florida.

Host Plants: Herbs including Saltwort (*Batis maritima*, p. 257) in the Saltwort family (Bataceae), Coastal Searocket (*Cakile lanceolata*), Pennsylvania Bittercress (*Cardamine pensylvanica*), Virginia Pepperweed (*Lepidium virginicum*, p. 260), occasionally Bayleaf Capertree (*Capparis flexuosa*, p. 259), and the exotic species Arugula (*Eruca vesicaria*), India Mustard (*Brassica juncea*), Abyssinian Mustard (*Brassica nigra*, p. 258) in the Mustard family (Brassicaceae), and Nasturtium (*Tropaeolum majus*) in the Nasturtium family (Tropaeolaceae).

Orangetips (subfamily Anthocharinae)

Paramidea midea (formerly *Anthocharis midea*)

Falcate Orangetip

Photo, p. 165

Description: To 0.8" in length. Head gray and white; body slender, yellowish green with a broad white stripe on the sides, a narrow orange stripe on the back, and numerous short black hairs arising from thick shiny bases.

Similar Species: None.

Habitat: Wetlands. Margins of swamps along streams and rivers.

U.S. Distribution: Florida Panhandle westward to eastern Texas and northward into Missouri, Illinois, Indiana, Ohio, Pennsylvania, and New Jersey.

Natural History: This extremely rare butterfly occurs sporadically in the Apalachicola River basin of the Florida Panhandle. There is only one generation per year. Females lay slender, orange colored eggs singly on the flower buds of the host. The caterpillars prefer to eat flower buds and immature fruit. The pupae overwinter.

Caterpillar Season: March and early April.

Host Plants: Probably Bulbous Bittercress (*Cardamine bulbosa*, p. 259), an herb in the Mustard family (Brassicaceae).

Sulphurs (subfamily Coliadinae)

Colias eurytheme
Orange Sulphur

Photo, p. 169

Description: To 1.3" in length. Head green; body green with a faint yellow stripe on the back, a white and pink or white and red stripe on the sides, sometimes with a broken black line lower on the sides, and numerous short hairs.

Similar Species: The Southern Dogface occasionally uses clover.

Habitat: Uplands. Pastures, roadsides, lawns, and open disturbed sites.

U.S. Distribution: All states except Alaska and Hawaii.

Natural History: This sulphur occurs throughout the state and is sometimes locally common, but the colonies are often ephemeral. At least three generations are produced per year in Florida. The slender, yellow eggs are laid singly on the leaves of the hosts. Hatchlings eat holes in the leaves while older larvae feed from the edges of the blades. Partly grown larvae overwinter.

Caterpillar Season: Throughout the year.

Host Plants: Herbs in the Pea family (Fabaceae) including the exotic species White Sweetclover (*Melilotus albus*, p. 279), White Clover (*Trifolium repens*, p. 286), Black Medick (*Medicago lupulina*, p. 279), and Alfalfa (*Medicago sativa*).

Zerene cesonia (formerly *Colias cesonia*)
Southern Dogface

Photo, p. 169

Description: To 1.3" in length. Head green; body color variable, typically green with a white or yellow stripe containing orange spots on the sides, with or without yellow and/or black transverse bands, and short hairs.

Similar Species: The Orange Sulphur also uses clover.

Habitat: Uplands. Scrubs, sandhills, and dry flatwoods.

U.S. Distribution: Florida westward to California and northward into Nevada, Colorado, Nebraska, Iowa, Illinois, Indiana, Ohio, and North Carolina.

Natural History: This sulphur is locally common in northern and central Florida, and infrequent in southern parts of the state. At least two generations are produced per year. The slender, yellow eggs are laid on the new growth of the hosts. The caterpillars eat young leaves.

Caterpillar Season: March to November.

Host Plants: Herbs and shrubs in the Pea family (Fabaceae) including Bastard Indigobush (*Amorpha fruticosa*, p. 266), Feay's Prairieclover (*Dalea feayi*, p. 272), Summer Farewell (*Dalea pinnata*, p. 273), and occasionally the exotic White Clover (*Trifolium repens*, p. 286).

Phoebis sennae

Cloudless Sulphur

Photo, p. 171

Description: To 1.5" in length. Color variable, typically green with a yellow stripe and blue patches on the sides, and numerous small dark spines arranged in transverse bands or yellow with black transverse bands and less conspicuous dark spines.

Similar Species: The Orange-barred Sulphur and Sleepy Orange also use sennas.

Habitat: Uplands. Found in many different habitats, but breeds mostly in disturbed areas such as roadsides, agricultural fields, weed lots, and gardens.

U.S. Distribution: Florida westward to California and strays northward into Nevada, Colorado, Nebraska, Iowa, Illinois, Indiana, and New Jersey.

Natural History: This sulphur migrates southward into Florida by the millions during late summer and fall. It occurs throughout the state and has three or more generations per year. The slender, yellow eggs are laid singly on the new growth of the hosts. The caterpillars feed on the young leaves and flowers. Small larvae often eat holes in the leaves, while older larvae feed from the edges. Larvae that eat mostly flowers become yellow. Eggs and young caterpillars may be eaten by ants attracted by nectar glands on the leaf petioles. The life stages of the Cloudless Sulphur are shown on p. 30.

Caterpillar Season: Throughout the year.

Host Plants: Herbs, shrubs, and trees in the Pea family (Fabaceae) including Partridge Pea (*Chamaecrista fasciculata*, p. 270), Sensitive Pea (*Chamaecrista nictitans*, p. 270), Privet Wild Sensitive Plant (*Senna ligustrina*), Maryland Wild Sensitive Plant (*Senna marilandica*), Chapman's Wild Sensitive Plant (*Senna mexicana* var. *chapmanii*, p. 282), and the exotic Candlestick Plant (*Senna alata*, p. 282), Africa Wild Sensitive Plant (*Senna didymobotrya*), Coffeeweed (*Senna obtusifolia*, p. 283), Septicweed (*Senna occidentalis*, p. 283), Valamuerto (*Senna pendula*), and Glossy Shower (*Senna surattensis*).

Phoebis philea

Orange-barred Sulphur

Photo, p. 171

Description: To 2.0" in length. Body typically olive green tinged with yellow, a chainlike band of triangular black spots on the sides, and many short black spines, or yellow with black patches on the sides.

Similar Species: The Cloudless Sulphur and Sleepy Orange also use sennas.

Habitat: Uplands. Mostly in urban areas and gardens.

U.S. Distribution: Peninsular Florida and occasionally southern Texas.

Natural History: This large sulphur is locally common near patches of the host plants throughout peninsular Florida. Three or more generations are produced each year. The slender, yellow eggs are laid singly on the new growth of the hosts. Caterpillars that eat leaves are green, while those that feed on the flowers become yellow. Eggs and young caterpillars may be eaten by ants attracted by nectar glands on the leaf petioles.

Caterpillar Season: Throughout the year.

Host Plants: Shrubs and trees in the Pea family (Fabaceae) including Chapman's Wild Sensitive Plant (*Senna mexicana* var. *chapmanii*, p. 282), as well as the exotic species Candlestick Plant (*Senna alata*, p. 282), Golden Shower (*Cassia fistula*), Africa Wild Sensitive Plant (*Senna didymobotrya*), Valamuerto (*Senna pendula*), and Glossy Shower (*Senna surattensis*).

Phoebis agarithe

Large Orange Sulphur

Photo, p. 171

Description: To 1.5" in length. Head green; body green with a pale yellow line along the sides. Some individuals also have numerous blue spots.

Similar Species: The Mimosa Yellow also uses False Tamarind.

Habitat: Uplands. Tropical hardwood hammocks.

U.S. Distribution: Central and southern Florida and southern Texas.

Natural History: This sulphur occurs commonly in coastal areas of southern Florida. At least three generations are produced per year. Females lay slender, whitish eggs on the new growth of the hosts. The caterpillars eat young leaves and are difficult to raise on cut food in captivity.

Caterpillar Season: Throughout the year.

Host Plants: Trees in the Pea family (Fabaceae) including False Tamarind (*Lysiloma latisiliquum*, p. 278), Florida Keys Blackbead (*Pithecellobium keyense*, p. 281), and Catclaw Blackbead (*Pithecellobium unguis-cati*).

Aphrissa statira (formerly *Phoebis statira*)

Statira Sulphur

Photo, p. 171

Description: To 1.5" in length. Head green with tiny blue dots; body green with blue dots, a pale yellow line on the sides, and very short hairs.

Similar Species: None.

Habitat: Uplands and wetlands. Coastal uplands and the margins of mangroves.

U.S. Distribution: Central and southern Florida and southern Texas.

Natural History: This sulphur is sometimes locally common around patches of the larval plant in coastal areas, but is usually infrequent and rarely strays inland. Three or more generations are produced per year. The slender, whitish eggs are laid on the new growth of the host. The caterpillars eat young leaves and are difficult to raise in captivity on cut food.

Caterpillar Season: Throughout the year.
Host Plants: Coinvine (*Dalbergia ecastaphyllum*, p. 272), a sprawling shrub in the Pea family (Fabaceae).

Kricogonia lyside
Lyside Sulphur
Photo, p. 165

Description: To 1.0" in length. Head green; body dark green with a white line on the back, a brown and white line on the sides, and very short hairs.
Similar Species: None.
Habitat: Uplands. Margins of tropical hardwood hammocks.
U.S. Distribution: Southern Texas and perhaps a temporary breeder in the Florida Keys.
Natural History: This rare species is only sporadically present in southern Florida, but is occasionally locally frequent. The caterpillars reportedly feed at night and hide on the branches or under bark during the daytime.
Caterpillar Season: Unknown.
Host Plants: Eats Holywood Lignumvitae (*Guajacum sanctum*, p. 312) in the Caribbean region. This shrub or small tree in the Caltrop family (Zygophyllaceae) occurs naturally in the Keys and is often used in landscaping in southern Florida.

Eurema daira
Barred Yellow
Photo, p. 167

Description: To 0.9" in length. Head green; body slender, green with a narrow whitish stripe on the sides, and short hairs.
Similar Species: None.
Habitat: Uplands. Scrubs, sandhills, flatwoods, margins of hammocks, roadsides, and open weedy areas.
U.S. Distribution: Florida westward to Louisiana and northward along the Atlantic coast into South Carolina. Occasionally seen in southern Texas and Arizona.
Natural History: This abundant sulphur occurs throughout Florida, and the adults are somewhat migratory in late summer and fall. At least three generations are produced each year. The slender, whitish eggs are laid singly on the new growth of the hosts. The caterpillars eat the young leaves.
Caterpillar Season: February through early November.
Host Plants: Herbs in the Pea family (Fabaceae) including Shyleaf (*Aeschynomene americana*, p. 266), Sticky Jointvetch (*Aeschynomene viscidula*), Sidebeak Pencilflower (*Stylosanthes biflora*, p. 284), Cheesytoes (*Stylosanthes hamata*, p.

285), Fourleaf Vetch (*Vicia acutifolia*), and occasionally the exotic Hairy Indigo (*Indigofera hirsuta*).

Eurema lisa
Little Yellow
Photo, p. 167

Description: To 0.9" in length. Head green; body slender, green with a narrow whitish line on the sides, faint darker lines on the back, and short hairs.
Similar Species: The Cloudless Sulphur also uses Partridge Pea.
Habitat: Uplands. Scrubs, sandhills, and flatwoods.
U.S. Distribution: Florida westward to western Texas; strays northward into Minnesota, Wisconsin, Michigan, and southern New York.
Natural History: This small sulphur is locally common throughout Florida. Adults in southern Florida sometimes disperse northward along the coasts in large numbers during late summer and fall. At least three generations are produced each year. The slender, whitish eggs are laid on the new growth of the hosts. The caterpillars eat young leaves.
Caterpillar Season: February through early November.
Host Plants: Herbs in the Pea family (Fabaceae) including Partridge Pea (*Chamaecrista fasciculata*, p. 270), Sensitive Pea (*Chamaecrista nictitans*, p. 270), and Powderpuff (*Mimosa strigillosa*, p. 280).

Eurema nise
Mimosa Yellow
Photo, p. 169

Description: To 0.8" in length. Head green; body slender, whitish green with a narrow whitish line on the sides, and short hairs.
Similar Species: The Large Orange Sulphur also uses False Tamarind.
Habitat: Uplands. Margins of tropical hardwood hammocks.
U.S. Distribution: Southern Florida, southern Texas, and occasionally southern Arizona.
Natural History: This rare species occurs sporadically in Florida, but is sometimes locally common. Females have been observed laying eggs on seedling False Tamarinds in the Homestead area of Miami-Dade County. The slender, whitish eggs are laid on the new growth. The caterpillars eat young leaves.
Caterpillar Season: Throughout the year.
Host Plants: False Tamarind (*Lysiloma latisiliquum*, p. 278), a tree in the Pea family (Fabaceae).

Eurema dina

Dina Yellow

Photo, p. 169

Description: To 1.0" in length. Head bluish green; body slender, bluish green with a narrow whitish stripe on the sides, and short hairs.
Similar Species: None.
Habitat: Uplands. Margins of tropical hardwood hammocks.
U.S. Distribution: Southeastern Florida and occasionally southern Texas and Arizona.
Natural History: This sulphur is locally common at just a few parks in southern Miami-Dade County, and is rarely seen elsewhere in Florida. There are at least three generations per year. The slender whitish eggs are laid on the new growth of the hosts. The caterpillars eat young leaves.
Caterpillar Season: Throughout the year.
Host Plants: Shrubs and trees in the Bitterbush family (Picramniaceae) including Mexican Alvaradoa (*Alvaradoa amorphoides*, p. 299) and Florida Bitterbush (*Picramnia pentandra*, p. 299).

Eurema nicippe

Sleepy Orange

Photo, p. 169

Description: To 1.0" in length. Head green; body slender, green with a narrow whitish stripe on the sides, and short hairs. Some of the hairs are enlarged at the tip and produce droplets of bitter tasting liquid.
Similar Species: The Cloudless Sulphur and Orange-barred Sulphur also use sennas.
Habitat: Uplands. Disturbed sites, especially agricultural fields, roadsides, and weed lots.
U.S. Distribution: Florida westward to southern California; strays northward into Nevada, Colorado, Nebraska, Missouri, Illinois, Indiana, Ohio, Pennsylvania, and New Jersey.
Natural History: This common sulphur occurs throughout the state, and is somewhat migratory during late summer and fall. At least three generations are produced each year. The slender, whitish eggs are laid on the new growth of the hosts. The caterpillars prefer to eat young leaves. Eggs and small caterpillars may be eaten by ants attracted by nectar glands on the leaf petioles.
Caterpillar Season: February through early November.
Host Plants: Shrubs in the Pea family (Fabaceae) including the exotic Coffeeweed (*Senna obtusifolia*, p. 283), Septicweed (*Senna occidentalis*, p. 283), and Valamuerto (*Senna pendula*).

Nathalis iole

Dainty Sulphur

Photo, p. 167

Description: To 0.6" in length. Head green; body slender, green, with a purple stripe on the sides and back, and short hairs; front of thorax with two short purplish projections. The purple stripes vary in width among individuals.
Similar Species: None.
Habitat: Uplands. Roadsides, weed lots, canal banks, and other disturbed sites.
U.S. Distribution: Florida westward to southern California; strays northward into Nevada, Utah, Colorado, Nebraska, Missouri, Illinois, and Indiana.
Natural History: This very small sulphur is common in southern Florida, but is more local northward. There are at least three generations per year. Females prefer to lay their slender, yellow eggs on seedlings or very small host plants. The caterpillars feed on young leaves and often rest on the stems. Their coloration perfectly matches the green and purple of the Beggarticks stems.
Caterpillar Season: Throughout the year.
Host Plants: Herbs including Beggarticks (*Bidens alba*, p. 254) in the Aster family (Asteraceae) and occasionally the exotic species Indian Chickweed (*Mollugo verticillata*) in the Carpetweed family (Molluginaceae).

Harvesters, Hairstreaks, and Blues (family Lycaenidae)

The lycaenids have small to tiny sluglike larvae that are covered with short hairs. The head is retracted into the prothorax. Although many hairstreaks and blues have distinctive caterpillars, others are very similar. Adding to the confusion, the color of individual larvae varies from green to red in some species, such as Henry's Elfin, White M Hairstreak, Gray Hairstreak, Mallow Scrub-Hairstreak, Cassius Blue, Nickerbean Blue, Ceraunus Blue, and the Eastern Tailed-Blue. Some species attract ants to help protect them. The caterpillars of hairstreaks and blues eat young leaves, flower buds, and the developing fruit and seeds of plants in the Bayberry, Bay Cedar, Beech, Buckthorn, Buckwheat, Cashew, Cedar, Hackberry, Heath, Holly, Mallow, Mistletoe, Pea, Pine, Soapberry, Spurge, Sweetleaf, Walnut, and Zamia families. The Harvester is unusual in that the caterpillar eats woolly aphids.

Harvesters (subfamily Miletinae)

Feniseca tarquinius
Harvester
Photo, p. 171

Description: To 0.8" in length. Body slug-shaped with short hairs; color varies from pink with no markings to shades of gray with white and brown, pink, or red streaks. The body is often coated with white wax from the host aphids.
Similar Species: None.
Habitat: Uplands and wetlands. Hammocks and the margins of streams and rivers.
U.S. Distribution: Florida westward to eastern Texas and northward into Minnesota, Wisconsin, Michigan, New York, and Maine.
Natural History: This uncommon species occurs in northern and central Florida. At least three generations are produced per year. The flat, whitish eggs are laid singly on leaves near colonies of woolly aphids. Because the Harvester caterpillar is carnivorous, development proceeds very rapidly, and the larval stage is completed in as little as eight days. Some Harvester caterpillars cover themselves with the remains of woolly aphids they have eaten. The carcasses are tied on with silk, perhaps to protect the caterpillars from ants, which tend and protect the aphids, and other natural enemies. Probably overwinters as a larva. The life stages of the Harvester are shown on p. 31.
Caterpillar Season: February through early November.
Hosts: Carnivorous on Woolly Maple Aphids (*Neoprociphilus aceris*) that suck sap from Earleaf Greenbrier (*Smilax auriculata*), Saw Greenbrier (*Smilax bonanox*), Cat Greenbrier (*Smilax glauca*), and Bristly Greenbrier (*Smilax tamnoides*, p. 236) in the Smilax family (Smilacaceae) as well as Woolly Alder Aphids (*Pro-*

ciphilus tesselatus) that feed on Hazel Alder (*Alnus serrulata*, p. 258) in the Birch family (Betulaceae).

Hairstreaks (subfamily Theclinae)

Eumaeus atala
Atala

Photo, p. 171

Description: To 1.0" in length. Body slug-shaped with short hairs, somewhat bumpy on top, bright red with two rows of yellow spots on the back.
Similar Species: None.
Habitat: Uplands. Tropical hardwood hammocks, pine rocklands, and gardens.
U.S. Distribution: Southeastern Florida.
Natural History: This beautiful hairstreak is locally common in coastal areas of Palm Beach, Broward, and Miami-Dade counties, but is rarely seen elsewhere in the state. There are three or more generations per year in Florida. The flat, whitish eggs are laid in clusters on the new growth of the host plant. The caterpillars feed on the young leaves and when mature often pupate together. The caterpillars store toxins from their Coontie hosts, and their bright coloration is a warning to potential predators that they are distasteful or poisonous. This butterfly declined in abundance during the last century, probably due to urban development and the harvesting of Coontie plants for the starch industry. By the late 1960s, the Atala was thought to be extinct in Florida. However, after one small colony was discovered near Miami, gardeners began propagating both the plant and the butterfly. Coontie is now a popular landscape plant, and the Atala has made a remarkable comeback. It is sometimes considered a pest by nurseries and botanic gardens.
Caterpillar Season: Throughout the year.
Host Plants: Coontie (*Zamia pumila*, p. 220), a small shrub in the Zamia family (Zamiaceae).

Atlides halesus
Great Purple Hairstreak

Photo, p. 173

Description: To 0.9" in length. Body slug-shaped, velvety, green with a small whitish shield on the thorax.
Similar Species: The White M Hairstreak and Oak Hairstreak are somewhat similar.
Habitat: Uplands and wetlands. Hammocks and swamps.
U.S. Distribution: Florida westward to California and northward into Nevada, Utah, Colorado, Oklahoma, Arkansas, Tennessee, and Virginia.

Natural History: This common hairstreak occurs in northern and central Florida. At least three generations are produced each year. Females lay flat, whitish eggs singly or in small groups on the leaves of the host. The larvae blend in very well with the plant and are very hard to find. Mature caterpillars wander away from the host plant to pupate under loose bark or in crevices. The pupae overwinter and make squeaking noises when handled.

Caterpillar Season: February through early November.

Host Plants: Oak Mistletoe (*Phoradendron leucarpum*, p. 312) in the family Viscaceae, a parasite of hardwood trees.

Chlorostrymon maesites
Amethyst Hairstreak

Not Shown

Description: To 0.5" in length. Body slug-shaped, green with paler chevrons on the back.

Similar Species: The Cassius Blue also eats leguminous trees.

Habitat: Uplands. The margins of tropical hardwood hammocks.

U.S. Distribution: The Florida Keys.

Natural History: This extremely rare hairstreak probably has three or more generations per year in Florida. It has recently been observed at Bahia Honda State Park. Little is known of its habits, but the caterpillars feed on the flowers and immature fruit of leguminous trees.

Caterpillar Season: Throughout the year.

Host Plants: Probably trees in the Pea family (Fabaceae).

Chlorostrymon simaethis
Silver-banded Hairstreak

Photo, p. 177

Description: To 0.6" in length. Head light brown; body slug-shaped, velvety, somewhat bumpy on top, light green with faint dark stripes.

Similar Species: The Miami Blue and occasionally the Gray Hairstreak also use Heartseed.

Habitat: Uplands. The margins of tropical hardwood hammocks.

U.S. Distribution: Southern Florida, southern Texas, and occasionally southern California and Arizona.

Natural History: This hairstreak is closely associated with the larval host plants, and is very local and uncommon in southern Florida. At least three generations are produced each year. The eggs are laid singly near the base of the developing fruit. Newly hatched larvae bore into the seedpods of their hosts and eat the immature, green seeds. Pods containing caterpillars may be recognized by the presence of the frass pellets that are visible through the thin walls of the pods. Pods containing caterpillars also have a tendency to drop from the plant.

Therefore, those that have fallen to the ground or those that fall when the plant is shaken are likely to contain caterpillars or show feeding damage. We have sometimes found the larvae tended by the exotic ant *Tapinoma melanocephalum*.

Caterpillar Season: Throughout the year.

Host Plants: Vines in the Soapberry family (Sapindaceae) including Heartseed (*Cardiospermum corindum*, p. 306), Small-fruited Balloonvine (*Cardiospermum microcarpum*), and probably the rare exotic species Love-In-A-Puff (*Cardiospermum halicacabum*).

Harkenclenus titus (formerly *Satyrium titus*)

Coral Hairstreak

Photo, p. 173

Description: To 0.8" in length. Head black; body slug- shaped with short hairs, green, the posterior and top of thorax purplish red.

Similar Species: None.

Habitat: Uplands. Sandhills and the margins of hammocks.

U.S. Distribution: Florida Panhandle westward to northern California and northward into Washington, Montana, North Dakota, Minnesota, Michigan, and Maine.

Natural History: This hairstreak is very rare and local in northern Florida. There is a single generation per year in early summer. The flat, whitish eggs are laid singly or in small groups on the twigs of the host. They hatch in the spring, when the leaves are young and tender and the flowers are produced. The caterpillars may rest at the base of the host tree during the daytime and climb the stems to feed on leaves and fruit at night. They are sometimes tended by ants. The larvae blend in very well with the plant and are very hard to find.

Caterpillar Season: March and April.

Host Plants: Black Cherry (*Prunus serotina*, p. 301) and Wild Plum (*Prunus* species), trees in the Rose family (Rosaceae).

Satyrium calanus

Banded Hairstreak

Photo, p. 175

Description: To 0.8" in length. Head light brown; body slug-shaped with short hairs, color variable, green or brownish, often with dark brown patches on top of the thorax and posterior, and faint dark lines on the sides.

Similar Species: The Oak Hairstreak and White M Hairstreak also eat oaks.

Habitat: Uplands. Scrubs, sandhills, and hammocks.

U.S. Distribution: Florida westward to eastern Texas and northward into North Dakota, Minnesota, Michigan, New York, and Maine. Also in western Colorado and northern New Mexico.

Natural History: This hairstreak is very local and generally uncommon in northern and central Florida. Only one generation is produced per year in late spring. The flat, brown eggs are laid singly or in small groups on the twigs of the host tree. The caterpillars eat very young leaves and flowers. The larvae often hide in curled leaves when not feeding. They blend in very well with the plant and are very hard to find. The eggs overwinter.

Caterpillar Season: February and March.

Host Plants: Trees in the Walnut family (Juglandaceae) including Mockernut Hickory (*Carya alba*), Scrub Hickory (*Carya floridana*), and Pignut Hickory (*Carya glabra*, p. 290), and sometimes Turkey Oak (*Quercus laevis*, p. 287) in the Beech family (Fagaceae).

Satyrium kingi

King's Hairstreak

Photo, p. 175

Description: To 0.8" in length. Head light brown; body slug-shaped with short hairs, green with faint stripes.

Similar Species: None.

Habitat: Uplands. Overgrown sandhills and dry hammocks.

U.S. Distribution: Florida Panhandle westward into eastern Texas and northward into southeastern Maryland.

Natural History: This hairstreak is very local and uncommon in northern Florida. Only one generation is produced per year in early summer. Females lay flat, brownish eggs singly or in small groups on the twigs of the host. The caterpillars feed on young leaves and buds. They blend in very well with the plant and are very hard to find. The eggs overwinter.

Caterpillar Season: March and April.

Host Plants: Common Sweetleaf (*Symplocos tinctoria*, p. 307), a shrub in the Sweetleaf family (Symplocaceae).

Satyrium liparops

Striped Hairstreak

Photo, p. 177

Description: To 0.8" in length. Head light brown; body slug-shaped with short hairs, green with faint stripes and a narrow yellow line on the sides.

Similar Species: None.

Habitat: Uplands. Dry hammocks.

U.S. Distribution: Florida to eastern Texas and northward into Colorado, Montana, North Dakota, Minnesota, Michigan, New York, and Maine.

Natural History: This hairstreak is very local and generally uncommon in northern and central Florida. Only one generation is produced per year in late

spring. The flat, brown eggs are laid singly or in small groups on the twigs of the host tree. The caterpillars eat very young leaves, buds, and immature fruits. They blend in very well with the plant and are very hard to find. The eggs overwinter.
Caterpillar Season: February and March.
Host Plants: Sparkleberry (*Vaccinium arboreum*, p. 262) in the Heath family (Ericaceae) and Parsley Hawthorn (*Crataegus marshallii*) in the Rose family (Rosaceae).

Fixsenia favonius (formerly *Satyrium favonius*)

Oak Hairstreak

Photo, p. 173

Description: To 0.8" in length. Head brown; body slug-shaped with short hairs, pale green with faint dark stripes.
Similar Species: The White M Hairstreak also uses oaks.
Habitat: Uplands. Scrubs, sandhills, dry flatwoods, coastal uplands, and hammocks.
U.S. Distribution: Florida westward to eastern Texas and northward into Kansas, Missouri, Illinois, Indiana, Ohio, Pennsylvania, and Massachusetts. Also in southeastern Colorado and northeastern New Mexico.
Natural History: This hairstreak is locally common throughout much of Florida, except for the extreme southern parts of the state. There is a single generation per year in late spring. The flat, brownish eggs are laid singly or in small groups on the twigs of the host tree. The caterpillars eat young leaves. They blend in very well with the plant and are very hard to find. The eggs overwinter.
Caterpillar Season: February and March.
Host Plants: Trees in the Beech family (Fagaceae) including Sand Live Oak (*Quercus geminata*) and other oaks.

Incisalia irus (formerly *Callophrys irus*)

Frosted Elfin

Photo, p. 175

Description: To 0.7" in length. Head light brown; body slug-shaped with short hairs, bluish green with very faint markings.
Similar Species: None.
Habitat: Uplands. Sandhills.
U.S. Distribution: Florida northward into Kentucky, West Virginia, Pennsylvania, and New York, and westward into Michigan and Wisconsin. Also found in eastern Texas, southern Oklahoma, Arkansas, and western Louisiana.
Natural History: This rare hairstreak occurs in close association with the host plant in northern Florida. There is only one generation per year in the spring. The flat, whitish eggs are laid singly on the flower buds. The caterpillars eat flow-

ers, buds, immature seeds, and sometimes the leaves. They blend in very well with the green lupine seed pods and are difficult to find. The pupae overwinter.

Caterpillar Season: March and April.

Host Plants: Sundial Lupine (*Lupinus perennis*, p. 278), an herb in the Pea family (Fabaceae).

Incisalia henrici (formerly *Callophrys henrici*)

Henry's Elfin

Photo, p. 177

Description: To 0.6" in length. Head brown; body slug-shaped with short hairs, color varies from green to red and green, or red with faint dark markings.

Similar Species: None.

Habitat: Uplands and wetlands. Hammocks, wet flatwoods, and swamps.

U.S. Distribution: Florida westward to eastern Texas and northward into Minnesota, Wisconsin, Michigan, southeastern Pennsylvania, and Massachusetts.

Natural History: This hairstreak is very local and usually uncommon in northern and central Florida. There is a single generation per year in the spring. Females lay the flat, whitish eggs singly or in small groups on the leaf buds of the host trees. The caterpillars eat young leaves. They may be found when the young holly leaves are the size of squirrels' ears. Mature larvae sometimes hide in patches of lichens on the branches or trunks of the hosts. The pupae overwinter.

Caterpillar Season: March and April.

Host Plants: Trees in the Holly family (Aquifoliaceae) including Dahoon (*Ilex cassine*, p. 250) and American Holly (*Ilex opaca*), and occasionally Eastern Redbud (*Cercis canadensis*, p. 269) in the Pea family (Fabaceae) in the Panhandle region.

Incisalia niphon (formerly *Callophrys niphon*)

Eastern Pine Elfin

Photo, p. 175

Description: To 0.7" in length. Body slug-shaped with very short hairs, green with white stripes.

Similar Species: None.

Habitat: Uplands. Scrubs and dry mixed pine and hardwood hammocks.

U.S. Distribution: Florida westward to eastern Texas and northward into Minnesota, Michigan, New York, and Maine.

Natural History: This hairstreak is very local and usually uncommon in northern and central Florida. There is a single generation per year in the spring. Females lay flat, whitish eggs singly or in small groups on the young pine shoots, especially of small trees. The caterpillars feed on the young leaves, later eating older needles starting at the tip. They blend in very well with the plant and are very hard to find. The pupae overwinter.

Caterpillar Season: March and April.

Host Plants: Sand Pine (*Pinus clausa*, p. 220) and perhaps Loblolly Pine (*Pinus taeda*) in the Pine family (Pinaceae).

Mitoura grynea (formerly *Callophrys gryneus*)

Juniper Hairstreak

Photo, p. 175

Description: To 0.7" in length. Body slug-shaped with very short hairs, green with white lines and broken oblique bars on the sides.

Similar Species: Hessel's Hairstreak is similar, but uses Atlantic White Cedar.

Habitat: Uplands. Coastal uplands, hammocks, and old fields with cedar trees.

U.S. Distribution: All states except Alaska and Hawaii.

Natural History: This beautiful hairstreak is very local and uncommon in northern and central Florida. There are three generations per year. Females lay flat, pale green eggs singly on the host foliage. The caterpillars feed on young leaves. They blend in very well with the plant and are very hard to find. The pupae overwinter.

Caterpillar Season: March through October.

Host Plants: Red Cedar (*Juniperus virginiana*, p. 219) a tree in the Cedar family (Cupressaceae).

Mitoura hesseli (formerly *Callophrys hesseli*)

Hessel's Hairstreak

Photo, p. 175

Description: To 0.7" in length. Body slug-shaped with very short hairs, dark green with white oblique bars and lines on the sides.

Similar Species: Juniper Hairstreak is similar, but uses Red Cedar.

Habitat: Wetlands. White Cedar swamps along blackwater streams and rivers.

U.S. Distribution: Florida Panhandle northward into Georgia, South Carolina, North Carolina, and along the coast into Virginia, Delaware, New Jersey, New York, Massachusetts, New Hampshire, and southern Maine.

Natural History: This rare hairstreak is exceedingly local near patches of its host plant in Florida. Three generations are produced each year. The flat, pale green eggs are laid singly on the foliage of the host tree. The caterpillars eat young leaves. Their cryptic coloration closely matches the color and pattern of their host plant. The pupae overwinter.

Caterpillar Season: March through October.

Host Plants: Atlantic White Cedar (*Chamaecyparis thyoides*, p. 219), a tree in the Cedar family (Cupressaceae).

Parrhasius m-album

White M Hairstreak

Photo, p. 177

Description: To 0.8" in length. Head brown; body slug-shaped with minute whitish hairs having broadened tips, color varies from green to red and green, or dull red with faint dark markings; thorax with a small pale shield on top; a dark spot on the back toward the posterior end.

Similar Species: The Oak Hairstreak also uses oaks.

Habitat: Uplands. Scrubs, sandhills, and hammocks.

U.S. Distribution: Florida westward to eastern Texas and northward into Missouri, Illinois, Indiana, Ohio, Pennsylvania, and Massachusetts.

Natural History: This hairstreak is common throughout Florida except the Keys. At least three generations are produced each year. Females lay the flat, whitish eggs on the leaves and twigs of oaks. The caterpillars eat the young leaves, which are often reddish in color, and blend in very well with the foliage. The pupae overwinter.

Caterpillar Season: March through October.

Host Plants: Trees in the Beech family (Fagaceae) including Sand Live Oak (*Quercus geminata*), Laurel Oak (*Quercus laurifolia*, p. 287), Water Oak (*Quercus nigra*, p. 288), Post Oak (*Quercus stellata*, p. 289), and Virginia Live Oak (*Quercus virginiana*, p. 289).

Strymon melinus

Gray Hairstreak

Photo, p. 177

Description: To 0.8" in length. Head brown; body slug-shaped with short hairs, color varies from whitish to green, green with red stripes, or all red with faint darker markings.

Similar Species: The Mallow Scrub-Hairstreak also eats Fanpetals and the Cassius Blue uses Hairypod Cowpea.

Habitat: Uplands. Many communities including scrubs, sandhills, flatwoods, prairies, pine savannas, as well as weedy disturbed sites.

U.S. Distribution: All states except Alaska and Hawaii.

Natural History: This hairstreak is common to abundant throughout Florida. There are three or more generations per year. The flat, whitish eggs are laid singly on the flower buds of the hosts. The caterpillars eat flower buds and immature seeds. They blend in very well with the plant and are very hard to find. The pupae overwinter.

Caterpillar Season: February through early November or perhaps all year in southern Florida.

Host Plants: Prefers herbs and vines in the Pea family (Fabaceae) including Partridge Pea (*Chamaecrista fasciculata*, p. 270), Coinvine (*Dalbergia ecastaphyllum*,

p. 272), Creeping Ticktrefoil (*Desmodium incanum*, p. 273), Panicledleaf Tick-trefoil (*Desmodium paniculatum*), Eastern Milkpea (*Galactia regularis*), Downy Milkpea (*Galactia volubilis*, p. 275), Sky-Blue Lupine (*Lupinus diffusus*), Hairy-pod Cowpea (*Vigna luteola*, p. 286), the exotic species Garden Bean (*Phaseolus vulgaris*) and Wild Bushbean (*Macroptilium lathyroides*); also sometimes Cottonweed (*Froelichia floridana*) in the Amaranth family (Amaranthaceae), Feay's Palafox (*Palafoxia feayi*) in the Aster family, Bladder Mallow (*Herissantia crispa*) and Common Fanpetals (*Sida acuta*, p. 293) in the Mallow family (Malvaceae), Tall Jointweed (*Polygonella gracilis*) and Pennsylvania Smartweed (*Polygonum pensylvanicum*) in the Buckwheat family (Polygonaceae), New Jersey Tea (*Ceanothus americanus*, p. 300) in the Buckthorn family (Rhamnaceae), and Heartseed (*Cardiospermum corindum*, p. 306) in the Soapberry family (Sapindaceae).

Strymon martialis

Martial Scrub-Hairstreak

Photo, p. 179

Description: To 0.7" in length. Head brown; body slug-shaped with very short hairs, light green.
Similar Species: The Mallow Scrub-Hairstreak sometimes uses Bay Cedar.
Habitat: Uplands. Coastal areas and margins of tropical hardwood hammocks.
U.S. Distribution: Southern Florida.
Natural History: This hairstreak is very local and uncommon. At least three generations are produced each year. The flat, whitish eggs are laid on the flower buds or new shoots of the host. The caterpillars eat flower buds, immature fruit, and young leaves. They blend in very well with the plant and are very hard to find.
Caterpillar Season: Throughout the year.
Host Plants: Mainly on Bay Cedar (*Suriana maritima*, p. 306), a shrub in the Bay Cedar family (Surianaceae), and occasionally Nettletree (*Trema micranthum*, p. 261) in the Hackberry family (Celtidaceae) and Buttonwood (*Conocarpus erectus*) in the Combretum family (Combretaceae).

Strymon acis

Bartram's Scrub-Hairstreak

Photo, p. 179

Description: To 0.7" in length. Head brown; body slug-shaped with short hairs, whitish to pale green with faint dark markings.
Similar Species: None.
Habitat: Uplands. Pine rocklands.
U.S. Distribution: Southern Florida.
Natural History: This rare hairstreak is very local near patches of its larval plant. There are three or more generations per year. The flat, whitish eggs are laid singly on the flower buds and young leaves of the host. Young caterpillars eat flowers

and immature fruit; older ones prefer young leaves. They live exposed on the host, but are hard to find because of their cryptic coloration.

Caterpillar Season: Throughout the year.

Host Plants: Pineland Croton (*Croton linearis*, p. 264), a small shrub in the Spurge family (Euphorbiaceae).

Strymon istapa (formerly *Strymon columella*)
Mallow Scrub-Hairstreak

Photo, p. 177

Description: To 0.6" in length. Head brown; body slug-shaped with short hairs, color varies from green to red and green, or all red with faint darker markings.

Similar Species: The Gray Hairstreak eats fanpetals and the Martial Scrub-Hairstreak uses Bay Cedar.

Habitat: Uplands. Coastal areas, weed lots, roadsides, and other disturbed sites.

U.S. Distribution: Southern Florida and southern Texas.

Natural History: This hairstreak is locally common and at least three generations are produced each year. The flat, whitish eggs are laid singly on the flower buds of the hosts. The caterpillars eat the flower buds and immature fruit. They blend in very well with the plant and are very hard to find.

Caterpillar Season: Throughout the year.

Host Plants: Herbs in the Mallow family (Malvaceae) including Common Fanpetals (*Sida acuta*, p. 293), Sleepy Morning (*Waltheria indica*, p. 294), and occasionally Bay Cedar (*Suriana maritima*, p. 306), a shrub in the Bay Cedar family (Surianaceae).

Electrostrymon angelia
Fulvous Hairstreak

Photo, p. 173

Description: To 0.6" in length. Head black; body slug-shaped with short hairs, olive green with reddish brown stripes, two rows of small pale spots on the back, and black spiracles.

Similar Species: The Red-banded Hairstreak also uses Brazilian Pepper.

Habitat: Uplands. Brazilian Pepper thickets in coastal uplands, canal banks, margins of hammocks, and shrubby disturbed sites.

U.S. Distribution: Southern Florida.

Natural History: This hairstreak is locally common and has at least three generations per year. The flat, pale green eggs are laid singly or in small clusters on the young leaves of the host. The caterpillars eat the new growth.

Caterpillar Season: Throughout the year.

Host Plants: Brazilian Pepper (*Schinus terebinthifolius*, p. 240), an invasive exotic shrub in the Cashew family (Anacardiaceae), as well as Florida Fishpoison Tree

(*Piscidia piscipula*, p. 280) and the exotic Karum Tree (*Pongamia pinnata*) in the Pea family (Fabaceae).

Calycopis cecrops
Red-banded Hairstreak
Photo, p. 173

Description: To 0.6" in length. Head dark; body slug-shaped with short hairs, pinkish-brown with faint darker markings, a small black shield on top of the thorax, and black spiracles.
Similar Species: The Fulvous Hairstreak also eats Brazilian Pepper.
Habitat: Uplands. Scrubs, sandhills, flatwoods, margins of hammocks, and shrubby disturbed areas.
U.S. Distribution: Florida westward to eastern Texas and northward into Missouri, Illinois, Indiana, Ohio, Pennsylvania, and New Jersey.
Natural History: This hairstreak is common throughout Florida. At least three generations are produced per year. The females lay flat, whitish eggs on dead leaves on the ground. The caterpillars mostly eat dead leaves, but can be raised on the young foliage of Southern Bayberry, oaks, and other plants. The pupae overwinter. The life stages of the Red-banded Hairstreak are shown on p. 32.
Caterpillar Season: February through early November.
Host Plants: Southern Bayberry (*Myrica cerifera*, p. 295) in the Bayberry family (Myricaceae), oaks in the Beech family (Fagaceae), and exotic species such as Brazilian Pepper (*Schinus terebinthifolius*, p. 240) and Mango (*Mangifera indica*) in the Cashew family (Anacardiaceae).

Ministrymon azia
Gray Ministreak
Photo, p. 173

Description: To 0.4" in length. Body slug-shaped, green with red and white markings and short tubercles on the back that bear several long hairs.
Similar Species: None.
Habitat: Uplands. Roadsides and disturbed sites.
U.S. Distribution: Southern and central Florida and southern Texas.
Natural History: This tiny hairstreak is very local and closely associated with the host plant. Three or more generations are produced each year. The flat, greenish eggs are laid singly on the flower buds. The caterpillars feed on the flower buds and are very hard to find because of their small size and cryptic coloration.
Caterpillar Season: Throughout the year.
Host Plants: White Leadtree (*Leucaena leucocephala*, p. 277), an exotic tree in the Pea family (Fabaceae).

Blues (subfamily Polyommatinae)

Brephidium isophthalma
Eastern Pygmy-Blue

Photo, p. 181

Description: To 0.4" in length. Head black; body slug-shaped with minute hairs, green.
Similar Species: None.
Habitat: Wetlands. Salt marshes.
U.S. Distribution: Florida westward along the Gulf coast to southern Texas and northward along the Atlantic coast into South Carolina.
Natural History: This tiny blue is locally common in coastal areas of Florida. At least three generations are produced each year. The flat, whitish eggs are laid on the stems of the host plant. The caterpillars eat the succulent stems of the host plants and are very difficult to find. They are often tended by the ant *Tapinoma sessile* in the Florida Keys.
Caterpillar Season: February through early November or throughout the year in southern Florida.
Host Plants: Herbs including Perennial Glasswort (*Sarcocornia perennis*, p. 240) and perhaps Annual Glasswort (*Salicornia bigelovii*) in the Amaranth family (Amaranthaceae) and possibly Saltwort (*Batis maritima*, p. 257) in the Saltwort family (Bataceae).

Leptotes cassius
Cassius Blue

Photo, p. 181

Description: To 0.5" in length. Head black; body slug-shaped with short hairs, color varies from uniform green with faint dark markings to highly patterned with red markings and white chevrons on the back.
Similar Species: The Gray Hairstreak also uses legumes.
Habitat: Uplands. Margins of hammocks, thickets, weedy areas, gardens, and disturbed sites.
U.S. Distribution: Peninsular Florida and southern Texas.
Natural History: This blue is locally common to abundant and has at least three generations per year in Florida. The flat, pale green eggs are laid singly on flower buds of the hosts. The caterpillars feed on flower buds and immature seeds. They blend in extremely well with the plant and are very hard to find. The life stages of the Cassius Blue are shown on p. 33.
Caterpillar Season: Throughout the year.
Host Plants: Vines, shrubs, and trees in the Pea family (Fabaceae) including Miami Lead Plant (*Amorpha herbacea* var. *crenulata*), Florida Hammock Milkpea

(*Galactia striata*, p. 275), Downy Milkpea (*Galactia volubilis*, p. 275), False Tamarind (*Lysiloma latisiliquum*, p. 278), Florida Keys Blackbead (*Pithecellobium keyense*, p. 281), Hairypod Cowpea (*Vigna luteola*, p. 286); associated with the invasive exotic species Rosary Pea (*Abrus precatorius*), and very fond of Cape Leadwort (*Plumbago auriculata*, p. 300), an exotic shrub in the Leadwort family (Plumbaginaceae) that is frequently grown in gardens.

Hemiargus thomasi
Miami Blue

Photo, p. 179

Description: To 0.6" in length. Head black; body slug-shaped with short hairs, usually green with faint dark markings but may also be green mottled with red or mostly red.
Similar Species: The Silver-banded Hairstreak and occasionally the Gray Hairstreak also use Heartseed.
Habitat: Uplands. Coastal uplands and the margins of tropical hardwood hammocks.
U.S. Distribution: Florida Keys.
Natural History: The Miami Blue was once a common butterfly of the Keys and coastal areas of the southern mainland, but has recently nearly disappeared from the state. It is now known to occur only in Bahia Honda State Park. Propagation efforts are under way at the University of Florida, McGuire Center for Lepidoptera Research, in order to reintroduce the butterfly into other areas of the Keys. The Miami Blue is an endangered species protected by state law. At least three generations are produced per year. The flat, bluish eggs are laid on the flower buds and young shoots of the host. The caterpillars feed on flower buds, immature fruit, and young leaves. The caterpillars are sometimes tended by carpenter ants (*Camponotus* spp.) and other ant species.
Caterpillar Season: Throughout the year.
Host Plants: Gray Nicker (*Caesalpinia bonduc*, p. 268), a shrubby vine in the Pea family (Fabaceae) and Heartseed (*Cardiospermum corindum*, p. 306), a vine in the Soapberry family (Sapindaceae).

Hemiargus ammon
Nickerbean Blue

Photo, p. 179

Description: To 0.5" in length. Head black; body slug-shaped with short hairs, color varies from uniform green with faint dark markings to highly patterned with red markings and white chevrons on the back.
Similar Species: The Cassius Blue also uses legumes.
Habitat: Uplands. Pine rocklands.

U.S. Distribution: Lower Florida Keys.

Natural History: This butterfly has only recently been found in Florida, and is now sometimes common on Big Pine Key. At least three generations are produced per year. The flat, bluish eggs are laid singly on the flower buds of the host. The caterpillars feed on the flower buds and immature seeds. They blend in very well with the plant and are very hard to find.

Caterpillar Season: Throughout the year.

Host Plants: Trees in the Pea family (Fabaceae) including Sweet Acacia (*Acacia farnesiana*) and Pineland Acacia (*Acacia pinetorum*, p. 265).

Hemiargus ceraunus

Ceraunus Blue

Photo, p. 181

Description: To 0.6" in length. Head black; body slug-shaped with short hairs, color varies from green to red with dark markings and a white stripe bounded by red on the sides.

Similar Species: The Nickerbean Blue and Eastern Tailed-Blue also eat legumes.

Habitat: Uplands. Scrubs, sandhills, flatwoods, and weedy, disturbed sites.

U.S. Distribution: Florida westward to southern California and northward along the Atlantic coast into the Carolinas.

Natural History: This blue is common throughout Florida. Three or more generations are produced each year. The flat, bluish eggs are laid singly on the flower buds of the hosts. The caterpillars eat flower buds and immature seeds. They blend in exceedingly well with the plant and are very hard to find.

Caterpillar Season: March through October or perhaps throughout the year in southern Florida.

Host Plants: Herbs in the Pea family (Fabaceae) including Partridge Pea (*Chamaecrista fasciculata*, p. 270), Sensitive Pea (*Chamaecrista nictitans, p.* 270), Alicia (*Chapmannia floridana*, p. 271), Carolina Indigo (*Indigofera caroliniana*, p. 276), Tropical Puff (*Neptunia pubescens*), Danglepod (*Sesbania herbacea*), and the exotic species Hairy Indigo (*Indigofera hirsuta*) and Trailing Indigo (*Indigofera spicata*, p. 276).

Everes comyntas

Eastern Tailed-Blue

Photo, p. 181

Description: To 0.5" in length. Head black; body slug-shaped with short hairs, color varies from dark green to red and green or mostly red with numerous tiny pale dots, faint dark markings, and a whitish stripe on the sides.

Similar Species: The Ceraunus Blue also uses legumes.

Habitat: Uplands. Sandhills.

U.S. Distribution: Florida westward to central Texas and northward to North Dakota, Minnesota, Michigan, New York, and Maine. Also in California, Oregon, Wyoming, Washington, Arizona, and New Mexico.

Natural History: This species is very local and rare in northern Florida. At least three generations are produced per year. The flat, pale green eggs are laid singly on the flower buds of the host. The caterpillars prefer flower buds and immature fruits but also eat very young leaves. They blend in very well with the plant and are very hard to find. The mature larvae overwinter.

Caterpillar Season: March through October.

Host Plants: Herbs in the Pea family (Fabaceae). Not reported in Florida, but uses clovers and other legumes elsewhere.

Celastrina ladon

'Edwards' Spring Azure

Photo, p. 179

Description: To 0.6" in length. Head black; body slug-shaped with short hairs, green with purple mottling, black markings, and white chevrons on the back.

Similar Species: The 'Summer' Spring Azure is extremely similar.

Habitat: Uplands and wetlands. Margins of hammocks and swamps along streams and rivers.

U.S. Distribution: Florida northward into Michigan, Ohio, Pennsylvania, and New York. Also in Missouri and Arkansas.

Natural History: This blue is local and uncommon in northern Florida. Only one generation is produced each year during early spring. The flat, pale green eggs are laid singly on the flower buds of the host. The caterpillars eat flowers and immature fruits. They are often tended by ants. The pupae overwinter.

Caterpillar Season: February and March.

Host Plants: Not observed in Florida, but one of main hosts in the eastern United States is Flowering Dogwood (*Cornus florida*).

Celastrina neglecta

'Summer' Spring Azure

Photo, p. 179

Description: To 0.6" in length. Head black; body slug-shaped with short hairs, green with purple mottling, black markings, and white chevrons on the back.

Similar Species: The 'Edwards' Spring Azure is nearly identical.

Habitat: Uplands and wetlands. Margins of hammocks and swamps along streams and rivers.

U.S. Distribution: Florida westward to eastern Texas and northward into Montana, North Dakota, Minnesota, Wisconsin, Michigan, New York, and Maine.

Natural History: This blue is locally common in northern Florida and less frequent in the central part of the state. There are three generations per year. The flat, pale green eggs are laid singly on the flower buds of the hosts. The caterpillars eat flower buds and immature seeds, and are often tended by ants. They blend in very well with the plant and are very hard to find. The pupae overwinter.

Caterpillar Season: March through October.

Host Plants: Sourwood (*Oxydendrum arboreum*, p. 262) in the Heath family (Ericaceae), the exotic garden ornamental David's Butterflybush (*Buddleja davidii*) in the family Buddlejaceae, and probably the flower buds of many other shrubs and trees.

Metalmarks (family Riodinidae)

The Metalmarks are a diverse tropical group of butterflies with close ties to the hairstreaks and blues. Only one species, the Little Metalmark, occurs in Florida. The caterpillars aren't as slug-shaped as the lycaenids, and the head is more visible.

Calephelis virginiensis

Little Metalmark

Photo, p. 181

Description: To 0.5" in length. Body stout with very long hairs on the back and sides, whitish green with small white dots and two rows of brownish green or reddish dashes on the back.

Similar Species: None.

Habitat: Uplands and marginal wetlands. Sandhills, flatwoods, pine savannas, prairies, and roadsides.

U.S. Distribution: Florida westward to eastern Texas and northward along the Atlantic coast into Virginia.

Natural History: This metalmark is common throughout Florida, except in the Keys. At least three generations are produced each year. The flat, brownish eggs are laid singly on the underside of the host foliage, where the caterpillars feed, leaving the translucent upper leaf cuticle intact. These translucent small circular windows in the leaves are a good sign to look for when searching for the larvae. Probably overwinter as partly grown larvae. The life stages of the Little Metalmark are shown on p. 34.

Caterpillar Season: March through early November.

Host Plants: Herbs in the Aster family (Asteraceae) including Vanillaleaf (*Carphephorus odoratissimus*), Yellow Thistle (*Cirsium horridulum*, p. 254), and sometimes Climbing Hempvine (*Mikania scandens*).

Brushfoots and Relatives (family Nymphalidae)

The Brushfooted Butterflies (family Nymphalidae) are a large and diverse group with many distinctive subfamilies. The true brushfoots (subfamily Nymphalinae) have slender larvae with uniform rows of branched spines and a pair of spines or horns on the top of the head. They sometimes make nests of leaves and silk. The caterpillars of the admirals and heliconians are similar to those of the true brushfoots. However, admiral caterpillars have spines of various sizes and shapes on the body, while heliconians have very long and slender spines.

The caterpillars of other brushfoots lack rows of branching spines on the body. Emperor larvae are green with yellow stripes. There is a pair of short branching spines on top of the head and the posterior end of the body is forked. The two Florida species of emperors feed on the leaves of hackberry trees. Satyr and Wood-nymph caterpillars also have a forked posterior, but the spines on top of the head are simple spikes. They eat only grasses and sedges. Leafwing Butterfly caterpillars have pebbly textured heads and eat crotons. Milkweed Butterfly larvae are boldly striped and have two or three pairs of long fleshy filaments on the body. As their name suggests, they eat only plants in the Dogbane family. The caterpillar of the American Snout eats hackberry leaves like the emperors, but resembles a Sulphur or a moth larva.

Snouts (subfamily Libytheinae)

Libytheana carinenta

American Snout

Photo, p. 181

Description: To 1.0" in length. Head green; body slender, green with numerous small yellow dots, narrow yellow stripes on the back and sides, and a pair of small black dots on top of the thorax.

Similar Species: The Hackberry Emperor and Tawny Emperor also eat Sugarberry.

Habitat: Uplands and marginal wetlands. Hammocks and urban areas.

U.S. Distribution: Florida westward to southern California and northward into Colorado, Nebraska, Missouri, Wisconsin, Michigan, New York, and Massachusetts.

Natural History: This butterfly is common in northern and central Florida, but is infrequent in the southern parts of the state. There are three or more generations each year. The tiny pale yellow eggs are laid singly in the leaf axils of the young shoots of the host tree. The caterpillars eat young leaves. The life stages of the American Snout are shown on p. 36.

Caterpillar Season: March through early November.

Host Plants: Sugarberry (*Celtis laevigata*, p. 261), a tree in the Hackberry family (Celtidaceae).

Heliconians (subfamily Heliconiinae)

Agraulis vanillae
Gulf Fritillary

Photo, p. 183

Description: To 1.5" in length. Head orange with black patches and a pair of long black horns on top; body slender, orange with greenish longitudinal stripes, and having rows of long, black, branched spines.

Similar Species: The Julia Heliconian, Zebra Heliconian, and Variegated Fritillary also eat passionflowers.

Habitat: Uplands. Scrubs, sandhills, coastal uplands, flatwoods, and weedy, disturbed sites.

U.S. Distribution: Florida westward to southern California and northward into Colorado, Kansas, Missouri, Illinois, Indiana, and New Jersey.

Natural History: This butterfly migrates southward by the millions during late summer and fall, and is common throughout the state. At least three generations are produced per year. The yellow eggs are laid singly on the new growth or sometimes at the tips of tendrils or even on nearby plants to avoid ant predators. The ants eat eggs as well as young larvae and are attracted by nectar glands on the leaf petioles of the host plant. The caterpillars prefer to eat young leaves but often defoliate entire vines. The life stages of the Gulf Fritillary are shown on p. 37.

Caterpillar Season: Throughout the year.

Host Plants: Vines in the Passionflower family (Passifloraceae) including Purple Passionflower (*Passiflora incarnata*, p. 297), Yellow Passionflower (*Passiflora lutea*, p. 298), and Corkystem Passionflower (*Passiflora suberosa*, p. 298), and an herb, Pitted Stripeseed (*Piriqueta cistoides*), in the Turnera family (Turneraceae).

Dryas iulia
Julia Heliconian

Photo, p. 183

Description: To 1.5" in length. Head orange with black patches and a pair of long black horns on top; body slender, black with white spots or lines on the back and sides, and having rows of long, black branched spines.

Similar Species: The Gulf Fritillary, Zebra Heliconian, and Variegated Fritillary also use passionflowers.

Habitat: Uplands. Margins of tropical hardwood hammocks, thickets, and shrubby, disturbed areas.

U.S. Distribution: Southern Florida and southern Texas.

Natural History: This butterfly is locally common. There are three or more generations per year in Florida. The yellow eggs are laid singly on the new growth of the host plants. The caterpillars eat young leaves. Eggs and young caterpillars may be eaten by ants attracted by nectar glands on the leaf petioles.

Caterpillar Season: Throughout the year.

Host Plants: Vines in the Passionflower family (Passifloraceae) including White-flower Passionflower (*Passiflora multiflora*) and Corkystem Passionflower (*Passiflora suberosa*, p. 298).

Heliconius charithonia

Zebra Heliconian

Photo, p. 183

Description: To 1.7" in length. Head white with black patches and a pair of long black horns on top; body slender, white with brown or black spots, and having rows of long, black, branched spines.

Similar Species: The Gulf Fritillary, Julia Heliconian, and Variegated Fritillary also use passionflowers.

Habitat: Uplands. Margins of hammocks, thickets, and shrubby, disturbed areas.

U.S. Distribution: Peninsular Florida, southern Texas, and occasionally southern Arizona. Seasonally present in coastal areas of Georgia and South Carolina.

Natural History: This butterfly is locally common in central and southern Florida and frequently strays northward during the summer and fall. At least three generations are produced each year. The yellow eggs are laid singly on the new growth of the host plants. The caterpillars eat young leaves at first. Eggs and young caterpillars may be eaten by ants attracted by nectar glands on the leaf petioles.

Caterpillar Season: Throughout the year.

Host Plants: Vines in the Passionflower family (Passifloraceae) including Purple Passionflower (*Passiflora incarnata*, p. 297), Yellow Passionflower (*Passiflora lutea*, p. 298), and Corkystem Passionflower (*Passiflora suberosa*, p. 298).

Euptoieta claudia

Variegated Fritillary

Photo, p. 183

Description: To 1.3" in length. Head orange with black patches and a pair of long black horns on top; body slender, orange with black and white lines, and having rows of long, bluish black, branched spines.

Similar Species: The Gulf Fritillary, Julia Heliconian, and Zebra Heliconian also use passionflowers.

Habitat: Uplands. Sandhills, flatwoods, and weedy areas.

U.S. Distribution: Florida westward to southern California and northward into Montana, North Dakota, Minnesota, Wisconsin, Michigan, New York, and southern Maine.

Natural History: This species is common in the Florida Panhandle but found less frequently in peninsular Florida. There are three or more generations per year. The pale green eggs are laid on the new growth of the hosts. The caterpillars eat young leaves.

Caterpillar Season: Throughout the year.

Host Plants: Florida Yellow Flax (*Linum floridanum*), an herb in the Flax family (Linaceae), Purple Passionflower (*Passiflora incarnata*, p. 297), a vine in the Passionflower family (Passifloraceae), and perhaps violets (*Viola* spp.) in the family Violaceae.

Brushfoots (subfamily Nymphalinae)

Chlosyne nycteis

Silvery Checkerspot

Photo, p. 187

Description: To 1.0" in length. Head black; body slender, black with tiny white dots, broad whitish stripes on the sides, and having rows of thick black or brown branched spines.

Similar Species: None.

Habitat: Margins of wetlands. Forest openings along streams and rivers.

U.S. Distribution: Florida Panhandle westward to eastern Texas and northward into North Dakota, Minnesota, Michigan, New York, and Maine. Also in Wyoming, Colorado, New Mexico, and Arizona.

Natural History: This butterfly occurs locally along the Chipola River near Marianna, especially at Florida Caverns State Park. There are two generations per year. The pale greenish yellow eggs are laid in clusters on the undersides of the host leaves. The young caterpillars live and feed together in a nest of silk on the underside of the leaves. Partly grown larvae overwinter.

Caterpillar Season: Throughout the year.

Host Plants: Not reported in Florida, but elsewhere in the Southeast uses Woodland Sunflower (*Helianthus divaricatus*) and Paleleaf Woodland Sunflower (*Helianthus strumosus*) in the Aster family (Asteraceae).

Anthanassa texana seminole (formerly *Phyciodes texana seminole*)

'Seminole' Texan Crescent

Photo, p. 187

Description: To 0.9" in length. Head black with white markings; body slender, black to dark brown with faint white dots, whitish stripes on the sides, and having rows of short, branched spines. The spines on the sides are pale brown.

Similar Species: The Phaon Crescent occasionally eats Looseflower Waterwillow.

Habitat: Wetlands. Wet hammocks and the margins of swamps along streams, rivers, and lakes.

U.S. Distribution: Florida westward to Arizona and northward along the Atlantic coast into South Carolina.

Natural History: This crescent is locally common in the Florida Panhandle, but uncommon elsewhere in the state. There are three or more generations per year. The pale greenish yellow eggs are laid in clusters on the undersides of the leaves of the host. The young caterpillars live and feed together in a silk nest on the undersides of the leaves. Partly grown larvae overwinter.

Caterpillar Season: Throughout the year.

Host Plants: Looseflower Waterwillow (*Justicia ovata*, p. 238), an herb in the Acanthus family (Acanthaceae).

Anthanassa frisia (formerly Phyciodes frisia)

Cuban Crescent

Photo, p. 187

Description: To 0.9" in length. Head brown with black patches; body slender, variegated brown and white with darker stripes, and having rows of short, branched spines. The spines on the prothorax are orange, those along the sides tan, and the spines on the dorsum are brown or blackish.

Similar Species: None.

Habitat: Uplands. Coastal uplands and margins of tropical hardwood hammocks.

U.S. Distribution: Southern Florida.

Natural History: This crescent is sometimes locally common in southern Florida, but colonies are often ephemeral. There are three or more generations per year. The pale greenish yellow eggs are laid in clusters on the undersides of the host leaves. The young caterpillars live and feed together in a silk nest on the undersides of the leaves.

Caterpillar Season: Throughout the year.

Host Plants: Sixangle Foldwing (*Dicliptera sexangularis*, p. 237), an herb in the Acanthus family (Acanthaceae).

Phyciodes phaon

Phaon Crescent

Photo, p. 187

Description: To 0.8" in length. Head brown with patches of black and white; body slender, dark brown with broad whitish bands, mottled with yellowish brown, and having rows of very short, branched spines.

Similar Species: The 'Seminole' Texan Crescent also eats Looseflower Waterwillow.

Habitat: Uplands and marginal wetlands. Pastures, roadsides, and weedy, disturbed areas.

U.S. Distribution: Florida westward to western Texas and northward into Kansas, Missouri, and North Carolina. Also occasionally seen in southern California, Arizona, and New Mexico.

Natural History: This crescent occurs abundantly throughout Florida. There are three or more generations per year. The pale greenish yellow eggs are laid in clusters on the undersides of the leaves of the host. The young caterpillars live and feed together in a silk nest on the undersides of the leaves.

Caterpillar Season: Throughout the year.

Host Plants: Turkey Tangle Fogfruit (*Phyla nodiflora*, p. 310), a herb in the Vervain family (Verbenaceae) and occasionally Looseflower Waterwillow (*Justicia ovata*, p. 238) in the Acanthus family (Acanthaceae).

Phyciodes tharos

Pearl Crescent

Photo, p. 187

Description: To 0.8" in length. Head black with whitish patches; body slender, dark brown with numerous tiny white dots, pale stripes, and having rows of short, branched spines.

Similar Species: None.

Habitat: Uplands. Sandhills, flatwoods, and weedy, disturbed sites.

U.S. Distribution: Florida westward to Arizona and northward into Montana, North Dakota, Minnesota, Michigan, New York, and Maine.

Natural History: This common crescent occurs throughout Florida. There are three or more generations per year. The pale greenish yellow eggs are laid in clusters on the undersides of the leaves of the host. The young caterpillars live and eat together in a silk nest on the underside of the leaves. Partly grown larvae overwinter. The life stages of the Pearl Crescent are shown on p. 35.

Caterpillar Season: Throughout the year.

Host Plants: Rice Button Aster (*Symphyotrichum dumosum*, p. 256) and probably other *Symphyotrichum* species in the Aster family (Asteraceae).

Polygonia interrogationis

Question Mark

Photo, p. 189

Description: To 1.4" in length. Head reddish brown with short spines and a pair of branched spines on top; body slender, black variegated with white or yellowish lines and spots, and having rows of branched spines. The spines range in color from yellow and orange to black.

Similar Species: The Eastern Comma and Mourning Cloak sometimes eat elms.

Habitat: Uplands and wetlands. Hammocks and swamps.

U.S. Distribution: Florida westward to Arizona and northward into North Dakota, Minnesota, Michigan, New York, and Maine.

Natural History: This common butterfly occurs mostly in northern and central Florida, but sometimes strays as far south as the Keys. There are two generations per year. The pale green eggs are laid singly or in short stacks on the underside of young leaves of the hosts. The caterpillars eat leaves and do not make nests, but occasionally may rest on the undersides of leaves on which the edges have been curled downward with silk.

Caterpillar Season: February through early November.

Host Plants: Trees, including Sugarberry (*Celtis laevigata*, p. 261) in the Hackberry family (Celtidaceae) as well as Winged Elm (*Ulmus alata*, p. 307) and American Elm (*Ulmus americana*, p. 308) in the Elm family (Ulmaceae).

Polygonia comma
Eastern Comma

Photo, p. 189

Description: To 1.2" in length. Head with short spines and a pair of branching spines on top; body slender, color and pattern vary from greenish white to black with white and red markings, with rows of black-tipped yellow spines.

Similar Species: The Red Admiral also uses nettles, and the Question Mark and Mourning Cloak eat elms.

Habitat: Uplands and wetlands. Hammocks and swamps.

U.S. Distribution: Florida westward to eastern Texas and northward into North Dakota, Minnesota, Michigan, New York, and Maine.

Natural History: This butterfly is infrequently observed in northern Florida, but seems to be established in the Panhandle area. The pale green eggs are laid singly or in short stacks on the undersides of the leaves of the hosts. The caterpillars eat leaves and make nests by tying the edges of a single leaf together with silk (p. 15).

Caterpillar Season: February through early November.

Host Plants: Uses elms (*Ulmus* spp.) and nettles (*Urtica* and *Laportea* spp.) elsewhere in the eastern United States.

Nymphalis antiopa
Mourning Cloak

Photo, p. 189

Description: To 2.0" in length. Head black with whitish hairs; body slender, black with numerous small white dots, a row of orange-red spots on the back, and having rows of long, branched spines.

Similar Species: The Question Mark and Eastern Comma also eat elms.

Habitat: Uplands and wetlands. Hammocks and swamps.

U.S. Distribution: All states except Hawaii.

Natural History: This butterfly is infrequently seen in northern Florida, but appears to breed in the state at least occasionally based on the abundance and condition of adults. The whitish eggs are laid in clusters that ring the tips of twigs of the hosts. The caterpillars eat tender leaves and feed together in groups when young.

Caterpillar Season: February through early November.

Host Plants: Uses willows (*Salix* spp.) and elms (*Ulmus* spp.) elsewhere, and these trees occur in northern Florida.

Vanessa virginiensis
American Lady

Photo, p. 189

Description: To 1.4" in length. Head black with short spines and hairs; body slender with narrow and broad black bands interspersed with narrow yellow bands, two rows of white spots on the back, and having rows of long, black branched spines with reddish bases.

Similar Species: None.

Habitat: Uplands. Sandhills, flatwoods, lawns, and weedy areas.

U.S. Distribution: All states except Alaska and only occasionally seen in Hawaii.

Natural History: This common butterfly is found throughout Florida. There are at least three generations per year. The pale green eggs are laid singly on the hosts. The caterpillars live in nests made of silk and chaff at the tips of the flower stalks (p. 15).

Caterpillar Season: February through early November.

Host Plants: Herbs in the Aster family (Asteraceae) including Narrowleaf Purple Everlasting (*Gamochaeta falcata*, p. 255), Pennsylvania Everlasting (*Gamochaeta pensylvanica*, p. 255), Spoonleaf Purple Everlasting (*Gamochaeta purpurea*), and Sweet Everlasting (*Pseudognaphalium obtusifolium*, p. 256).

Vanessa cardui
Painted Lady

Photo, p. 189

Description: To 1.5" inches in length. Body color pattern variable from pale brown to black with yellow bands and stripes, and having rows of long, branching dark or pale spines with red bases and scattered short white hairs.

Similar Species: None.

Habitat: Uplands. Sandhills, coastal uplands, flatwoods, and open weedy areas.

U.S. Distribution: All states except Alaska.

Natural History: This butterfly is sometimes seen in numbers, but usually is uncommon in Florida. It is most frequently seen in late summer and fall as adults migrate into the state as far south as the Keys. The Painted Lady appears to breed in Florida at least occasionally, based on the abundance and condition of adults. The pale green eggs are laid singly on the upperside of the leaves of the hosts. The caterpillars eat leaves and live in nests made by tying leaves together with silk. The Painted Lady is one of the few butterflies that will eat an artificial diet of soybeans and other ingredients. Kits to raise the Painted Lady from eggs sent from a laboratory are available for purchase on the Internet.

Caterpillar Season: February through early November.

Host Plants: Thistles such as Yellow Thistle (*Cirsium horridulum*, p. 254), an herb in the Aster family (Asteraceae), and many other kinds of plants, especially those in the Mallow family (Malvaceae) and Pea family (Fabaceae).

Vanessa atalanta

Red Admiral

Photo, p. 189

Description: To 1.4" in length. Head black with short spines and hairs; body slender, color pattern variable from pale brown with a yellowish stripe on the sides to black with small white spots and a broken white stripe on the sides, and having rows of long branching dark or pale spines with red bases.

Similar Species: The Eastern Comma also eats nettles.

Habitat: Uplands and wetlands. Hammocks, swamps, marshes, and weedy areas.

U.S. Distribution: All states.

Natural History: This common butterfly occurs throughout Florida. There are probably two to three generations per year. The pale green eggs are laid singly on the uppersides of the leaves of the host plants. The caterpillar makes a shelter by folding over several leaves and tying them together with silk. On the large-leaved nettles, the larva ties the edges of a single leaf together (p. 15).

Caterpillar Season: February through early November.

Host Plants: Herbs in the Nettle family (Urticaceae), including False Nettle (*Boehmeria cylindrica*, p. 308), Florida Pellitory (*Parietaria floridana*, p. 309), and Heartleaf Nettle (*Urtica chamaedryoides*, p. 309) as well as the naturalized exotics, Stinging Nettle (*Urtica dioica*) and Burning Nettle (*Urtica urens*).

Junonia coenia

Common Buckeye

Photo, p. 185

Description: To 1.4" in length. Head orange and black with short spines, and a short pair of branched spines on top; body slender, black with white spots and lines, the legs orange or black, with bluish black, branched spines, the bases of those on the sides orange, and having rows of branched spines.

Similar Species: None.

Habitat: Uplands. Scrubs, sandhills, flatwoods, pine savannas, prairies, and weedy disturbed places.

U.S. Distribution: Florida westward to California and northward into Oregon, Nevada, Utah, Colorado, South Dakota, Minnesota, Wisconsin, Michigan, New York, and Massachusetts.

Natural History: The Common Buckeye migrates southward into Florida by the millions during late summer and fall. This common butterfly occurs throughout the state. At least three generations are produced per year. The green eggs are laid singly on the host plant. The caterpillars eat leaves and frequently hide at the bases of the plants near the ground.

Caterpillar Season: Throughout the year.

Host Plants: Herbs including Oblongleaf Twinflower (*Dyschoriste oblongifolia*, p. 238) and Swamp Twinflower (*Dyschoriste humistrata*) in the Acanthus family (Acanthaceae), Beach False Foxglove (*Agalinis fasciculata*, p. 296), Saltmarsh False Foxglove (*Agalinis maritima*), Purple False Foxglove (*Agalinis purpurea*), American Bluehearts (*Buchnera americana*), Yaupon Blacksenna (*Seymeria cassioides*, p. 297), and Piedmont Blacksenna (*Seymeria pectinata*) in the Broom-rape family (Orobanchaceae), Virginia Plantain (*Plantago virginica*) and the naturalized exotic English Plantain (*Plantago lanceolata*) and Common Plantain (*Plantago major*) in the Plantain family (Plantaginaceae), occasionally Turkey Tangle Fogfruit (*Phyla nodiflora*, p. 310) in the Vervain family (Verbenaceae), as well as Canada Toadflax (*Linaria canadensis*, p. 311) and Apalachicola Toadflax (*Linaria floridana*) in the Speedwell family (Veronicaceae).

Junonia evarete

Mangrove Buckeye

Photo, p. 185

Description: To 1.5" in length. Head black in front, orange in back with short spines, and a pair of short, branched spines on top; body slender, black with small white dots, the legs orange, and having rows of bluish black branched spines, the bases of those on the sides orange.

Similar Species: None.

Habitat: Wetlands. Salt marshes and the edges of mangrove swamps.

U.S. Distribution: Coastal areas of central and southern Florida.

Natural History: This buckeye is locally common around mangroves in Florida. There are at least three generations per year. The green eggs are laid singly on the young leaves of small host trees. The caterpillars eat young leaves.

Caterpillar Season: Throughout the year.

Host Plants: Black Mangrove (*Avicennia germinans*, p. 257), a tree in the Black Mangrove family (Avicenniaceae), but the larvae also accept plantains (*Plantago* spp.) in captivity.

Junonia genoveva

Tropical Buckeye

Photo, p. 185

Description: To 1.4" in length. Head black with short spines and a pair of short, branched spines on top; body slender, black with rows of bluish black branched spines.

Similar Species: None.

Habitat: Uplands. Weedy, disturbed sites.

U.S. Distribution: Southern Florida, Texas, New Mexico, and Arizona.

Natural History: This buckeye is extremely local and rare in southern Florida. At least three generations are produced per year. The green eggs are laid singly on the leaves of the host. The caterpillars eat leaves and do not make nests.

Caterpillar Season: Throughout the year.

Host Plants: Blue Porterweed (*Stachytarpheta jamaicensis*, p. 310), an herb in the Vervain family (Verbenaceae).

Anartia jatrophae

White Peacock

Photo, p. 185

Description: To 1.4" in length. Head black with a pair of long horns that are knobbed at the tips; body slender, black with small white dots and having rows of branched spines, those on the back of the abdomen and the bases of those on the sides orange.

Similar Species: None.

Habitat: Uplands and wetlands. Wet flatwoods, pine savannas, prairies, margins of marshes, ditches, ponds, and weedy disturbed areas.

U.S. Distribution: Peninsular Florida and southern Texas.

Natural History: This butterfly occurs abundantly in southern and central Florida and colonizes further north, especially along the coasts, during summer and fall. There are at least three generations per year. The green eggs are laid singly on the leaves of the hosts. The caterpillars eat leaves and often hide near the ground during the daytime.

Caterpillar Season: Throughout the year.

Host Plants: Herbs including Herb-of-Grace (*Bacopa monnieri*, p. 311) in the Speedwell family (Veronicaceae) and Turkey Tangle Fogfruit (*Phyla nodiflora*, p. 310) in the Vervain family (Verbenaceae).

Siproeta stelenes

Malachite

Photo, p. 187

Description: To 1.6" in length. Head black with a pair of long, branched spines that are knobbed at the tips; body slender, black with rows of long branched spines, those on the back orange.
Similar Species: None.
Habitat: Uplands. Hammocks, thickets, groves, and shrubby disturbed places.
U.S. Distribution: Southern Florida and southern Texas.
Natural History: This beautiful butterfly is locally common in Palm Beach, Broward, and Miami-Dade counties, and sometimes strays into other parts of southern and central Florida. There are three or more generations per year. The green eggs are laid on the flower bracts and leaves of the host. The caterpillars eat leaves and flower bracts. Small larvae hide among the bracts, while larger larvae rest near the ground.
Caterpillar Season: Throughout the year.
Host Plants: Herbs including Browne's Blechum (*Blechum pyramidatum*, p. 237) a naturalized, exotic species and perhaps occasionally Carolina Wild Petunia (*Ruellia caroliniensis*) in the Acanthus family (Acanthaceae).

Admirals (subfamily Limenitidinae)

Basilarchia arthemis astyanax (formerly *Limenitis arthemis astyanax*)

Red-spotted Purple

Photo, p. 183

Description: To 1.6" in length. Head brown, fringed with short spines and cleft on top; body slender, olive green to greenish brown with a pinkish white saddle and a white lateral line, a pair of long, thick, branched spines on the top of the prothorax, a small pair of branched spines on the top of the posterior end, and having several humps on the back.
Similar Species: The Viceroy also uses willows.
Habitat: Uplands and margins of wetlands. Hammocks and occasionally shrub swamps.
U.S. Distribution: Florida westward to eastern Texas and northward into Minnesota, Wisconsin, Michigan, New York, Vermont, and New Hampshire.
Natural History: This common butterfly occurs in northern and central Florida. Two generations are produced per year. The pale green eggs are laid singly on the uppersides of leaves near the tips. The young caterpillar eats most of the leaf tip, except for the midrib, on which it rests (p. 22). The larva attaches pieces of leaves and fecal pellets to the base of the exposed midrib with silk, presumably to protect itself from predators. Older caterpillars resemble bird droppings. Third

stage caterpillars overwinter in a small leaf shelter that is anchored to the stem with silk. The life stages of the Red-spotted Purple are shown on p. 38.

Caterpillar Season: Throughout the year.

Host Plants: Trees and shrubs including Deerberry (*Vaccinium stamineum*, p. 263) in the Heath family (Ericaceae), Black Cherry (*Prunus serotina*, p. 301) in the Rose family (Rosaceae), occasionally Carolina Willow (*Salix caroliniana*, p. 305) in the Willow family (Salicaceae), and probably trees in the Birch family (Betulaceae).

Basilarchia archippus (formerly *Limenitis archippus*)

Viceroy

Photo, p. 183

Description: To 1.6" in length. Head brown, fringed with short spines and cleft on top; body slender, olive green to greenish brown with a pinkish white saddle and a white lateral line, a pair of long, branched spines (the spines longer than those on the Red-spotted Purple) on the dorsum of the prothorax, small spines on the top of the thorax and beginning abdominal segments, and a small pair of branched spines on the posterior end, the back with several humps.

Similar Species: The Red-spotted Purple sometimes uses willows.

Habitat: Wetlands. Marshes and shrub swamps.

U.S. Distribution: Florida westward to southern California and northward into Washington, Montana, North Dakota, Minnesota, Michigan, New York, and Maine.

Natural History: This common butterfly occurs throughout Florida. There are two to three generations produced each year. The pale green eggs are laid singly on the upperside of the leaves near the tips. Young caterpillars eat leaves and rest on the exposed midribs. The larva attaches pieces of leaves and fecal pellets with silk to the base of the midrib on which it rests. Third-stage caterpillars overwinter in a small leaf shelter that is attached to the stem with silk (p. 11).

Caterpillar Season: Throughout the year.

Host Plants: Shrubs and trees in the Willow family (Salicaceae) including Carolina Willow (*Salix caroliniana*, p. 305), Black Willow (*Salix nigra*), the exotic Weeping Willow (*Salix babylonica*), and probably cottonwoods (*Populus* spp.).

Eunica monima

Dingy Purplewing

Photo, p. 185

Description: To 1.0" in length. Head orange, lower part of face bluish black; body slender, greenish orange with a narrow, yellow lateral stripe and widely spaced tiny black spines. Also having a row of small, bluish black spines on the sides, a larger pair of spines on the back near the posterior end of the body, and a small bluish black patch on top of the prothorax and above the anus.

Similar Species: None.

Habitat: Uplands. Tropical hardwood hammocks.

U.S. Distribution: Southern Florida, Texas, and occasionally southern Arizona.

Natural History: This rare species occurs in a few parks in southern Miami-Dade County. Three or more generations are produced each year. The pale green eggs are laid in clusters on the undersides of the host leaves. The caterpillars eat young leaves and live in a messy nest of silk and frass (p. 15).

Caterpillar Season: Throughout the year.

Host Plants: Gumbo-Limbo (*Bursera simaruba*, p. 260), a tree in the Gumbo-Limbo family (Burseraceae).

Eunica tatila

Florida Purplewing

Photo, p. 185

Description: To 1.3" in length. Head orange and black with short spines and a pair of long, branched spines on top that are knobbed at the tips; body slender, greenish orange, the posterior end black, and having black branched spines.

Similar Species: None.

Habitat: Uplands. Tropical hardwood hammocks.

U.S. Distribution: Upper Florida Keys and occasionally southern Texas.

Natural History: This beautiful butterfly was locally common in the Upper Florida Keys, but has become very rare in recent years. Lignumvitae Key State Botanical Site is the best place to see the Florida Purplewing. There are three or more generations each year. The pale green eggs are laid singly on the upperside of leaves of the host. The young caterpillar eats the tip of the leaf and rests on the exposed midrib that is extended by attaching fecal pellets with silk (p. 22).

Caterpillar Season: Throughout the year.

Host Plants: Crabwood (*Gymnanthes lucida*, p. 265), a small tree in the Spurge family (Euphorbiaceae).

Marpesia petreus

Ruddy Daggerwing

Photo, p. 191

Description: To 1.4" in length. Head orange and black with an enormously long pair of black spines on top; body slender, orange and white with pale blue and black markings, and having a long bluish black spine on the top of abdominal segments 2, 4, 6, and 8.

Similar Species: None.

Habitat: Uplands and wetlands. Hammocks and swamps.

U.S. Distribution: Central and southern Florida, southern Texas, and occasionally southern Arizona.

Natural History: This butterfly is locally common in southern Florida. At least three generations are produced each year. The yellowish eggs are laid singly on the new growth. The caterpillars eat young leaves.

Caterpillar Season: Throughout the year.

Host Plants: Trees including Strangler Fig (*Ficus aurea*, p. 294) and Wild Banyan Tree (*Ficus citrifolia*, p. 295) in the Mulberry family (Moraceae).

Leafwings (subfamily Charaxinae)

Anaea troglodyta floridalis

Florida Leafwing

Photo, p. 191

Description: To 1.4" in length. Head green with short, rounded orange spines, those on top of the head orange and black; body slender, green with numerous tiny whitish spines, a yellow lateral stripe curved upward to a pair of dark spots on the top of the second abdominal segment, and some small dark patches on top of the posterior end.

Similar Species: None.

Habitat: Uplands. Pine rocklands.

U.S. Distribution: Southern Florida.

Natural History: This rare butterfly occurs on Big Pine Key and in Everglades National Park. There are three or more generations produced each year. The pale green eggs are laid on the leaves of the host. Caterpillars eat young leaves and live exposed on the plant.

Caterpillar Season: Throughout the year.

Host Plants: Pineland Croton (*Croton linearis*, p. 264), a small shrub in the Spurge family (Euphorbiaceae).

Anaea andria

Goatweed Leafwing

Photo, p. 191

Description: To 1.3" in length. Head green with short rounded yellowish spines; body slender, green, covered with small whitish spines that produce a granular appearance, and sometimes marked with red spots on the back.

Similar Species: None.

Habitat: Uplands. Sandhills and dry flatwoods.

U.S. Distribution: Florida westward to Arizona and northward to Colorado, Nebraska, Iowa, Illinois, and Indiana.

Natural History: This butterfly occurs sporadically in northern and central Florida, but may sometimes be locally common. There are two generations per year. The pale green eggs are laid on the new growth of the host plant. The young caterpillar eats the leaf tip except for the midrib, upon which it rests. The larvae attach fecal pellets to their backs (p. 22) and to the base of the leaf midrib with silk, probably to repel ants and other predators. Older caterpillars tie the edges of leaves together with silk to form a nest (p. 15). The larva rests with the heavily sclerotized head blocking the entrance of the nest during the day, and exits the shelter at night to feed. The life stages of the Goatweed Leafwing are shown on p. 39.

Caterpillar Season: March through early November.

Host Plants: Silver Croton (*Croton argyranthemus*, p. 263) and Woolly Croton (*Croton capitatus*), herbs in the Spurge family (Euphorbiaceae).

Emperors (subfamily Apaturinae)

Asterocampa celtis

Hackberry Emperor

Photo, p. 191

Description: To 1.4" in length. Head green with faint white stripes, the upper half black, short spines on the sides, and a pair of short horns on top; body stout, green with numerous tiny yellow dots, two narrow yellow stripes on the back, narrow longitudinal and oblique yellow stripes on the sides, and two short tails on the posterior end.

Similar Species: The Tawny Emperor and American Snout also eat hackberries.

Habitat: Uplands. Hammocks.

U.S. Distribution: Florida westward to Arizona and northward into Colorado, Nebraska, Minnesota, Wisconsin, Michigan, New York, and Massachusetts.

Natural History: This butterfly occurs abundantly near the host trees in northern and central Florida, but is infrequent in the southern parts of the state. There are three generations each year. Females lay their pale yellow eggs one at a time on the undersides of the host leaves. The caterpillars rest on the undersides of leaves when not feeding. They are highly visible with a beam from a flashlight at night. Young larvae overwinter in a leaf shelter. The life stages of the Hackberry Emperor are shown on p. 40.

Caterpillar Season: Throughout the year.

Host Plants: Trees in the Hackberry family (Celtidaceae), including Sugarberry (*Celtis laevigata*, p. 261) and Hackberry (*Celtis occidentalis*).

Asterocampa clyton

Tawny Emperor

Photo, p. 191

Description: To 1.5" in length. Head green with faint white stripes, short spines on the sides, and a pair of short, black horns on top; body stout, green with broad yellow and white stripes, and a pair of short tails on the posterior.

Similar Species: The Hackberry Emperor and American Snout also use hackberries.

Habitat: Uplands. Hammocks.

U.S. Distribution: Florida westward to southern Arizona and northward into Nebraska, Minnesota, Wisconsin, Michigan, New York, and Massachusetts.

Natural History: This butterfly occurs abundantly near the host trees in northern and central Florida, but is more local in southern parts of the state. There are three generations each year. Females lay large clusters of eggs on the undersides of the host leaves. The caterpillars are gregarious at first (p. 18), but become more solitary as they mature. They eat leaves and live in shelters of leaves tied together with silk. When disturbed, they twitch their bodies from side to side to deter predators. Partly grown larvae overwinter in a large group in a shelter made of two leaves tied together and lined with silk (p. 11).

Caterpillar Season: Throughout the year.

Host Plants: Trees in the Hackberry family (Celtidaceae), including Sugarberry (*Celtis laevigata*, p. 261) and Hackberry (*Celtis occidentalis*).

Satyrs and Wood-Nymphs (subfamily Satyrinae)

Enodia portlandia

Southern Pearly-eye

Photo, p. 195

Description: To 1.5" in length. Head green with two red-tipped horns on top; body slender, green mottled with yellow and narrow pale yellow lines on the sides, and two red-tipped tails at the posterior end, or the head and body brown with black lines and dashes on the back. The horns are shorter than the length of the head.

Similar Species: None.

Habitat: Wetlands. Wet hammocks, lower slopes of seeps, and margins of swamps, streams, and rivers.

U.S. Distribution: Florida westward to eastern Texas and northward into Missouri, Kentucky, and Virginia.

Natural History: This butterfly occurs in northern and central Florida and is locally common. There are three generations produced each year. The pale green eggs are laid singly on the host leaves. The caterpillars rest on the underside of the host leaves when not feeding. Partly grown larvae overwinter. The life stages of the Southern Pearly-eye are shown on p. 41.

Caterpillar Season: Throughout the year.

Host Plants: Switchcane (*Arundinaria gigantea*, p. 228), a small bamboo in the Grass family (Poaceae).

Satyrodes appalachia
Appalachian Brown
Photo, p. 195

Description: To 1.3" in length. Head green with two red-tipped horns on top; body slender, green overcast with yellow, narrow pale yellow lines on the sides, and two red-tipped tails at the posterior end. The horns are about as long as the length of the head.

Similar Species: None.

Habitat: Wetlands. Wet hammocks and swamps.

U.S. Distribution: Florida westward to Mississippi and northward into Minnesota, Wisconsin, Michigan, New York, Vermont, and New Hampshire.

Natural History: This uncommon butterfly occurs in northern and central Florida, but is very local. Probably three generations are produced each year. The pale green eggs are laid singly on the leaves of the host. The caterpillars hide on the undersides of the host leaves. Partly grown larvae overwinter.

Caterpillar Season: Throughout the year.

Host Plants: Atlantic Sedge (*Carex atlantica*) and Narrowfruit Horned Beaksedge (*Rhynchospora inundata*, p. 225) in the Sedge family (Cyperaceae).

Cyllopsis gemma
Gemmed Satyr
Photo, p. 195

Description: To 1.0" in length. Head green with dark stripes and a pair of black-tipped horns on top; body slender, green with faint yellow lines, and a pair of tails on the posterior end, or head and body brown with pale brown lines and black spots. The horns are longer than the length of the head.

Similar Species: None.

Habitat: Uplands and wetlands. Wet hammocks and margins of swamps.

U.S. Distribution: Florida westward to eastern Texas and northward into Missouri, Illinois, Indiana, Ohio, West Virginia, and Virginia.

Natural History: This secretive butterfly occurs in low abundance in northern and central Florida. There are three or more generations produced each year. The pale green eggs are laid singly on the leaves of the host. The caterpillars hide on the underside of the host leaves and are difficult to find. Partly grown larvae overwinter.

Caterpillar Season: Throughout the year.

Host Plants: Slender Woodoats (*Chasmanthium laxum*, p. 228) and probably related grasses (family Poaceae).

Hermeuptychia sosybius

Carolina Satyr

Photo, p. 193

Description: To 1.0" in length. Head green with a pair of very short pinkish spikes on top; body slender, green covered with numerous tiny white dots, a row of tiny white spots along the sides, and having a pair of short tails on the posterior end.

Similar Species: None.

Habitat: Uplands and wetlands. Hammocks, flatwoods, margins of swamps, and shady yards.

U.S. Distribution: Florida westward to eastern Texas and northward into Missouri, Indiana, Ohio, West Virginia, Virginia, and Delaware.

Natural History: This butterfly occurs abundantly throughout the state, except in the Keys. At least three generations are produced each year. The pale green eggs are laid singly on the host leaves. The caterpillars rest on the undersides of the leaves and are difficult to find. Partly grown larvae overwinter.

Caterpillar Season: Throughout the year.

Host Plants: Grasses (family Poaceae) including Common Carpetgrass (*Axonopus fissifolius*), Woodsgrass (*Oplismenus hirtellus*), St. Augustinegrass (*Stenotaphrum secundatum*, p. 234), and the naturalized exotic Tropical Signalgrass (*Urochloa distachya*).

Neonympha areolata

Georgia Satyr

Photo, p. 193

Description: To 1.0" in length. Head green with a pair of short pink spikes on top; body slender, green overcast with yellow and sprinkled with tiny yellow dots, and having a pair of short tails on the posterior end.

Similar Species: The Common Wood-Nymph also uses bluestems.

Habitat: Uplands and wetlands. Sandhills, flatwoods, pine savannas, prairies, and pitcher plant seeps. Locally common.

U.S. Distribution: Florida westward to eastern Texas and northward along the Atlantic coast into southern New Jersey.

Natural History: This satyr is local, but often common throughout Florida except in the Keys. Two to three generations are produced each year. The pale green eggs are laid singly on the host leaves. The caterpillars rest on the undersides of the leaves and are difficult to find. Partly grown larvae overwinter.

Caterpillar Season: Throughout the year.

Host Plants: Grasses (family Poaceae) and sedges (family Cyperaceae). Probably mostly on bluestems (*Andropogon* spp.).

Megisto cymela

Little Wood-Satyr

Photo, p. 193

Description: To 1.2" in length. Head brown with a pair of very short spikes on top; body stout, light brown with darker brown stripes and short hairs, and having a pair of short tails on the posterior end.
Similar Species: None.
Habitat: Uplands and wetlands. Hammocks and the margins of swamps.
U.S. Distribution: Florida westward to eastern Texas and northward into North Dakota, Minnesota, Michigan, New York, and Maine.
Natural History: This butterfly is locally common in northern and central Florida. Only one generation is produced each year. The pale green eggs are laid on the host leaves. The caterpillars rest on the undersides of the leaves and are very difficult to find. Partly grown larvae overwinter.
Caterpillar Season: Throughout the year.
Host Plants: Grasses (family Poaceae).

Cercyonis pegala

Common Wood-Nymph

Photo, p. 193

Description: To 1.5" in length. Head green and rounded; body stout, green with short hairs, two pale yellow lines on the sides, and a pair of short reddish tails at the posterior end.
Similar Species: The Georgia Satyr probably also uses bluestems.
Habitat: Uplands and wetlands. Sandhills, flatwoods, pine savannas, prairies, and pitcher plant seeps.
U.S. Distribution: All states except Alaska and Hawaii.
Natural History: This butterfly is locally common in northern Florida but becomes infrequent farther south, to the Orlando area. Only one generation is produced each year. The pale yellow eggs are laid on the leaves of the host. The caterpillars rest on the undersides of the leaves. Hatchling larvae overwinter.
Caterpillar Season: Throughout the year.
Host Plants: Broomsedge Bluestem (*Andropogon virginicus*, p. 227) and other grasses (family Poaceae).

Milkweed Butterflies (subfamily Danainae)

Danaus plexippus
Monarch

Photo, p. 191

Description: To 2.0" in length. Head whitish with black stripes; body stout, banded with yellow, white, and black, a pair of black fleshy filaments on top of the second thoracic segment and also on top of the eighth abdominal segment.
Similar Species: The Queen and Soldier use milkweeds as well.
Habitat: Uplands and wetlands. Scrubs, sandhills, coastal uplands, flatwoods, pine savannas, prairies, marshes, citrus groves, pastures, and gardens.
U.S. Distribution: All states except Alaska.
Natural History: In northern Florida, Monarchs are seasonal, occurring in low numbers during the spring and by the millions during late summer and fall. In central and southern Florida, Monarchs breed all year. Two or more generations are produced each year. The whitish eggs are laid on the leaves and flower buds of the milkweed hosts, which vary by species in the amount of cardenolid toxins they contain. The caterpillars eat young leaves and flowers, storing the poisonous chemicals and becoming poisonous themselves. Their bright coloration warns predators that they are dangerous to eat. Milkweed butterflies prefer to lay their eggs on the most toxic species, thus ensuring that their offspring will be well protected. The milkweed plants also protect themselves with latex that sticks to the mouthparts of herbivores. Milkweed butterfly caterpillars often cut the leaves near the base of the blade to drain out the latex before eating.
Caterpillar Season: Throughout the year.
Host Plants: Herbs and vines in the Dogbane family (Apocynaceae) especially Curtiss' Milkweed (*Asclepias curtissii*), Pinewoods Milkweed (*Asclepias humistrata*, p. 246), Pink Swamp Milkweed (*Asclepias incarnata*, p. 247), Fewflower Milkweed (*Asclepias lanceolata*), Longleaf Milkweed (*Asclepias longifolia*), White Swamp Milkweed (*Asclepias perennis*, p. 247), Velvetleaf Milkweed (*Asclepias tomentosa*), Butterflyweed (*Asclepias tuberosa*) as well as the exotic Scarlet Milkweed (*Asclepias curassavica*, p. 246) and Giant Milkweed (*Calotropis gigantea*, p. 248).

Danaus gilippus
Queen

Photo, p. 193

Description: To 1.8" in length. Head white with black stripes; body slender, transversely banded with black and white, having bright yellow spots or bars on the back within the broad black bands, and pairs of black fleshy filaments on top of the second thoracic and second and eighth abdominal segments.
Similar Species: The Monarch and Soldier also eat milkweeds.

Habitat: Uplands and wetlands. Sandhills, coastal areas, pine savannas, prairies, marshes, citrus groves, pastures, and gardens.

U.S. Distribution: Florida westward to southern California and northward into Nevada, Utah, Colorado, and Kansas, and along the Atlantic coast to North Carolina.

Natural History: This butterfly is locally common in central and southern Florida. During late summer and fall, the Queen migrates and colonizes northward, especially along the coasts. At least three generations are produced each year. The whitish eggs are laid singly on the host leaves and flowers. The caterpillars eat young leaves and flowers. Their bright coloration warns predators that they are not good to eat. The life stages of the Queen are shown on p. 42.

Caterpillar Season: Throughout the year.

Host Plants: Herbs and vines in the Dogbane family (Apocynaceae) such as Curtiss' Milkweed (*Asclepias curtissii*), Pinewoods Milkweed (*Asclepias humistrata*, p. 246), Pink Swamp Milkweed (*Asclepias incarnata*, p. 247), Fewflower Milkweed (*Asclepias lanceolata*), Longleaf Milkweed (*Asclepias longifolia*), White Swamp Milkweed (*Asclepias perennis*, p. 247), Velvetleaf Milkweed (*Asclepias tomentosa*), rarely Butterflyweed (*Asclepias tuberosa*), Gulf Coast Swallowwort (*Cynanchum angustifolium*, p. 248), Florida Milkvine (*Matelea floridana*, p. 249), White Twinevine (*Sarcostemma clausum*, p. 250), as well as the exotic Scarlet Milkweed (*Asclepias curassavica*, p. 246) and Latexplant (*Morrenia odorata*, p. 249).

Danaus eresimus

Soldier

Photo, p. 193

Description: To 1.8" in length. Head white with black stripes; body slender, brown, banded with black and white, with a broad white stripe on the sides, and pairs of black fleshy filaments on top of the second thoracic and second and eighth abdominal segments.

Similar Species: The Monarch and Queen also use milkweeds.

Habitat: Uplands and wetlands. Mostly in prairies, marshes, citrus groves, pastures, gardens, and weedy disturbed sites.

U.S. Distribution: Florida, southern Texas, and occasionally southern Arizona.

Natural History: This butterfly is locally common to abundant in southern and central Florida. Three or more generations are produced each year. The whitish eggs are laid singly on the host. The caterpillars eat young leaves and flowers.

Caterpillar Season: Throughout the year.

Host Plants: Herbs and vines in the Dogbane family (Apocynaceae) especially White Twinevine (*Sarcostemma clausum*, p. 250), swallowwort (*Cynanchum* spp.), and the exotic Latexplant (*Morrenia odorata*, p. 249), as well as milkweeds (*Asclepias* spp.).

Skippers (family Hesperiidae)

Skipper caterpillars usually live in distinctive shelters of folded pieces of leaf or leaves tied together. Some moths, especially in the family Pyralidae, also make shelters, but the leaves are rolled and tied with silk, or several leaves are tied together in a messy manner. The most diagnostic feature of skipper larvae is their large head, which is usually more constricted at the back than that of other caterpillars. There are three subfamilies of skippers in Florida. Spread-winged Skipper larvae are thick-bodied and may be green, brown, or brightly colored. Some species have yellow or red eye patches on the head. In Florida, they eat plants in the Amaranth, Beech, Buckthorn, Mallow, Red Mangrove, and Pea families. The caterpillars of Grass-Skippers are more slender than those of the Spread-winged Skippers. They are usually green or brown, and some species develop white wax glands on the underside of the body in the last larval stage. Grass-Skipper larvae eat monocots (plants with one seed leaf). Most eat grasses and sedges, but a few also use hosts in the Arrowroot, Canna, Ginger, and Palm families. Giant-Skippers have large, thick-bodied caterpillars that are white or brown with reddish brown heads. These larvae are usually difficult to find because they bore into the stems and roots of yuccas. The most distinctive sign is the cigar-shaped tent that the caterpillar constructs from silk and plant fibers.

Spread-winged Skippers (subfamily Pyrginae)

Phocides pigmalion
Mangrove Skipper
Photo, p. 199

Description: To 2.0" in length. Head reddish brown, darker around the mouth, rounded with large yellow eye patches; body stout, waxy white with small dark spots. Young larvae are red with transverse yellow stripes.
Similar Species: None.
Habitat: Wetlands. Mangrove swamps and nearby areas.
U.S. Distribution: Coastal areas of central and southern Florida.
Natural History: This large skipper is locally common near mangroves. At least three generations are produced each year. The green eggs are laid singly on the leaves of the host. The caterpillars cut and fold over flaps of leaf to make a shelter in which they hide.
Caterpillar Season: Throughout the year.
Host Plants: Red Mangrove (*Rhizophora mangle*, p. 301), a tree in the Red Mangrove family (Rhizophoraceae).

Epargyreus zestos

Zestos Skipper

Photo, p. 197

Description: To 2.0" in length. Head dark brown, rounded with large yellow eye patches; body stout, green overcast with whitish green, forming faint transverse lines, the thorax reddish below, the prothoracic shield broad and brown, the thoracic legs brown, and the prolegs pale orange.

Similar Species: The Long-tailed Skipper also uses legumes.

Habitat: Uplands. Tropical hardwood hammocks.

U.S. Distribution: Florida Keys.

Natural History: This skipper was once locally common in the Keys, but has become very rare in recent years. At least three generations are produced each year. The green eggs are laid singly on the leaves of the host. The caterpillar eats leaves and lives in a shelter of leaves tied together with silk.

Caterpillar Season: Throughout the year.

Host Plants: Florida Hammock Milkpea (*Galactia striata*, p. 275), a vine in the Pea family (Fabaceae).

Epargyreus clarus

Silver-spotted Skipper

Photo, p. 197

Description: To 2.0" in length. Head dark reddish brown, rounded with large yellow eye patches; body stout, yellow with narrow dark stripes and spots, thorax reddish below, the prothoracic shield broad and brown, the thoracic legs brown, and the prolegs orange.

Similar Species: The Long-tailed Skipper and Golden-banded Skipper also use legumes and have bright colors.

Habitat: Uplands and wetlands. Sandhills, margins of hammocks and swamps.

U.S. Distribution: All states except Alaska and Hawaii.

Natural History: This large skipper is locally common in northern and central Florida, but is infrequent in the southern part of the state. Three generations are produced each year. Females lay the green eggs singly on the leaves of the host or sometimes on other nearby plants. The young caterpillar makes a shelter by eating two narrow channels in a leaf along the edge of the blade. The resulting flap is then shaped into a cone, folded over, and tied with silk. The young caterpillars rest upside down on the underside of the flap. Older caterpillars make baggy shelters by folding over large leaves or tying two or more leaves together with silk (p. 15). When provoked, they spit a bitter-tasting greenish fluid. The pupae overwinter.

Caterpillar Season: March through early November.

Host Plants: Herbs, vines, shrubs, and trees in the Pea family (Fabaceae), including Bastard Indigobush (*Amorpha fruticosa*, p. 266), American Hogpeanut (*Amphicarpaea bracteata*, p. 267), Groundnut (*Apios americana*, p. 267), American Wisteria (*Wisteria frutescens*), and the introduced Dixie Ticktrefoil (*Desmodium tortuosum*, p. 274), Kudzu (*Pueraria montana*), Black Locust (*Robinia pseudoacacia*, p. 281), and Chinese Wisteria (*Wisteria sinensis*).

Polygonus leo

Hammock Skipper

Photo, p. 199

Description: To 1.5" in length. Head flattened, somewhat triangular, white with a black line on the sides and two black spots on the upper face; body stout, pale green with numerous tiny yellow spots, a narrow yellow line on the upper sides, the prothoracic shield indistinct, and the thoracic legs pale brown.
Similar Species: None.
Habitat: Uplands. Tropical hardwood hammocks and gardens.
U.S. Distribution: Florida, southern Texas, and occasionally southern Arizona.
Natural History: This skipper is locally common in southern Florida. At least three generations are produced each year. The green eggs are laid singly on the leaves of the hosts. The caterpillar eats leaves and lives in a shelter of leaves tied together with silk. When provoked, they spit a bitter-tasting greenish fluid.
Caterpillar Season: Throughout the year.
Host Plants: Florida Fishpoison Tree (*Piscidia piscipula*, p. 280) and the exotic Karum Tree (*Pongamia pinnata*), both in the Pea family (Fabaceae).

Urbanus proteus

Long-tailed Skipper

Photo, p. 197

Description: To 1.5" in length. Head brown, black on the lower face and in back, rounded with reddish orange eye patches; body stout, yellowish green with small black spots, a wide yellow line on the upper sides that becomes orange near the posterior end, the prothorax red below, prothoracic shield broad and brown, the first pair of thoracic legs darker brown than the others, and the prolegs orange.
Similar Species: The Silver-spotted Skipper and Golden-banded Skipper also use legumes and have bright colors.
Habitat: Uplands. Scrubs, sandhills, coastal uplands, flatwoods, margins of hammocks, roadsides, and weedy disturbed sites.
U.S. Distribution: Florida westward to southern Texas and northward into Missouri and Tennessee, and along the Atlantic coast to New Jersey.
Natural History: This common skipper occurs throughout Florida and migrates southward into the state by the millions during late summer and fall. At least three generations are produced each year. Females lay pale yellow eggs singly or

in short stacks on the undersides of the host leaves. Young caterpillars make shelters by cutting, folding over, and tying pieces of leaves together with silk (p. 15). Older larvae make shelters by tying whole leaves together. Caterpillars of this species, called bean leaf rollers, are sometimes pests on planted beans. When provoked, they spit a bitter-tasting greenish fluid. The life stages of the Long-tailed Skipper are shown on p. 43.

Caterpillar Season: Throughout the year.

Host Plants: Herbs and vines in the Pea family, including Pineland Butterfly Pea (*Centrosema arenicola*), Spurred Butterfly Pea (*Centrosema virginianum*, p. 269), Atlantic Pigeonwings (*Clitoria mariana*, p. 271), Florida Ticktrefoil (*Desmodium floridanum*), Creeping Ticktrefoil (*Desmodium incanum*, p. 273), Panicledleaf Ticktrefoil (*Desmodium paniculatum*), Slimleaf Ticktrefoil (*Desmodium tenuifolium*), Velvetleaf Ticktrefoil (*Desmodium viridiflorum*), Elliott's Milkpea (*Galactia elliottii*, p. 274), Florida Hammock Milkpea (*Galactia striata*, p. 275), Eastern Milkpea (*Galactia regularis*), Downy Milkpea (*Galactia volubilis*, p. 275), Least Snoutbean (*Rhynchosia minima*), Hairypod Cowpea (*Vigna luteola*, p. 286), American Wisteria (*Wisteria frutescens*), and the exotic species White Moneywort (*Alysicarpus vaginalis*), Asian Pigeonwings (*Clitoria ternatea*), Dixie Ticktrefoil (*Desmodium tortuosum*, p. 274), Soybean (*Glycine max*), Wild Bush-bean (*Macroptilium lathyroides*), Garden Bean (*Phaseolus vulgaris*), Rattlebox (*Sesbania punicea*), and Kudzu (*Pueraria montana*). Females also lay eggs on Woolly Dutchman's-Pipe (*Aristolochia tomentosa*), Garden Radish (*Raphanus sativus*), and Showy Rattlebox (*Crotalaria spectabilis*); the young caterpillars will make small shelters on the leaves, but are unable to survive on these plants.

Urbanus dorantes

Dorantes Longtail

Photo, p. 197

Description: To 1.5" in length. Head dark brown or black, rounded with a few small spines on top; body stout with short hairs, usually green overcast with whitish green or occasionally brown with yellowish brown markings, a dark line down the back and a chainlike band of spots on the sides, the prothorax reddish below, prothoracic shield broad and dark brown, and the first pair of thoracic legs darker brown than the others.

Similar Species: The Hoary Edge and cloudywings also use legumes and are drably colored.

Habitat: Uplands. Margins of hammocks and roadsides and weedy, disturbed places.

U.S. Distribution: Florida, southern Texas, and southern Arizona.

Natural History: This skipper is common in southern and central Florida and disperses northward, especially along the coasts, in numbers during late summer and fall. At least three generations are produced each year. The greenish eggs are laid singly on the flower stalks and leaves. The caterpillar eats leaves and lives in a shelter of leaves tied together with silk.

Caterpillar Season: Throughout the year.

Host Plants: Herbs and vines in the Pea family (Fabaceae) including Creeping Ticktrefoil (*Desmodium incanum*, p. 273) and occasionally Hairypod Cowpea (*Vigna luteola*, p. 286), as well as the exotic species Dixie Ticktrefoil (*Desmodium tortuosum*, p. 274) and Threeflower Ticktrefoil (*Desmodium triflorum*).

Autochton cellus

Golden Banded-Skipper

Photo, p. 197

Description: To 1.4" in length. Head reddish brown, rounded with large pale orange eye patches; body stout, translucent green with numerous tiny yellow spots and a wide yellow band on the sides, prothorax reddish below, prothoracic shield broad and dark brown, and the first pair of thoracic legs darker brown than the others.

Similar Species: The Silver-spotted Skipper and Long-tailed Skipper also use legumes and have bright colors.

Habitat: Uplands and wetlands. Moist hammocks and the margins of swamps along streams and rivers.

U.S. Distribution: Florida westward to Arizona and northward into Missouri, southern Indiana, West Virginia, and Maryland.

Natural History: This rare skipper occurs in highly localized colonies in the Panhandle and north-central Florida. There are two generations each year. The pale yellow eggs are laid singly or in short stacks on the undersides of the leaves. The caterpillar eats leaves and lives in a shelter of leaves tied together with silk. The pupae overwinter.

Caterpillar Season: March through early November.

Host Plants: Vines in the Pea (*Fabaceae*) family including American Hogpeanut (*Amphicarpaea bracteata*, p. 267) and occasionally the invasive exotic Kudzu (*Pueria montana*).

Achalarus lyciades

Hoary Edge

Photo, p. 195

Description: To 1.4" in length. Head dark brown or black, rounded with a few small spines on top; body stout with short hairs, greenish overcast and heavily spotted with yellowish brown, the posterior end slightly darkened, a yellowish brown line on the upper sides, prothorax reddish below, the prothoracic shield broad and dark brown, and the first pair of thoracic legs darker brown than the others.

Similar Species: The Dorantes Longtail and cloudywings also use legumes and are drably colored.

Habitat: Uplands. Sandhills and dry flatwoods.

U.S. Distribution: Florida westward to eastern Texas and northward into Iowa, Illinois, Michigan, New York, Vermont, and New Hampshire.

Natural History: This uncommon skipper occurs in northern Florida. Two generations are produced each year. The whitish eggs are laid singly on the undersides of the leaves of the hosts. The caterpillar eats leaves and lives in a shelter of leaves tied together with silk. Fully grown larvae overwinter.

Caterpillar Season: Throughout the year.

Host Plants: Herbs and vines in the Pea family (Fabaceae) including Atlantic Pigeonwings (*Clitoria mariana*, p. 271) and Creeping Ticktrefoil (*Desmodium incanum*, p. 273).

Thorybes bathyllus
Southern Cloudywing

Photo, p. 195

Description: To 1.4" in length. Head dark brown or black, rounded; body stout with short hairs, olive green to brown, a dark line on the back and a pinkish brown line on the sides above the spiracles, prothorax reddish below, the prothoracic shield broad and dark brown, and the thoracic legs all dark brown. The younger stages are green.

Similar Species: The Dorantes Longtail, Hoary Edge, and other cloudywings also use legumes and are drably colored.

Habitat: Uplands. Sandhills and dry flatwoods.

U.S. Distribution: Florida westward to eastern Texas and northward into Nebraska, Iowa, Wisconsin, Michigan, New York, and Maine.

Natural History: This skipper is locally common in northern and central Florida. There are two generations each year. The pale green eggs are laid singly on the leaves of the host. The caterpillar eats leaves and lives in a shelter of leaves tied together with silk. Fully grown larvae overwinter.

Caterpillar Season: Throughout the year.

Host Plants: Herbs and vines in the Pea family (Fabaceae) including Atlantic Pigeonwings (*Clitoria mariana*, p. 271), Pine Barren Ticktrefoil (*Desmodium strictum*), Velvetleaf Ticktrefoil (*Desmodium viridiflorum*), and Hairy Lespedeza (*Lespedeza hirta*, p. 277).

Thorybes pylades
Northern Cloudywing

Page 000: Photo 233

Description: To 1.5" in length. Very similar to the Southern Cloudywing, but the body color usually pinkish brown.

Similar Species: The Dorantes Longtail, Hoary Edge, and other cloudywings also use legumes and are drably colored.

Habitat: Uplands. Scrubs, sandhills, and dry flatwoods.

U.S. Distribution: All states except Alaska and Hawaii.

Natural History: This skipper is locally common in northern and central Florida. Two generations are produced each year. The pale green eggs are laid singly on the leaves of the hosts. The caterpillar eats leaves and lives in a shelter of leaves tied together with silk. Fully grown larvae overwinter.

Caterpillar Season: Throughout the year.

Host Plants: Herbs and vines in the Pea family including Groundnut (*Apios americana*, p. 267), Pineland Butterfly Pea (*Centrosema arenicola*), Spurred Butterfly Pea (*Centrosema virginianum*, p. 269), Velvetleaf Ticktrefoil (*Desmodium viridiflorum*), Elliott's Milkpea (*Galactia elliottii*, p. 274), Eastern Milkpea (*Galactia regularis*), Hairy Lespedeza (*Lespedeza hirta*, p. 277), and Florida Hoarypea (*Tephrosia florida*, p. 285).

Thorybes confusis
Confused Cloudywing

Photo, p. 197

Description: To 1.5" in length. Very similar to the Southern Cloudywing, but the body paler brown.

Similar Species: The Dorantes Longtail, Hoary Edge, and other cloudywings also use legumes and are drably colored.

Habitat: Uplands. Sandhills and dry flatwoods.

U.S. Distribution: Florida westward to eastern Texas and northward into Kansas, Missouri, Illinois, Indiana, Ohio, and Pennsylvania.

Natural History: This skipper is locally common in northern and central Florida. Two generations are produced each year. The pale green eggs are laid singly on the leaves of the hosts. The caterpillar eats leaves and lives in a shelter of leaves tied together with silk. Fully grown larvae overwinter.

Caterpillar Season: Throughout the year.

Host Plants: Herbs and vines in the Pea family (Fabaceae) including *Lespedeza* species and Florida Hoarypea (*Tephrosia florida*, p. 285).

Staphylus hayhurstii
Hayhurst's Scallopwing

Photo, p. 201

Description: To 1.0" in length. Head black, rounded with short feathery hairs; body somewhat stout, translucent green with short hairs, numerous tiny white spots and thin broken white lines on the sides, prothoracic shield broad, pale brown, and the thoracic legs pale brown.

Similar Species: None.

Habitat: Uplands. Margins of hammocks.

U.S. Distribution: Florida westward to central Texas and northward to Nebraska, Iowa, Illinois, Indiana, Ohio, West Virginia, and Pennsylvania.

Natural History: This uncommon skipper occurs throughout Florida. Two to three generations are produced each year. The brownish eggs are laid singly on the leaves of the host. The caterpillar eats leaves and lives in a shelter of leaves tied together with silk. Partly grown larvae overwinter.

Caterpillar Season: Throughout the year.

Host Plants: Juba's Bush (*Iresine diffusa*, p. 239), an herb in the Amaranth family (Amaranthaceae).

Ephyriades brunneus
Florida Duskywing

Photo, p. 199

Description: To 1.1" in length. Head black with orange patches on the sides and upper face; body somewhat stout, translucent green with numerous tiny yellow spots, a dark line narrowly outlined with yellow on the back, narrow yellow lines on the sides, prothoracic shield indistinct, and the thoracic legs pale.

Similar Species: None.

Habitat: Uplands. Pine rocklands and margins of tropical hardwood hammocks.

U.S. Distribution: Southern Florida.

Natural History: This skipper is locally common on Big Pine Key and Long Pine Key in Everglades National Park. At least three generations are produced each year. The pale green eggs are laid singly on the leaves of the host. The caterpillar eats leaves and lives in a shelter of leaves tied together with silk.

Caterpillar Season: Throughout the year.

Host Plants: Shrubs in the Barbados Cherry family (Malpighiaceae). Primarily Long Key Locustberry (*Byrsonima lucida*, p. 292) and occasionally the exotic Barbados Cherry (*Malpighia emarginata*).

Erynnis brizo
Sleepy Duskywing

Photo, p. 201

Description: To 1.1" in length. Head brown with small yellowish eye patches; body somewhat stout, green with short hairs, numerous tiny yellow spots, a dark line on the back, a narrow yellow line on the sides, prothoracic shield indistinct, and the thoracic legs pale. The larvae change color from green to brown in the fall as they stop feeding and prepare to overwinter (p. 12).

Similar Species: Juvenal's Duskywing and Horace's Duskywing also eat oaks.

Habitat: Uplands. Scrubs, sandhills, and dry flatwoods.

U.S. Distribution: Florida westward to California and northward into Utah, Colorado, Minnesota, Michigan, and New York.

Natural History: This skipper is locally common in northern and central Florida, and infrequent in southern parts of the state. There is only one generation produced each year in the spring. The pale green eggs are laid on the leaves of oaks. The caterpillar eats leaves and lives in a shelter formed by tying the edges of a leaf together with silk (p. 16). Fully grown larvae overwinter.

Caterpillar Season: Throughout the year.

Host Plants: Trees in the Beech family (Fagaceae) including Chapman's Oak (*Quercus chapmanii*), Scrub Oak (*Quercus inopina*), Turkey Oak (*Quercus laevis*, p. 287), and Myrtle Oak (*Quercus myrtifolia*, p. 288).

Erynnis juvenalis

Juvenal's Duskywing

Photo, p. 199

Description: To 1.3" in length. Head flattened and triangular in shape, brown, dark around the mouth with pale orange eye patches and pale orange spots on top and on the sides of face; body somewhat stout, bluish green with numerous tiny white spots, a faint dark line on the back, a yellow line on the sides, the prothoracic shield indistinct, and the thoracic legs pale.

Similar Species: The Sleepy Duskywing and Horace's Duskywing also eat oaks.

Habitat: Uplands. Scrubs, sandhills, dry flatwoods, and margins of xeric hammocks.

U.S. Distribution: Florida westward to central Texas and northward into Wyoming, North Dakota, Minnesota, Wisconsin, Michigan, New York, and Maine. Also in southern Arizona and New Mexico.

Natural History: This skipper is locally common in northern and central Florida, and infrequent in southern parts of the state. There is only one generation produced each year in the spring. The pale green eggs are laid singly on the leaves of oaks. The caterpillar eats leaves and lives in a shelter formed by tying leaves or parts of leaves together with silk. Fully grown larvae overwinter.

Caterpillar Season: Throughout the year.

Host Plants: Trees in the Beech family (Fagaceae) including Chapman's Oak (*Quercus chapmanii*), Southern Red Oak (*Quercus falcata*), Scrub Oak (*Quercus inopina*), Turkey Oak (*Quercus laevis*, p. 287), and other oaks.

Erynnis horatius

Horace's Duskywing

Photo, p. 199

Description: To 1.3" in length. Very similar to Juvenal's Duskywing, but the yellow line on the sides is faint or absent.

Similar Species: The Sleepy Duskywing and Juvenal's Duskywing also eat oaks.

Habitat: Uplands. Scrubs, sandhills, flatwoods, and margins of hammocks, thickets, and swamps.

U.S. Distribution: Florida westward to New Mexico and northward into Utah, Colorado, Nebraska, Minnesota, Wisconsin, Michigan, New York, and Massachusetts.

Natural History: This skipper is locally common throughout Florida, except for the Keys. At least three generations are produced each year. The pale green eggs are laid singly on the new growth of oaks. The caterpillar eats leaves and lives in a shelter formed by tying leaves or parts of leaves together with silk. Fully grown larvae overwinter.

Caterpillar Season: Throughout the year.

Host Plants: Trees in the Beech family (Fagaceae) including Chapman's Oak (*Quercus chapmanii*), Sand Live Oak (*Quercus geminata*), Scrub Oak (*Quercus inopina*), Turkey Oak (*Quercus laevis*, p. 287), Laurel Oak (*Quercus laurifolia*, p. 287), Myrtle Oak (*Quercus myrtifolia*, p. 288), Water Oak (*Quercus nigra*, p. 288), Virginia Live Oak (*Quercus virginiana*, p. 289), and other oaks.

Erynnis martialis
Mottled Duskywing

Photo, p. 199

Description: To 1.2" in length. Head flattened and triangular in shape with small knobs near the top, dark brown with small orange eye patches, orange spots on the sides, and orange patches on the upper face; body somewhat stout with short hairs, green with numerous tiny white spots, a faint dark line on the back, a whitish line on the sides, the prothoracic shield indistinct, and the thoracic legs pale.

Similar Species: None.

Habitat: Uplands. Sandhills and dry flatwoods.

U.S. Distribution: Florida Panhandle westward to central Texas and northward into Minnesota, Wisconsin, Michigan, New York, Vermont, and New Hampshire. Also in Colorado and Nebraska.

Natural History: This rare skipper has occurred in the Panhandle region, but has not been observed in recent years. Two generations are produced each year. The pale green eggs are laid singly on the leaves of the host. The caterpillar eats leaves and lives in a shelter formed by tying leaves or parts of leaves together with silk. Fully grown larvae overwinter.

Caterpillar Season: Throughout the year.

Host Plants: New Jersey Tea (*Ceanothus americanus*, p. 300), a small shrub in the Buckthorn family (Rhamnaceae).

Erynnis zarucco

Zarucco Duskywing

Photo, p. 201

Description: To 1.3" in length. Head flattened and triangular in shape, dark brown to black with pale orange spots on the sides and pale orange patches on the upper face, the pattern often forming a dark W on the face; body somewhat stout, green with numerous tiny white spots, a faint dark line on the back, a narrow whitish line containing a pale yellow spot at the start of each segment on the sides, the prothoracic shield indistinct, and the thoracic legs pale.

Similar Species: The Wild Indigo Duskywing also eats legumes.

Habitat: Uplands and margins of wetlands. Scrubs, sandhills, coastal uplands, flatwoods, pine savannas, margins of hammocks and marshes.

U.S. Distribution: Florida westward to central Texas and northward into Oklahoma, Arkansas, Georgia, and the Carolinas.

Natural History: This common skipper occurs throughout most of Florida, but is infrequent in the extreme south and Keys. At least three generations are produced each year. The pale green eggs are laid singly on the new growth of the hosts. The caterpillar eats leaves and lives in a shelter formed by tying leaves or parts of leaves together with silk. Fully grown larvae overwinter.

Caterpillar Season: Throughout the year.

Host Plants: Herbs, vines, and shrubs in the Pea family (Fabaceae) including White Wild Indigo (*Baptisia alba*, p. 268), Elliott's Milkpea (*Galactia elliottii*, p. 274), Eastern Milkpea (*Galactia regularis*), Downy Milkpea (*Galactia volubilis*, p. 275), Carolina Indigo (*Indigofera caroliniana*, p. 276), Danglepod (*Sesbania herbacea*), Bladderpod (*Sesbania vesicaria*, p. 284), and the exotic plants Trailing Indigo (*Indigofera spicata*, p. 276) and Rattlebox (*Sesbania punicea*).

Erynnis baptisiae

Wild Indigo Duskywing

Photo, p. 201

Description: To 1.1" in length. Head flattened and triangular in shape, dark brown to black with small orange eye patches, orange-brown spots on the sides, and an orange-brown patch on the upper face, the pattern sometimes forming a black W on the face or occasionally the head entirely black; body somewhat stout, green with numerous tiny white spots, a faint dark line on the back, a narrow whitish line on the sides, the prothoracic shield indistinct, and the thoracic legs pale.

Similar Species: The Zarucco Duskywing eats similar legumes.

Habitat: Uplands. Sandhills and dry flatwoods.

U.S. Distribution: Florida Panhandle westward to central Texas and northward into Nebraska, Minnesota, Wisconsin, Michigan, New York, and Massachusetts.

Natural History: This skipper has been reported from the Panhandle region, but has not been observed in recent years. It is easily confused with the Zarucco Duskywing. There are two or three generations each year. The pale green eggs are laid singly on the leaves of the host. The caterpillar eats leaves and lives in a shelter formed by tying leaves or parts of leaves together with silk. Fully grown larvae overwinter.

Caterpillar Season: Throughout the year.

Host Plants: Not known for Florida, but probably White Wild Indigo (*Baptisia alba*, p. 268), an herb in the Pea family (Fabaceae).

Pyrgus communis
Common Checkered-Skipper

Photo, p. 203

Description: To 1.0" in length. Head black, rounded with short feathery hairs; body slender with short hairs that are sometimes enlarged at the tips, green with faint dark lines, the ones on the sides outlined with white, the prothoracic shield light brown at the front, black in back, and interrupted on top by a whitish line, the first pairs of thoracic legs darker brown than the last.

Similar Species: The White Checkered-Skipper and Tropical Checkered-Skipper also use mallows.

Habitat: Uplands. Pastures, roadsides, weed lots, and disturbed places.

U.S. Distribution: All states except Vermont, New Hampshire, Maine, Alaska, and Hawaii.

Natural History: This once common skipper has become rare in recent times. It is easily confused with the White Checkered-Skipper. The Common Checkered-Skipper occurs in northern and central Florida. At least three generations are produced each year. The pale green eggs are laid singly on the leaves of the hosts. The caterpillar eats leaves and lives in a shelter formed by tying living and/or dead leaves together with silk. Fully grown larvae overwinter.

Caterpillar Season: Throughout the year.

Host Plants: Herbs in the Mallow family (Malvaceae) including Common Fanpetals (*Sida acuta*, p. 293), Cuban Jute (*Sida rhombifolia*, p. 293), and occasionally Woodland Poppymallow (*Callirhoe papaver*).

Pyrgus albescens
White Checkered-Skipper

Photo, p. 201

Description: To 1.0" in length. Very similar to the Common Checkered-Skipper, but the body more frosted with white.

Similar Species: The Common Checkered-Skipper and Tropical Checkered-Skipper also use mallows.

Habitat: Uplands. Pastures, groves, roadsides, weed lots, and disturbed places.

U.S. Distribution: Florida westward to southern California and northward into Nevada and Utah.

Natural History: This species has only recently expanded its range eastward into Florida and is now locally common throughout the state, except for the Keys. There are three or more generations produced each year. The pale green eggs are laid singly on the leaves of the host. The caterpillar eats leaves and lives in a shelter formed by tying living and/or dead leaves together with silk (p. 16). Fully grown larvae overwinter.

Caterpillar Season: Throughout the year.

Host Plants: Herbs in the Mallow family (Malvaceae) including Common Fanpetals (*Sida acuta*, p. 293) and Cuban Jute (*Sida rhombifolia*, p. 293).

Pyrgus oileus

Tropical Checkered-Skipper

Photo, p. 203

Description: To 1.0" in length. Very similar to the other checkered skippers, but the prothoracic shield is interrupted by three whitish lines.

Similar Species: The Common Checkered-Skipper and White Checkered-Skipper also use mallows.

Habitat: Uplands. Pastures, groves, roadsides, weed lots, and disturbed places.

U.S. Distribution: Florida westward along the Gulf Coast into southern Texas. Also occasionally found in southern Arizona.

Natural History: This skipper is locally common in peninsular Florida, and infrequent in the Panhandle region. At least three generations are produced each year. The pale green eggs are laid singly on the leaves of the host. The caterpillar eats leaves and lives in a shelter formed by tying living and dead leaves together with silk.

Caterpillar Season: Throughout the year.

Host Plants: Herbs in the Mallow family (Malvaceae) including Common Fanpetals (*Sida acuta*, p. 293), Cuban Jute (*Sida rhombifolia*, p. 293), probably False Mallow (*Malvastrum corchorifolium*) and other mallows.

Pholisora catullus

Common Sootywing

Photo, p. 201

Description: To 0.8" in length. Head black, rounded with short feathery hairs; body somewhat stout with short hairs, green with numerous small white spots and faint dark lines, the ones on the sides outlined with white, the prothoracic shield broad and black, and the thoracic legs brown.

Similar Species: Hayhurst's Scallopwing also eats plants in the Amaranth family.

Habitat: Uplands. Pastures, agricultural fields, gardens, and weedy disturbed areas.

U.S. Distribution: All states except Vermont, New Hampshire, Maine, Alaska, and Hawaii.

Natural History: This skipper is local and uncommon in the Panhandle region and very rare in northern and central Florida. There are three generations per year. The brownish eggs are laid singly on the leaves of the host. The caterpillar eats leaves and lives in a shelter formed by tying leaves or parts of leaves together with silk. Fully grown larvae overwinter.

Caterpillar Season: Throughout the year.

Host Plants: Lamb's quarters (*Chenopodium album*, p. 239), an herb in the Amaranth family (Amaranthaceae).

Grass-Skippers (subfamily Hesperiinae)

Nastra lherminier
Swarthy Skipper

Photo, p. 205

Description: To 1.1" in length. Head somewhat conical, pale brown with reddish brown stripes around the margin and on the face; body slender, green overcast with pale yellow, a dark line on the back and sides highlighted with pale yellow, the prothoracic shield indistinct, and the thoracic legs pale green. Develops wax glands in lateral patches on the underside of abdominal segments 7 and 8 just prior to pupation.

Similar Species: The Neamathla Skipper and Arogos Skipper.

Habitat: Uplands. Sandhills, flatwoods, pine savannas, prairies, and weedy areas.

U.S. Distribution: Florida westward to central Texas and northward into Kansas, Missouri, Illinois, Indiana, Ohio, Pennsylvania, New York, and Connecticut.

Natural History: This skipper is locally common in northern and central Florida, and infrequent in the southern part of the state. At least three generations are produced each year. The whitish eggs are laid singly on the leaves of the hosts. The caterpillar may live in a tubular leaf shelter, or often simply exposed on the leaf blade.

Caterpillar Season: Throughout the year.

Host Plants: Grasses (family Poaceae) including Broomsedge Bluestem (*Andropogon virginicus*, p. 227), Lopsided Indiangrass (*Sorghastrum secundum*, p. 233), and the invasive exotic Cogongrass (*Imperata cylindrica*).

Nastra neamathla
Neamathla Skipper

Photo, p. 205

Description: Nearly identical to the Swarthy Skipper, but the reddish brown stripes on the face are wider.

Similar Species: The Swarthy Skipper and Arogos Skipper.

Habitat: Uplands. Sandhills, flatwoods, pine savannas, prairies, and weedy areas.

U.S. Distribution: Peninsular Florida and eastern Texas.

Natural History: This skipper is locally common in southern and central Florida. At least three generations are produced each year. The whitish eggs are laid singly on the leaves of the hosts. The caterpillar lives in a tubular leaf shelter.

Caterpillar Season: Throughout the year.

Host Plants: Grasses (family Poaceae) including Broomsedge Bluestem (*Andropogon virginicus*, p. 227) and Bearded Skeletongrass (*Gymnopogon ambiguus*).

Cymaenes tripunctus
Three-spotted Skipper

Photo, p. 203

Description: To 1.1" in length. Head somewhat conical, white with black stripes on the edges and down the center of the face; body slender, green frosted with white, faint dark lines on the back and sides outlined with white, the prothoracic shield indistinct, and the thoracic legs pale. Develops wax glands in lateral patches on the underside of abdominal segments 7 and 8 just prior to pupation.

Similar Species: The Clouded Skipper.

Habitat: Uplands. Margins of hammocks.

U.S. Distribution: Southern Florida.

Natural History: This species is locally common near patches of the host plants. Three or more generations are produced each year. The whitish eggs are laid singly on the leaves of the hosts. The young larva cuts and folds over a flap of leaf near the tip of the blade to make a shelter. The larger caterpillar makes a tubular leaf shelter, and frequently partly cuts the midrib at the base such that the shelter dangles downward from the tip of the leaf.

Caterpillar Season: Throughout the year.

Host Plants: Grasses (family Poaceae) including Southern Crabgrass (*Digitaria ciliaris*), Thin Paspalum (*Paspalum setaceum*), Eastern Gamagrass (*Tripsacum dactyloides*, p. 235) as well as the exotic Guineagrass (*Panicum maximum*, p. 231) and Paragrass (*Urochloa mutica*).

Lerema accius
Clouded Skipper

Photo, p. 203

Description: To 1.4" in length. Head somewhat conical, white with black stripes on the edges, three black stripes on the face, and a short brown line at the top; body slender, bluish green frosted with white, faint dark lines on back and sides outlined with white, the prothoracic shield a narrow dark band, and the thoracic legs pale. Develops wax glands in lateral patches on the underside of abdominal segments 7 and 8 just prior to pupation.

Similar Species: The Three-spotted Skipper and Byssus Skipper.

Habitat: Uplands and wetlands. Flatwoods, hammocks, swamps, agricultural fields, weed lots, and gardens.

U.S. Distribution: Florida westward to Texas and occasionally southern Arizona and northward into Oklahoma, Missouri, Kentucky, Pennsylvania, New Jersey, and Rhode Island.

Natural History: This common species occurs throughout Florida and is particularly abundant during late summer and fall. At least three generations are produced each year. The whitish eggs are laid singly on the leaves of the hosts. The young larva cuts and folds over a flap of leaf near the tip of the blade to make a shelter. The larger caterpillar makes a tubular leaf shelter (p. 16), and frequently partly cuts the midrib at the base such that the shelter dangles downward from the tip of the leaf.

Caterpillar Season: Throughout the year.

Host Plants: Coarse grasses (family Poaceae) including Switchcane (*Arundinaria gigantea*, p. 228), Indian Woodoats (*Chasmanthium latifolium*), Slender Woodoats (*Chasmanthium laxum*, p. 228), Deertongue Witchgrass (*Dichanthelium clandestinum*), Rough Barnyardgrass (*Echinochloa muricata*), Coast Cockspur (*Echinochloa walteri*), Beaked Panicum (*Panicum anceps*), Fall Panicgrass (*Panicum dichotomiflorum*), Maidencane (*Panicum hemitomon*, p. 231), Redtop Panicum (*Panicum rigidulum*, p. 232), Egyptian Paspalidium (*Paspalidium geminatum*), Florida Paspalum (*Paspalum floridanum*), Water Paspalum (*Paspalum repens*), Thin Paspalum (*Paspalum setaceum*), Savannah Panicum (*Phanopyrum gymnocarpon*), Sugarcane Plumegrass (*Saccharum giganteum*, p. 232), Coral Bristlegrass (*Setaria macrosperma*), St. Augustinegrass (*Stenotaphrum secundatum*, p. 234), Tall Redtop (*Tridens flavus*), Eastern Gamagrass (*Tripsacum dactyloides*, p. 235), and Southern Wild Rice (*Zizaniopsis miliacea*, p. 235), as well as the exotic species Giant Reed (*Arundo donax*), Common Bamboo (*Bambusa vulgaris*), Barnyardgrass (*Echinochloa crusgalli*), Sweet Tanglehead (*Heteropogon melanocarpus*), Brazilian Satintail (*Imperata braziliensis*), Cogongrass (*Imperata cylindrica*), Guineagrass (*Panicum maximum*, p. 231), Dallisgrass (*Paspalum dilatatum*), Elephantgrass (*Pennisetum purpureum*), Fountaingrass (*Pennisetum setaceum*), Golden Bamboo (*Phyllostachys aurea*), Sugarcane (*Saccharum officinarum*), Johnsongrass (*Sorghum halepense*), Paragrass (*Urochloa mutica*), and Corn (*Zea mays*).

Ancyloxypha numitor
Least Skipper
Photo, p. 205

Description: To 0.9" in length. Head light brown with a black stripe around the edges, and broad brown lines on the face; body slender, green with numerous small yellow dots, a faint dark line on the back, the prothoracic shield white with a narrow black band at the posterior edge, and the thoracic legs pale.

Similar Species: Young larvae of the Clouded Skipper.

Habitat: Wetlands. Marshes, swamps, ditches, and the margins of ponds and lakes.

U.S. Distribution: Florida westward to Texas and northward into North Dakota, Minnesota, Michigan, New York, Vermont, New Hampshire, and Maine.

Natural History: This skipper is locally common throughout Florida, except for the Keys. At least three generations are produced each year. The yellowish eggs are laid singly on the leaves of the hosts. The larvae live in tubular leaf shelters. Partly grown larvae overwinter.

Caterpillar Season: Throughout the year.

Host Plants: Grasses (family Poaceae) including Southern Cutgrass (*Leersia hexandra*, p. 230), American Cupscale (*Sacciolepis striata*), and Southern Wild Rice (*Zizaniopsis miliacea*, p. 235).

Copaeodes minimus

Southern Skipperling

Photo, p. 213

Description: To 0.7" in length. Head green with two small points together at the center top; body slender, green frosted with white, a faint dark line on the back, the prothoracic shield indistinct, and the thoracic legs pale.

Similar Species: None.

Habitat: Uplands. Pastures, roadsides, and weedy areas.

U.S. Distribution: Florida westward to southern Texas and northward into Oklahoma, Arkansas, Georgia, and the Carolinas.

Natural History: This species is locally common in southern and central Florida, but is less frequent in the northern part of the state. At least three generations are produced each year. The whitish eggs are laid singly on the leaves of the hosts. The larvae live in tubular leaf shelters.

Caterpillar Season: Throughout the year.

Host Plants: Weedy grasses (family Poaceae), especially the exotic Bermudagrass (*Cynodon dactylon*, p. 229).

Hylephila phyleus

Fiery Skipper

Photo, p. 209

Description: To 1.3" in length. Head black with pale eye patches and two pale lines on the upper face; body slender, brown with tiny dark spots, the heart line dark, the prothoracic shield and the thoracic legs dark brown to black. Develops wax glands in transverse patches on the underside of abdominal segments 7 and 8 just prior to pupation.

Similar Species: The Dotted Skipper, Meske's Skipper, and Sachem.

Habitat: Uplands. Scrubs, sandhills, flatwoods, pine savannas, prairies, and weedy places.

U.S. Distribution: Florida westward to central California and northward into Nevada, Kansas, Nebraska, Iowa, Illinois, Indiana, Ohio, Pennsylvania, and New Jersey. Also established in Hawaii.

Natural History: This skipper is common throughout Florida. There are three or more generations each year. The greenish white eggs are laid singly on the leaves of the hosts. The caterpillar lives in a tube of silk and detritus at the soil line near the base of the host grass and is very difficult to find. Partly grown larvae overwinter.

Caterpillar Season: Throughout the year.

Host Plants: Grasses (family Poaceae) including St. Augustinegrass (*Stenotaphrum secundatum*, p. 234) and the exotic Bermudagrass (*Cynodon dactylon*, p. 229).

Hesperia attalus
Dotted Skipper

Photo, p. 211

Description: To 1.3" in length. Head black with two pale lines on the upper face; body stout, olive green with a faint dark heart line, dark spiracles, the prothoracic shield black, and the first pairs of thoracic legs darker than the last. Develops wax glands in transverse patches on the underside of abdominal segments 7 and 8 just prior to pupation.

Similar Species: The Whirlabout.

Habitat: Uplands. Sandhills and dry flatwoods.

U.S. Distribution: Florida westward into eastern Louisiana. Also in the Carolinas, New Jersey, Texas, Oklahoma, and Kansas.

Natural History: This skipper is local and uncommon in northern and central Florida. Two or three generations are produced each year. The whitish eggs are laid singly on the leaves of the hosts. The caterpillar lives in a tube of silk and detritus at the soil line near the base of the host grass and is very difficult to find. Partly grown larvae overwinter.

Caterpillar Season: Throughout the year.

Host Plants: Grasses (family Poaceae), possibly Bluestems (*Andropogon* spp.).

Hesperia meskei
Meske's Skipper

Photo, p. 211

Description: To 1.4" in length. Head black with two pale lines on the upper face; body stout, brown with a faint dark heart line, dark spiracles, the prothoracic shield black, and first two pairs of thoracic legs darker than the last. Develops wax glands in transverse patches on the underside of abdominal segments 7 and 8 just prior to pupation.

Similar Species: The Fiery Skipper, Dotted Skipper, and Sachem.

Habitat: Uplands. Sandhills, dry flatwoods, and pine rocklands.

U.S. Distribution: Florida northward into Alabama, Georgia, and the Carolinas. Also in central Texas and Arkansas.

Natural History: This skipper is local and uncommon in northern and central Florida and very rare on Big Pine Key. Two or three generations are produced each year. The whitish eggs are laid singly on the leaves of the hosts. The caterpillar lives in a tube of silk and detritus at the soil line near the base of the host grass and is very difficult to find. Partly grown larvae overwinter.

Caterpillar Season: Throughout the year.

Host Plants: Grasses (family Poaceae), possibly Bluestems (*Andropogon* spp.).

Polites baracoa

Baracoa Skipper

Photo, p. 211

Description: To 0.9" in length. Head brown with short white and black lines on the upper face and small pale areas around the eyes; body somewhat stout, brown, with dark lines on the back and sides, the prothoracic shield black with a narrow white band at the front, the thoracic legs dark, and having three short black stripes on the posterior end. Develops wax glands in transverse patches on the underside of abdominal segments 7 and 8 just prior to pupation.

Similar Species: The Tawny-edged Skipper.

Habitat: Uplands. Sandhills and dry flatwoods in the northern and central part of the state, and weedy disturbed sites in southern Florida.

U.S. Distribution: Peninsular Florida into southern Georgia.

Natural History: This skipper is locally common in southern and central Florida, but infrequent in the northern part of the state. There are three or more generations each year. The whitish eggs are laid singly on the leaves of the hosts. The caterpillar lives in a tubular shelter at the base of the host grass.

Caterpillar Season: Throughout the year.

Host Plants: Grasses (family Poaceae).

Polites themistocles

Tawny-edged Skipper

Photo, p. 211

Description: To 1.1" in length. Head black; body somewhat stout, brown with small dark spots and dark lines on the back and sides, the prothoracic shield black with a narrow white band at the front, the thoracic legs dark, and the posterior end with three short black stripes. Develops wax glands in transverse patches on the underside of abdominal segments 7 and 8 just prior to pupation.

Similar Species: The Baracoa Skipper and Crossline Skipper.

Habitat: Uplands. Sandhills, flatwoods, pine savannas, and prairies.

U.S. Distribution: All states except Idaho, Nevada, Alaska, and Hawaii; very local in Washington, Oregon, and California.

Natural History: This common skipper occurs in northern Florida, and less frequently in the central part of the state. There are two or three generations each year. The whitish green eggs are laid singly on the leaves of the hosts. The caterpillar lives in a tubular shelter constructed at the base of the host grass and is very difficult to find. Partly grown larvae overwinter.

Caterpillar Season: Throughout the year.

Host Plants: Grasses (family Poaceae) including Needleleaf Witchgrass (*Dichanthelium aciculare*, p. 229) and the exotic Centipedegrass (*Eremochloa ophiuroides*).

Polites origenes

Crossline Skipper

Photo, p. 211

Description: To 1.2" in length. Head black; body somewhat stout, brown, the heart line dark, the prothoracic shield black, the thoracic legs dark, and the posterior end with only a few small black spots. Develops wax glands in transverse patches on the underside of abdominal segments 7 and 8 just prior to pupation.

Similar Species: The Baracoa Skipper and Tawny-edged Skipper.

Habitat: Uplands and wetlands. Pine savannas, prairies, and pitcher plant seeps.

U.S. Distribution: Florida westward to eastern Texas and northward into Colorado, the Dakotas, Minnesota, Wisconsin, Michigan, New York, Vermont, New Hampshire, and Maine.

Natural History: This uncommon skipper is very local in distribution in northern and central Florida. There are two generations each year. The whitish green eggs are laid singly on the leaves of the hosts. The caterpillar lives in a tubular shelter at the base of the host grass and is very difficult to find. Partly grown larvae overwinter.

Caterpillar Season: Throughout the year.

Host Plants: Grasses (family Poaceae) including Chalky Bluestem (*Andropogon virginicus* var. *glaucus*, p. 227).

Polites vibex

Whirlabout

Photo, p. 211

Description: To 1.2" in length. Head black, sometimes mottled with white, two pale lines on the upper face and pale around the eyes; body slender, green with small dark spots, the heart line dark, dark spiracles, the prothoracic shield black, and the thoracic legs dark. Develops wax glands in transverse patches on the underside of abdominal segments 7 and 8 just prior to pupation.

Similar Species: The Dotted Skipper is similar but lives near the ground.

Habitat: Uplands. Scrubs, sandhills, coastal uplands, flatwoods, pine savannas, prairies, and weedy disturbed areas.

U.S. Distribution: Florida westward to southern Texas and northward into Arkansas, Georgia, and the Carolinas.

Natural History: This common skipper occurs throughout Florida. At least three generations are produced each year. The whitish eggs are laid singly on the leaves of the hosts, or frequently on other nearby plants. The caterpillar lives in a tubular leaf shelter.

Caterpillar Season: Throughout the year.

Host Plants: Weedy grasses (family Poaceae) including Southern Crabgrass (*Digitaria ciliaris*) and St. Augustinegrass (*Stenotaphrum secundatum*, p. 234).

Wallengrenia otho

Southern Broken-Dash

Photo, p. 213

Description: To 1.2" in length. Head black; body slender, pinkish brown with small dark spots and faint dark lines on the back and sides, a pale orange line on the side of the thorax that fades out on the abdomen, the prothoracic shield black, and the thoracic legs dark. Develops wax glands in transverse patches on the underside of abdominal segments 7 and 8 just prior to pupation.

Similar Species: The Northern Broken-Dash.

Habitat: Uplands. Flatwoods and margins of hammocks.

U.S. Distribution: Florida westward to southern Texas and northward into Kansas, Missouri, Georgia, the Carolinas, Virginia, and Maryland.

Natural History: This common skipper occurs throughout Florida. There are two or three generations each year. The whitish eggs are laid singly on the leaves of the hosts. The caterpillar lives in a case of grass clippings and silk (p. 16). Partly grown larvae overwinter.

Caterpillar Season: Throughout the year.

Host Plants: Grasses (family Poaceae) such as the exotic Indian Goosegrass (*Eleusine indica*).

Wallengrenia egeremet

Northern Broken-Dash

Photo, p. 213

Description: To 1.2" in length. Head black; body slender, pinkish brown with small dark spots and faint dark lines on the back and sides, a very pale orange line on the side of the thorax that fades out on the abdomen, the prothoracic shield black with a narrow whitish band in front, the thoracic legs dark, and the posterior end blackish. Develops wax glands in transverse patches on the underside of abdominal segments 7 and 8 just prior to pupation.

Similar Species: The Southern Broken-Dash.

Habitat: Uplands. Margins of hammocks and swamps.

U.S. Distribution: Florida westward to eastern Texas and northward into the Dakotas, Minnesota, Wisconsin, Michigan, New York, Vermont, New Hampshire, and Maine.

Natural History: This skipper is locally common in northern Florida and infrequent in the central part of the state. There are two generations each year. The whitish eggs are laid singly on the leaves of the hosts. The caterpillar lives in a case of grass clippings and silk. Partly grown larvae overwinter.

Caterpillar Season: Throughout the year.

Host Plants: Grasses (family Poaceae).

Pompeius verna

Little Glassywing

Photo, p. 215

Description: To 1.2" in length. Head shiny black, body slender, green with small dark spots and faint dark lines on the back and sides, the spiracles dark, the prothoracic shield black with a narrow whitish band in front, and the first pair of thoracic legs darker than the others. Develops wax glands in transverse patches on the underside of abdominal segments 7 and 8 just prior to pupation.

Similar Species: The Whirlabout and Dotted Skipper.

Habitat: Uplands. Margins of hammocks and swamps.

U.S. Distribution: Florida westward to eastern Texas and northward into Nebraska, Iowa, Minnesota, Wisconsin, Michigan, New York, and Massachusetts.

Natural History: This skipper is locally common in the Panhandle and infrequent elsewhere in northern and central Florida. There are two generations each year. The whitish eggs are laid singly on the leaves of the hosts. The caterpillar lives in a tubular shelter near the base of the host plant and is difficult to find. Partly grown larvae overwinter.

Caterpillar Season: Throughout the year.

Host Plants: Grasses (family Poaceae).

Atalopedes campestris

Sachem

Photo, p. 209

Description: To 1.4" in length. Head black with two brown lines on the upper face; body somewhat stout, greenish brown with a faint dark heart line, the prothoracic shield dark brown, and the first pairs of thoracic legs darker brown than last. Develops wax glands in transverse patches on the underside of abdominal segments 7 and 8 just prior to pupation.

Similar Species: The Fiery Skipper, Dotted Skipper, and Meske's Skipper.

Habitat: Uplands and wetlands. Sandhills, flatwoods, prairies, salt marshes, and pastures.

U.S. Distribution: Florida westward into California and northward into Oregon, Colorado, South Dakota, Minnesota, Illinois, Indiana, Ohio, Pennsylvania, and New Jersey.

Natural History: This skipper is common, but local in distribution. It occurs throughout Florida. At least three generations are produced each year. The whitish eggs are laid singly on the leaves of the hosts. The caterpillar lives in a tube of silk and detritus at the soil line near the base of the host grass and is very difficult to find. Partly grown larvae overwinter.

Caterpillar Season: Throughout the year.

Host Plants: Grasses (family Poaceae).

Atrytone arogos

Arogos Skipper

Photo, p. 205

Description: To 1.1" in length. Head light brown with pale reddish brown stripes around the edge and on the face; body slender, bluish white with a dark heart line, the prothoracic shield a narrow black band, and the thoracic legs pale.

Similar Species: The Swarthy Skipper and Neamathla Skipper.

Habitat: Uplands and wetlands. Sandhills, flatwoods, pine savannas, prairies, and pitcher plant seeps.

U.S. Distribution: Florida westward to eastern Louisiana, also North Carolina, New Jersey, and Midwestern states from central Texas to North Dakota.

Natural History: This very rare skipper occurs in northern and central Florida. The Arogos Skipper is known from fewer than ten sites in the state, and is often associated with the equally rare Dusted Skipper. There are three generations each year. The whitish eggs are laid singly on the leaves of the hosts. The caterpillar lives in a tubular leaf shelter. Partly grown larvae overwinter.

Caterpillar Season: Throughout the year.

Host Plants: Grasses (family Poaceae). Uses Lopsided Indiangrass (*Sorghastrum secundum*, p. 233) in peninsular Florida and Toothachegrass (*Ctenium aromaticum*) in the Panhandle.

Anatrytone logan

Delaware Skipper

Photo, p. 207

Description: To 1.4" in length. Head whitish with broad black stripes around the edge and on the face; body slender, bluish green with a slightly darker heart line, the prothoracic shield black, the first pair of thoracic legs dark and the others pale, and having two black crescents on the posterior end of the body.

Similar Species: The Reversed Roadside-Skipper and Lace-winged Roadside-Skipper also use Switchcane.

Habitat: Uplands and wetlands. Sandhills, flatwoods, pine savannas, prairies, margins of marshes and pitcher plant seeps.

U.S. Distribution: Florida westward to New Mexico and northward into Montana, North Dakota, Minnesota, Michigan, New York, and Maine.

Natural History: This skipper is locally common throughout Florida, except for the Keys. There are two (possibly three) generations each year. The pale green eggs are laid singly on the leaves of the hosts. The caterpillar lives in a tubular leaf shelter. Partly grown larvae overwinter.

Caterpillar Season: Throughout the year.

Host Plants: Grasses (family Poaceae) including Broomsedge Bluestem (*Andropogon virginicus*, p. 227), Switchcane (*Arundinaria gigantea*, p. 228), Maidencane (*Panicum hemitomon*, p. 231), Redtop Panicum (*Panicum rigidulum*, p. 232), Lopsided Indiangrass (*Sorghastrum secundum*, p. 233), and the invasive exotic Cogongrass (*Imperata cylindrica*).

Problema byssus

Byssus Skipper

Photo, p. 207

Description: To 1.6" in length. Head whitish with a narrow black stripe around the edge and three black stripes on the face; body somewhat stout, whitish with a yellowish cast to the thorax and posterior segments, the heart line dark, the prothoracic shield whitish in front and black in back, the first pair of thoracic legs darker than the others. Young caterpillars have a black patch on the posterior end of the body. Wax glands form ventral transverse patches on the undersides of abdominal segments 7 and 8.

Similar Species: The Clouded Skipper.

Habitat: Uplands and wetlands. Flatwoods and margins of hammocks, marshes, and swamps along streams and rivers.

U.S. Distribution: Florida westward to eastern Louisiana, northward into Georgia and the Carolinas; also in Colorado, Iowa, Missouri, Illinois, and Indiana.

Natural History: This skipper is locally common throughout Florida, except for the extreme southern part of the state. There are two generations each year. The whitish eggs are laid singly on the leaves of the hosts. The caterpillar lives in a tubular leaf shelter. Partly grown larvae overwinter.

Caterpillar Season: Throughout the year.

Host Plants: Coarse grasses (family Poaceae) including Slender Woodoats (*Chasmanthium laxum*, p. 228), Silver Plumegrass (*Saccharum alopecuroides*), Sugarcane Plumegrass (*Saccharum giganteum*, p. 232), and Eastern Gamagrass (*Tripsacum dactyloides*, p. 235), as well as the invasive species Brazilian Satintail (*Imperata braziliensis*) and Cogongrass (*Imperata cylindrica*).

Poanes zabulon

Zabulon Skipper

Photo, p. 215

Description: To 1.2" in length. Head dark reddish brown; body somewhat stout, pinkish brown with diffuse dark lines on the back and sides, the prothoracic shield narrow and black, and the thoracic legs light brown.

Similar Species: The Yehl Skipper.

Habitat: Uplands and wetlands. Hammocks and margins of swamps along streams and rivers.

U.S. Distribution: Florida westward to central Texas and northward into Nebraska, Iowa, Illinois, Indiana, Ohio, Pennsylvania, New York, and Massachusetts.

Natural History: This skipper is very local and uncommon in northern Florida. There are probably two or three generations each year. The whitish eggs are laid singly on the leaves of the hosts. The caterpillar lives in a tubular leaf shelter. Partly grown larvae overwinter.

Caterpillar Season: Throughout the year.

Host Plants: Grasses (family Poaceae), probably Slender Woodoats (*Chasmanthium laxum*, p. 228).

Poanes aaroni

Aaron's Skipper

Photo, p. 215

Description: To 1.3" in length. Head pale brown with three dark stripes on the upper face and black around the eyes; body somewhat stout, pinkish brown with dark lines on the back and sides, the spiracles dark, the prothoracic shield narrow and black, and the thoracic legs light brown.

Similar Species: The Broad-winged Skipper.

Habitat: Wetlands. Freshwater marshes, marshy edges of ponds, lakes, and sluggish streams as well as salt marshes.

U.S. Distribution: Florida westward along the Gulf coast to eastern Texas and northward along the Atlantic coast to New Jersey.

Natural History: This skipper is very local in distribution, but may be common where it does occur. It is found throughout much of Florida, but is infrequent in the Panhandle and absent from the Keys. Two generations are produced each year. The whitish eggs are laid singly on the leaves of the hosts. The caterpillar lives in a tubular leaf shelter. Partly grown larvae overwinter.

Caterpillar Season: Throughout the year.

Host Plants: Grasses (family Poaceae). Uses Maidencane (*Panicum hemitomon*, p. 231) in freshwater wetlands and an undetermined grass in salt marshes.

Poanes yehl
Yehl Skipper

Photo, p. 215

Description: To 1.5" in length. Head black with short hairs and small orange patches around the eyes; body somewhat stout, whitish green with faint dark lines on the back and sides, the prothoracic shield narrow and black, and the thoracic legs light brown.

Similar Species: The Zabulon Skipper.

Habitat: Uplands. Margins of hammocks and swamps.

U.S. Distribution: Florida westward to eastern Texas and northward into Arkansas, Kentucky, Georgia, the Carolinas, and Virginia.

Natural History: This skipper is very local and uncommon in northern Florida. There are two generations each year. The whitish eggs are laid singly on the leaves of the hosts. The caterpillar lives in a tubular leaf shelter. Partly grown larvae overwinter.

Caterpillar Season: Throughout the year.

Host Plants: Grasses (family Poaceae). Possibly Switchcane (*Arundinaria gigantea*, p. 228) or Slender Woodoats (*Chasmanthium laxum*, p. 228).

Poanes viator
Broad-winged Skipper

Photo, p. 215

Description: To 1.6" in length. Head pale brown with a dark stripe, two dark spots on the upper face, and black around the eyes; body somewhat stout, greenish brown with dark lines on the sides, the heart line dark with a row of faint dark spots on each side, the prothoracic shield narrow and black, and the thoracic legs light brown.

Similar Species: Aaron's Skipper.

Habitat: Wetlands. Freshwater marshes and margins of streams and rivers.

U.S. Distribution: Florida westward along the Gulf coast to central Texas and northward along the Atlantic coast to Massachusetts, then westward into New York, Michigan, Wisconsin, Minnesota, the Dakotas, and Nebraska.

Natural History: This skipper is very local in northern Florida, but may be common where it does occur. Two generations are produced each year. The whitish eggs are laid singly on the leaves of the hosts. The caterpillars live in tubular shelters on the leaves when small and later construct simple shelters in the leaf axils or curled leaves when they are more mature. Partly grown larvae overwinter.

Caterpillar Season: Throughout the year.

Host Plants: Large aquatic grasses (family Poaceae) including Southern Wild Rice (*Zizaniopsis miliacea*, p. 235) and probably Wild Rice (*Zizania aquatica*).

Euphyes arpa

Palmetto Skipper

Photo, p. 207

Description: To 1.7" in length. Head blocky, pale brown with a wide brown stripe around the margin, a brown **M** on the lower face, and an elongate black spot surrounded by white on the upper face; body somewhat stout, green mottled with pale yellow, two narrow dark lines on the back, the spiracles black, the prothoracic shield white with a black posterior, the thoracic legs pale. Develops wax glands in transverse patches on the underside of abdominal segments 7 and 8 just prior to pupation.

Similar Species: None.

Habitat: Uplands. Flatwoods, pine savannas, prairies, and occasionally sandhills and scrubs.

U.S. Distribution: Florida westward along the Gulf coast to Mississippi and northward along the Atlantic coast into Georgia.

Natural History: This skipper is very local in distribution but may be common where it does occur. It is found throughout the state but is extirpated from the Keys. Two or three generations are produced each year. The pale green eggs are laid singly on the leaves of the hosts. The caterpillar lives in a tubular shelter constructed by folding over part of a palmetto leaf and tying it with silk (p. 16) and overwinters as a partly grown larva. The fully mature last instar blocks the entrance to the shelter with a plug of wax flakes produced by the wax glands and then pupates.

Caterpillar Season: Throughout the year.

Host Plants: Palmettos (family Arecaceae) including Scrub Palmetto (*Sabal etonia*) and Saw Palmetto (*Serenoa repens*, p. 223).

Euphyes pilatka

Palatka Skipper

Photo, p. 207

Description: To 1.7" in length. Head pale brown with a brown stripe around the margin, and three black stripes separated by white on the face; body somewhat stout, bluish green mottled with pale yellow, two narrow dark lines on the back, the spiracles black, the prothoracic shield greenish with a black posterior, and the thoracic legs pale. Develops wax glands in transverse patches on the underside of abdominal segments 7 and 8 just prior to pupation.

Similar Species: None.

Habitat: Wetlands. Freshwater marshes, as well as wet flatwoods and prairies.

U.S. Distribution: Florida westward along the Gulf coast to Louisiana and northward along the Atlantic coast to Virginia.

Natural History: This skipper is very local in distribution, but it may be common where it does occur. It is found throughout the state. Two or three generations are produced each year. The pale green eggs are laid singly on the leaves of the host. The caterpillar lives in a tubular leaf shelter and overwinters as a partly grown larva. The fully mature last instar blocks the entrance to the shelter with a plug of wax flakes produced by the wax glands and then pupates.

Caterpillar Season: Throughout the year.

Host Plants: Jamaica Swamp Sawgrass (*Cladium jamaicense*, p. 225), a large sedge (family Cyperaceae).

Euphyes dion

Dion Skipper

Photo, p. 209

Description: To 1.5" in length. Head blocky, pale brown with a wide brown stripe around the margin, a wide brown M on the lower face, and an elongate black spot surrounded by white on the upper face; body somewhat stout, bluish green mottled with white, two narrow dark lines on the back, the spiracles dark, the prothoracic shield greenish with a black posterior, and the thoracic legs pale. Develops wax glands in transverse patches on the underside of abdominal segments 7 and 8 just prior to pupation.

Similar Species: Dukes' Skipper, Berry's Skipper, and the Dun Skipper.

Habitat: Wetlands. Wet flatwoods, pine savannas, and margins of swamps.

U.S. Distribution: Florida westward to eastern Texas and northward into Nebraska, North Dakota, Minnesota, Wisconsin, Michigan, New York, and Massachusetts.

Natural History: This skipper is very local and uncommon in northern Florida. There are two generations each year. The pale green eggs are laid singly on the leaves of the hosts. The caterpillar lives in a tubular leaf shelter and overwinters while partly grown.

Caterpillar Season: Throughout the year.

Host Plants: Sedges (family Cyperaceae) such as Clustered Sedge (*Carex glaucescens*, p. 224), Warty Sedge (*Carex verrucosa*), and Woolgrass (*Scirpus cyperinus*, p. 226).

Euphyes dukesi

Dukes' Skipper

Photo, p. 209

Description: Very similar to the Dion Skipper, but the stripes on the head are not as wide and the body color is greener.
Similar Species: The Dion Skipper, Berry's Skipper, and Dun Skipper.
Habitat: Wetlands. Swamps.
U.S. Distribution: Florida northward along the Atlantic coast to North Carolina and also from Louisiana northward into Illinois, Indiana, and Ohio.
Natural History: This skipper is usually very local and uncommon in northern and central Florida. There are two generations each year. The pale green eggs are laid singly on the leaves of the hosts. The caterpillar lives in a tubular leaf shelter and overwinters while partly grown.
Caterpillar Season: Throughout the year.
Host Plants: Sedges (family Cyperaceae) including False Hop Sedge (*Carex lupuliformis*, p. 224), Narrowfruit Horned Beaksedge (*Rhynchospora inundata*, p. 225), and Millet Beaksedge (*Rhynchospora miliacea*).

Euphyes berryi

Berry's Skipper

Photo, p. 209

Description: Very similar to Dukes' Skipper, but the brown stripe on the margin of the head is wider and the body color is more bluish.
Similar Species: The Dion Skipper, Dukes' Skipper, and Dun Skipper.
Habitat: Wetlands. Wet flatwoods, pine savannas, and margins of swamps.
U.S. Distribution: Florida, Georgia, and South Carolina.
Natural History: This skipper is very local in distribution, but may be common where it does occur. It is found throughout Florida, except for the Keys. There are two generations each year. The pale green eggs are laid singly on the leaves of the hosts. The caterpillar lives in a tubular leaf shelter and overwinters while partly grown.
Caterpillar Season: Throughout the year.
Host Plants: Sedges (family Cyperaceae). Undetermined *Carex* species.

Euphyes vestris

Dun Skipper

Photo, p. 209

Description: To 1.3" in length. Very similar to other *Euphyes* species, but the prothoracic shield is edged with white and there is a black crescent on the posterior end of the body.

Similar Species: The Dion Skipper, Dukes' Skipper, and Berry's Skipper.

Habitat: Uplands and wetlands. Margins of hammocks and swamps.

U.S. Distribution: All states except Nevada, Utah, Alaska, and Hawaii.

Natural History: This skipper is local and usually uncommon in northern and central Florida. There are two generations each year. The pale green eggs are laid singly on the leaves of the hosts. The caterpillar lives in a tubular leaf shelter and overwinters while partly grown.

Caterpillar Season: Throughout the year.

Host Plants: Sedges (family Cyperaceae). Undetermined *Carex* species.

Asbolis capucinus
Monk Skipper

Photo, p. 217

Description: To 2.2" in length. Head rounded, orange; body somewhat stout, whitish green, the spiracles dark, the prothoracic shield a narrow black band, the thoracic legs pale, and the posterior end edged with black. Develops wax glands in small round patches behind each of the middle prolegs just prior to pupation.

Similar Species: None.

Habitat: Uplands. Hammocks and urban areas.

U.S. Distribution: Peninsular Florida.

Natural History: This skipper is locally common in southern and central Florida. There are three or more generations each year. The greenish eggs are laid singly on the leaves of the hosts. The caterpillar lives in a tubular leaf shelter constructed by tying the edges of a leaflet or leaf tip together with silk. Partly grown larvae overwinter.

Caterpillar Season: Throughout the year.

Host Plants: Palms (family Arecaceae) including Everglades Palm (*Acoelorrhaphe wrightii*), Florida Silver Palm (*Coccothrinax argentata*), Florida Royal Palm (*Roystonea regia*), Scrub Palmetto (*Sabal etonia*), Cabbage Palm (*Sabal palmetto*, p. 222), Saw Palmetto (*Serenoa repens*, p. 223), Brittle Thatch Palm (*Thrinax morrisii*), and Florida Thatch Palm (*Thrinax radiata*) as well as the exotic Coconut Palm (*Cocos nucifera*, p. 222), Areca Palm (*Chrysalidocarpus lutescens*), Hurricane Palm (*Dictyosperma album*), Date Palm (*Phoenix dactylifera*), and Manila Palm (*Veitchia merrillii*).

Atrytonopsis hianna
Dusted Skipper

Photo, p. 215

Description: To 1.3" in length. Head brown; body somewhat stout with long wispy hairs, translucent green with a pink tinge, the prothoracic shield a narrow black band, and the thoracic legs pale. Develops wax glands in transverse patches on the underside of abdominal segments 7 and 8 just prior to pupation.

Similar Species: The Twin-spot Skipper.

Habitat: Uplands. Sandhills, flatwoods, pine savannas, and prairies.

U.S. Distribution: Florida westward into northern Texas and northward into Montana, North Dakota, Minnesota, Wisconsin, Michigan, New York, and Massachusetts.

Natural History: This very rare skipper occurs in highly localized colonies in northern and central Florida. The Dusted Skipper is known from fewer than ten sites in the state, and is often associated with the equally rare Arogos Skipper. There are two generations each year. The pinkish brown eggs are laid singly on the leaves of the hosts. The caterpillar lives in a tubular leaf shelter. Partly grown larvae overwinter.

Caterpillar Season: Throughout the year.

Host Plants: Lopsided Indiangrass (*Sorghastrum secundum*, p. 233) in the family Poaceae.

Amblyscirtes hegon
Pepper and Salt Skipper

Photo, p. 203

Description: To 0.9" in length. Head whitish with a brown line around the margin and two convergent brown stripes on the face, a small point on each side of clypeus; body somewhat stout, green densely frosted with white, a dark line on the back and sides, the prothoracic shield black, and the thoracic legs pale. Develops wax glands in lateral patches on the underside of abdominal segments 7 and 8 just prior to pupation.

Similar Species: Young larvae of the Clouded Skipper.

Habitat: Uplands. Margins of hammocks and swamps.

U.S. Distribution: Florida Panhandle westward to eastern Texas and northward into Minnesota, Wisconsin, Michigan, New York, Vermont, New Hampshire, and Maine.

Natural History: This very rare skipper is known from Torreya State Park and a few other sites in the Panhandle. There is a single generation each year. The whitish eggs are laid singly on the leaves of the hosts. The caterpillar lives in a tubular leaf shelter. Mature larvae clip the shelter from the host and overwinter in the leaf litter on the ground inside this cocoon.

Caterpillar Season: Throughout the year.

Host Plants: Grasses (family Poaceae). Probably Fowl Managrass (*Glyceria striata*).

Amblyscirtes aesculapius

Lace-winged Roadside-Skipper

Photo, p. 203

Description: To 1.1" in length. Head pale with a black line around the margin and two convergent black lines on the face, a small point on each side of clypeus; body somewhat stout, green mottled with white, a dark line on the back, the prothoracic shield black, and the thoracic legs pale. Develops wax glands in lateral patches on the underside of abdominal segments 7 and 8 just prior to pupation.

Similar Species: The Clouded Skipper, Delaware Skipper, and Reversed Roadside-Skipper also eat Switchcane.

Habitat: Wetlands. Wet hammocks and edges of swamps.

U.S. Distribution: Florida westward to eastern Texas and northward into Oklahoma, Missouri, Kentucky, and Virginia.

Natural History: This skipper is local and uncommon in northern and central Florida. There are two or three generations each year. The whitish eggs are laid singly on the leaves of the hosts. The caterpillar lives in a tubular leaf shelter. Mature larvae clip the shelter from the host and overwinter in the leaf litter on the ground inside this cocoon.

Caterpillar Season: Throughout the year.

Host Plants: Switchcane (*Arundinaria gigantea*, p. 228), a small bamboo in the Grass family (Poaceae).

Amblyscirtes vialis

Common Roadside-Skipper

Photo, p. 205

Description: To 1.1" in length. Head pale brown with a brown line around the margin and two convergent brown lines on the face, a small point on each side of clypeus; body somewhat stout, green overcast with greenish white, the heart line dark, the prothoracic shield black, and the thoracic legs pale. Develops wax glands in lateral patches on the underside of abdominal segments 7 and 8 just prior to pupation.

Similar Species: Young larvae of the Clouded Skipper.

Habitat: Uplands. Margins of hammocks.

U.S. Distribution: All states except Nevada, Arizona, Alaska, and Hawaii.

Natural History: This very rare skipper is found in the Florida Panhandle region. A small colony was recently found at Eglin Air Force Base. There are two generations each year. The whitish eggs are laid singly on the leaves of the hosts. The caterpillar lives in a tubular leaf shelter. Mature larvae clip the shelter from the host and overwinter among the leaf litter on the ground inside this cocoon.

Caterpillar Season: Throughout the year.

Host Plants: Grasses (family Poaceae). Possibly Indian Woodoats (*Chasmanthium latifolium*) or Silver Plumegrass (*Saccharum alopecuroides*).

Amblyscirtes reversa
Reversed Roadside-Skipper
Photo, p. 207

Description: To 1.1" in length. Head whitish with a wide black line around the margin and a black triangular patch on the face, a small point on each side of clypeus; body somewhat stout, whitish, a faint dark line on the back, the prothoracic shield black, and the thoracic legs pale. Develops wax glands in lateral patches on the underside of abdominal segments 7 and 8 just prior to pupation.
Similar Species: The Clouded Skipper, Delaware Skipper, and Lace-winged Roadside-Skipper also eat Switchcane.
Habitat: Wetlands. Pitcher plant seeps with canebrakes.
U.S. Distribution: Florida Panhandle westward along the Gulf coast to Mississippi and northward into Georgia, the Carolinas, and Virginia.
Natural History: This very rare skipper is found in the western Panhandle of Florida. A small colony was recently discovered in the Blackwater River State Forest. There are two or three generations each year. The whitish eggs are laid singly on the leaves of the hosts. The caterpillar lives in a tubular leaf shelter. Mature larvae clip the shelter from the host and overwinter among the leaf litter on the ground inside this cocoon.
Caterpillar Season: Throughout the year.
Host Plants: Switchcane (*Arundinaria gigantea*, p. 228), a small bamboo in the Grass family (Poaceae).

Amblyscirtes alternata
Dusky Roadside-Skipper
Photo, p. 205

Description: To 0.8" in length. Head pale brown with a brown line around the margin and three brown lines separated by white on the face, a small point on each side of clypeus; body somewhat stout, green densely frosted with white, a faint dark line on the back, the prothoracic shield black, and the thoracic legs pale. Develops wax glands in lateral patches on the underside of abdominal segments 7 and 8 just prior to pupation.
Similar Species: The Swarthy Skipper, Neamathla Skipper, Pepper and Salt Skipper, and Eufala Skipper.
Habitat: Uplands. Sandhills, flatwoods, pine savannas, and prairies.
U.S. Distribution: Florida westward to eastern Texas and northward along the Atlantic coast into Virginia.
Natural History: This tiny skipper is extremely local and uncommon through-

out much of Florida, except for the southern part of the state. There are two generations each year. The whitish eggs are laid singly on the leaves of the hosts. The caterpillar lives in a tubular leaf shelter. Mature larvae clip the shelter from the host and overwinter among the leaf litter on the ground inside this cocoon.

Caterpillar Season: Throughout the year.

Host Plants: Bearded Skeletongrass (*Gymnopogon ambiguous*) (family Poaceae).

Lerodea eufala

Eufala Skipper

Photo, p. 207

Description: To 1.1" in length. Head whitish with a brown line around the edges and a triangular brown patch on the face; body slender, green with faint dark lines, the prothoracic shield indistinct, and the thoracic legs pale. Develops wax glands in lateral patches on the underside of abdominal segments 7 and 8 just prior to pupation.

Similar Species: The Swarthy Skipper and Neamathla Skipper.

Habitat: Uplands. Sandhills, flatwoods, and weedy disturbed sites.

U.S. Distribution: Florida westward to central California and northward into Nevada, Kansas, Georgia, the Carolinas, and Virginia.

Natural History: This common skipper is found throughout Florida. At least three generations are produced each year. The greenish eggs are laid singly on the leaves of the hosts. The caterpillar lives in a tubular leaf shelter.

Caterpillar Season: Throughout the year.

Host Plants: Grasses (family Poaceae) including Pinewoods Fingergrass (*Eustachys petraea*) and Lopsided Indiangrass (*Sorghastrum secundum*, p. 233) as well as the exotic species Cogongrass (*Imperata cylindrica*), Vaseygrass (*Paspalum urvillei*), and Tropical Signalgrass (*Urochloa distachya*).

Oligoria maculata

Twin-spot Skipper

Photo, p. 217

Description: To 1.3" in length. Head pale brown; body somewhat stout with short hairs, pinkish green, the prothoracic shield black, and the thoracic legs pale. Develops wax glands in transverse patches on the underside of abdominal segments 7 and 8 just prior to pupation.

Similar Species: The Dusted Skipper.

Habitat: Uplands. Flatwoods, pine savannas, prairies, and pine rocklands.

U.S. Distribution: Florida westward along the Gulf coast to eastern Texas and northward along the Atlantic coast into North Carolina and occasionally New Jersey.

Natural History: This skipper is locally common throughout Florida. There are two or three generations each year. The pinkish brown eggs are laid singly on the leaves of the hosts. The caterpillar lives in a tubular leaf shelter and overwinters while partly grown.

Caterpillar Season: Throughout the year.

Host Plants: Grasses (family Poaceae) including Broomsedge Bluestem (*Andropogon virginicus*, p. 227), Lopsided Indiangrass (*Sorghastrum secundum*, p. 233), and the invasive exotic Cogongrass (*Imperata cylindrica*).

Calpodes ethlius

Brazilian Skipper

Photo, p. 217

Description: To 2.5" inches in length. Head blocky, pale brown with a black spot on the face and black patches around the eyes; body somewhat stout, transparent but appearing green because of the gut contents, the prothoracic shield pale on top and brown on the sides, and the first two pairs of thoracic legs darker than the last. Develops wax glands in lateral patches on the underside of abdominal segments 7 and 8 just prior to pupation.

Similar Species: None.

Habitat: Uplands and wetlands. Wet flatwoods, freshwater marshes, swamps, and gardens.

U.S. Distribution: Florida westward along the Gulf coast to central Texas and occasionally northward along the Atlantic coast as far as southern New Jersey.

Natural History: This common skipper is found throughout Florida, but is less frequent in the Panhandle region. At least three generations are produced each year. The grayish eggs are laid singly on the leaves of the hosts. The young caterpillar cuts two channels near the edge of the leaf, folds over the flap, and secures it with silk strands to make a shelter (p. 16). Older larvae often tie the edges of a single small leaf together with silk. The life stages of the Brazilian Skipper are shown on p. 44.

Caterpillar Season: Throughout the year.

Host Plants: Herbs in the Canna family (Cannaceae) including Bandana-of-the-Everglades (*Canna flaccida*, p. 223), exotic species such as Indian Shot (*Canna indica*) and Garden Canna (*Canna x generalis*), as well as Alligatorflag (*Thalia geniculata*, p. 226) in the Arrowroot family (Marantaceae) and occasionally Zedoary (*Curcuma zedoaria*) and other exotic gingers (family Zingiberaceae).

Panoquina panoquin

Salt Marsh Skipper

Photo, p. 213

Description: To 1.1" in length. Head blocky, green, sometimes with faint reddish stripes; body slender, green, the heart line dark, a pale yellow line on the sides, the prothoracic shield indistinct, the thoracic legs pale, and having the posterior end of the body somewhat pointed.

Similar Species: The Obscure Skipper.

Habitat: Wetlands. Salt marshes and the margins of mangrove swamps.

U.S. Distribution: Florida westward along the Gulf Coast to southern Texas and northward along the Atlantic coast to New Jersey and Rhode Island.

Natural History: This skipper is locally abundant in coastal areas of Florida. At least three generations are produced each year. The whitish eggs are laid singly on the leaves of the hosts. The caterpillar lives exposed on the leaves.

Caterpillar Season: Throughout the year.

Host Plants: Grasses (family Poaceae) including Saltgrass (*Distichlis spicata*, p. 230) and Saltmarsh Cordgrass (*Spartina alterniflora*, p. 233).

Panoquina panoquinoides

Obscure Skipper

Photo, p. 213

Description: To 1.1" in length. Head blocky, green, sometimes with faint reddish stripes; body slender, green with a narrow pale yellow line on the sides and a faint dark heart line, the prothoracic shield indistinct, the thoracic legs pale, and the posterior end of the body somewhat pointed.

Similar Species: The Salt Marsh Skipper.

Habitat: Wetlands. Salt marshes and the margins of mangrove swamps.

U.S. Distribution: Coastal areas of peninsular Florida, Texas, and Louisiana.

Natural History: This skipper is locally abundant in central and southern Florida. At least three generations are produced each year. The whitish eggs are laid singly on the leaves of the hosts. The caterpillar lives exposed on the leaves.

Caterpillar Season: Throughout the year.

Host Plants: Grasses (family Poaceae) including Coral Dropseed (*Sporobolus domingensis*), Seashore Dropseed (*Sporobolus virginicus*, p. 234), and probably Saltgrass (*Distichlis spicata*, p. 230).

Panoquina ocola

Ocola Skipper

Photo, p. 213

Description: To 1.3" in length. Head blocky, green; body slender, green overcast with pale yellow, faint dark lines edged with narrow pale yellow lines, the prothoracic shield indistinct, the thoracic legs pale, and the posterior end of the body somewhat pointed.

Similar Species: The Least Skipper also eats Southern Cutgrass.

Habitat: Uplands and wetlands. Wet prairies, freshwater marshes, roadside ditches, and the margins of ponds, lakes, and sluggish streams.

U.S. Distribution: Florida westward to southern Texas and northward into Georgia and the Carolinas, occasionally straying into Arkansas, Illinois, Indiana, Ohio, Pennsylvania, and New Jersey.

Natural History: This common skipper occurs throughout Florida. It migrates southward into the state by the millions during late summer and fall. At least three generations are produced each year. The whitish eggs are laid singly on the leaves of the hosts. The caterpillar usually lives exposed on the leaves.

Caterpillar Season: Throughout the year.

Host Plants: Wetland grasses (family Poaceae) including Southern Cutgrass (*Leersia hexandra*, p. 230) and the invasive exotic Torpedograss (*Panicum repens*).

Giant-Skippers (subfamily Megathyminae)

Megathymus yuccae

Yucca Giant-Skipper

Photo, p. 217

Description: To 2.6" in length. Head dark reddish brown; body stout, pale brown, the spiracles brown, the prothoracic shield black, the thoracic legs brown, and the posterior end blackish. Develops wax glands in transverse patches on the underside of abdominal segments 7 and 8 just prior to pupation.

Similar Species: The Cofaqui Giant-Skipper.

Habitat: Uplands. Scrubs, sandhills, coastal uplands, and dry flatwoods.

U.S. Distribution: Florida westward to southern California and northward into Nevada, Utah, Colorado, Nebraska, Kentucky, and North Carolina.

Natural History: This large skipper is local and usually uncommon. It occurs in central and northern Florida. There is only one generation per year in the spring. The pale brown eggs are laid singly on the leaves of the hosts. The young caterpillars make a nest of silk and plant fragments for a short time, then begin boring into the center of the plant. The larva builds a cigar-shaped pouch in the center of the host rosette (p. 16) and expels frass from the open tip of the pouch or tent. Prior to pupation, the larva produces quantities of white wax from special glands on the underside of the abdomen, coating the inside of the excavated feeding tunnel.

Caterpillar Season: Throughout the year.

Host Plants: Shrubs in the Agave family (Agavaceae) including Adam's Needle (*Yucca filamentosa*, p. 221) and the exotic Spanish Bayonet (*Yucca aloifolia*, p. 221).

Megathymus cofaqui

Cofaqui Giant-Skipper

Photo, p. 217

Description: To 2.4" in length. Head blackish, body stout, whitish to pale brown, the spiracles brown, the prothoracic shield black, the thoracic legs brown, and the posterior end blackish. Develops wax glands in transverse patches on the underside of abdominal segments 7 and 8 just prior to pupation.

Similar Species: The Yucca Giant-Skipper.

Habitat: Uplands. Scrubs, sandhills, coastal uplands, and dry flatwoods.

U.S. Distribution: Florida, Georgia, and the Carolinas.

Natural History: This secretive skipper is local and usually uncommon. It occurs in central and northern Florida. There are two or three generations per year. The whitish eggs are laid singly on the leaves of the hosts. After hatching from the eggs, the young caterpillars begin boring into the center of the plant. They drop their frass at the end of the tunnels as they eat their way downward into the roots. Prior to pupation, the larva burrows upward through the soil and makes a small tent near the base of the plant (p. 16). The life stages of the Cofaqui Giant-Skipper are shown on p. 45.

Caterpillar Season: Throughout the year.

Host Plants: Shrubs in the Agave family (Agavaceae) including Adam's Needle (*Yucca filamentosa*, p. 221) and the exotic Spanish Bayonet (*Yucca aloifolia*, p. 221).

Plates

Size scale (maximum length) used in the caterpillar descriptions.

Very small (less than ¾")   ——————

Small (¾" to 1¼")   ————————

Medium (1¼" to 2")   —————————————

Large (greater than 2")   ————————————————————

The ranges shown are for caterpillars and do not necessarily represent the distributions of the adults. In making a correct identification it is very important to match host plant, range, and picture, but some species may require rearing to the adult stage for final determination.

Normal larval range

Extended range in favorable years

Possibly present   ?

Figure 9. Color code for caterpillar distribution maps.

Swallowtails

Battus philenor Pipevine Swallowtail

Large size; body with long black tubercles, osmeterium yellow. Page 67. Eats the leaves and flowers of pipevines, especially Virginia Snakeroot.

Battus polydamas Polydamas Swallowtail

Large size; body with short fleshy tubercles, orange with black tips, osmeterium yellow. The younger caterpillars live and feed communally. Page 68.
Eats the leaves and flowers of pipevines.

Eurytides marcellus Zebra Swallowtail

Medium size; yellow, black, and blue transverse stripes on the back that are usually hidden; body various shades of green or brown, osmeterium yellow. Page 68.
Eats the leaves and flowers of pawpaws.

Pterourus troilus Spicebush Swallowtail

Large size, large eyespots on the thorax, orange patch on back with a blue spot inside, osmeterium yellow; hides in a curled leaf nest. Page 73.
Eats the leaves of many shrubs and trees in the Laurel family, especially bays and Sassafras.

Pterourus glaucus Eastern Tiger Swallowtail

Large size; small eyespots on thorax, transverse yellow and black stripes on the back that are usually hidden from view, osmeterium orange; hides in a curled leaf nest. Page 71.
Eats only the leaves of Sweet Bay in peninsular Florida but also uses ashes and Wild Cherry in northern Florida.

Pterourus palamedes Palamedes Swallowtail

Large size, large eyespots on the thorax, orange patch on back with a blue spot along leading edge, osmeterium yellow; no nest. Page 72.
Eats the leaves of bay trees (*Persea* spp.).

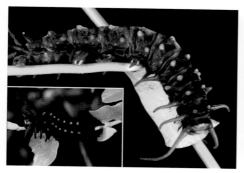

Battus philenor Pipevine Swallowtail

Battus polydamas Polydamas Swallowtail

Eurytides marcellus Zebra Swallowtail

Pterourus troilus Spicebush Swallowtail

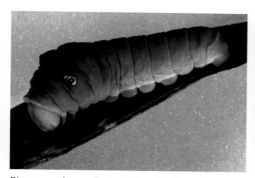

Pterourus glaucus Eastern Tiger Swallowtail

Pterourus palamedes Palamedes Swallowtail

163

Swallowtails, Orangetips, and Sulphurs

Papilio polyxenes Black Swallowtail

Medium size; transverse black bands with yellow spots, osmeterium orange. Page 71.
Eats the leaves and seeds of many plants in the Carrot family, especially Fennel, Dill, Parsley, and Water Cowbane.

Heraclides aristodemus Schaus' Swallowtail

Large size; white spots and blotches along the sides, osmeterium white. Page 70.
Eats the young leaves of Torchwood.

Heraclides cresphontes Giant Swallowtail

Large size, white saddle patch long; leading edge of thorax rounded, osmeterium bright red. Page 69.
Eats the leaves of many shrubs and trees in the Citrus family.

Heraclides andraemon Bahamian Swallowtail

Medium size; white saddle patch short, leading edge of thorax with small "ears," osmeterium white. Page 70.
Eats the leaves of Torchwood, Wild Lime, and Key Lime.

Paramidea midea Falcate Orangetip

Small and slender; wide white stripe on sides. Page 76.
Eats the leaves and flowers of Bittercress.

Kricogonia lyside Lyside Sulphur

Small size; narrow white stripes on sides and back, brownish side stripes. Page 80.
Possibly eats the leaves of Lignumvitae.

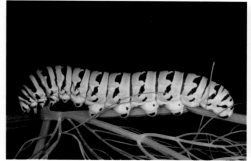

Papilio polyxenes Black Swallowtail

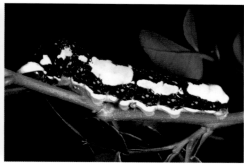

Heraclides aristodemus Schaus' Swallowtail

Heraclides cresphontes Giant Swallowtail

Heraclides andraemon Bahamian Swallowtail

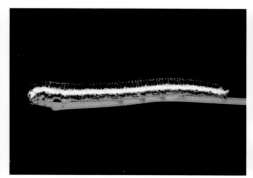

Paramidea midea Falcate Orangetip

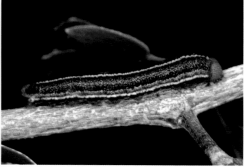

Kricogonia lyside Lyside Sulphur

Orangetips, Whites, and Sulphurs

Ascia monuste Great Southern White

Medium size; head yellowish, body with small black spots. Page 75.
Eats Saltwort and Pepperweed.

Pontia protodice Checkered White

Small size; head gray with yellow patches, body with small black spots.
Page 74.
Eats the leaves of Pepperweed.

Pieris rapae Cabbage White

Small size; narrow broken yellow line on sides and back, body with tiny
blue spots. Page 75.
Eats the leaves of Cabbage, Broccoli, Collards, and related crops.

Nathalis iole Dainty Sulphur

Very small size; thorax with a pair of short projections on leading edge,
body green with or without purple stripes. Page 83.
Eats the leaves of Spanish Needles.

Eurema daira Barred Yellow

Small and slender; bright green with a narrow, yellowish line on sides.
Page 80.
Eats the leaves of jointvetches and pencilflowers.

Eurema lisa Little Yellow

Small and slender; bright green with a narrow, yellowish line on sides,
narrow faint dark lines on upper sides and back. Page 81.
Eats the leaves of partridge peas.

Ascia monuste Great Southern White

Pontia protodice Checkered White

Pieris rapae Cabbage White

Nathalis iole Dainty Sulphur

Eurema daira Barred Yellow

Eurema lisa Little Yellow

167

Sulphurs and Whites

Eurema nise Mimosa Yellow

Small and slender; green, frosted with white, narrow whitish line on sides. Page 81.
Eats the leaves of False Tamarind.

Eurema dina Dina Yellow

Small and slender; bluish green with whitish line on sides. Page 82.
Eats the leaves of Mexican Alvaradoa and Florida Bitterbush.

Eurema nicippe Sleepy Orange

Small size; green with yellowish line on sides, with glandular hairs that exude small droplets. Page 82.
Eats the leaves of sennas.

Colias eurytheme Orange Sulphur

Medium size; green with a white and pink-spotted line on sides and a narrow yellow line on back. Page 77.
Eats the leaves of clovers, medicks, and sweet clovers.

Zerene cesonia Southern Dogface

Medium size; green with a white and pink-spotted line on the sides and transverse bands of yellow and blackish-blue. Page 77.
Eats the leaves of Indigobush and prairieclovers.

Appias drusilla Florida White

Medium size; bluish-green with tiny dark blue and yellow spots, posterior with a pair of short tails. Page 74.
Eats the young leaves of Bayleaf Capertree and Guiana Plum.

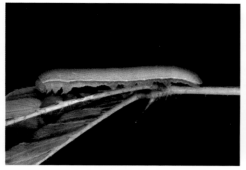

Eurema nise Mimosa Yellow

Eurema dina Dina Yellow

Eurema nicippe Sleepy Orange

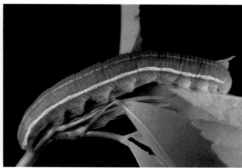

Colias eurytheme Orange Sulphur

Zerene cesonia Southern Dogface

Appias drusilla Florida White

Sulphurs, Harvesters, and Hairstreaks

Phoebis sennae Cloudless Sulphur

Medium size; green with a yellow line and blue patches on the sides or yellow with blackish blue transverse bands, body with short black or blue spikes. Page 78.
Eats the leaves of partridge peas and sennas.

Phoebis agarithe Large Orange Sulphur

Medium size; green with a pale yellow line on the sides, no spikes. Page 79.
Eats the leaves of False Tamarind and blackbeads.

Aphrissa statira Statira Sulphur

Medium size; green with a pale yellow line on sides and body with tiny blue spikes. Page 79.
Eats the leaves of Coinvine.

Phoebis philea Orange-barred Sulphur

Medium size; yellowish green with a chain of large black spots on sides, body covered with black spikes. Page 78.
Eats the leaves of woody sennas.

Feniseca tarquinius Harvester

Small and sluglike; brightly patterned with gray, yellow, and white, and covered with bristly hairs; the pattern is often obscured with the white wax produced by the prey. Page 84.
Carnivorous. Eats woolly aphids on alders and greenbriers.

Eumaeus atala Atala

Small and sluglike; bright red with yellow spots. Page 85.
Eats the leaves of Coontie.

Phoebis sennae Cloudless Sulphur

Phoebis agarithe Large Orange Sulphur

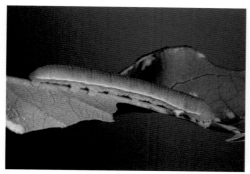

Aphrissa statira Statira Sulphur

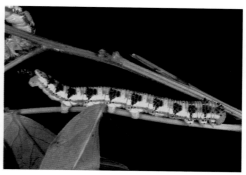

Phoebis philea Orange-barred Sulphur

Feniseca tarquinius Harvester

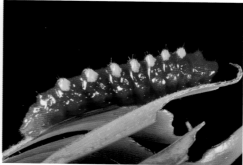

Eumaeus atala Atala

Hairstreaks

Electrostrymon angelia Fulvous Hairstreak

Very small and sluglike; greenish mottled with reddish brown and two rows of small pale spots on back, spiracles black. Page 94.
Eats the flower buds and young shoots of Brazilian Pepper and Florida Fishpoison Tree.

Calycopis cecrops Red-banded Hairstreak

Very small and sluglike; pinkish brown with black spiracles and a small shield on thorax. Page 95.
Eats dead leaves under Brazilian Pepper, Wax Myrtle, oaks, and other shrubs and trees.

Harkenclenus titus Coral Hairstreak

Small and sluglike; bright green with purple on top of thorax and posterior end. Page 87.
Eats the young leaves of Wild Cherry.

Ministrymon azia Gray Ministreak

Very small and sluglike; green mottled with red, two rows of bumps on back. Page 95.
Eats the flower buds of White Leadtree.

Atlides halesus Great Purple Hairstreak

Small and sluglike; bright green with short velvety hairs and a small whitish shield on top of the thorax. Page 85.
Eats the young leaves of Mistletoe.

Fixsenia favonius Oak Hairstreak

Small and sluglike; pale green with faint diagonal markings. Page 89.
Eats the young leaves of oaks.

Electrostrymon angelia Fulvous Hairstreak

Calycopis cecrops Red-banded Hairstreak

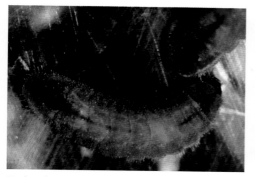

Harkenclenus titus Coral Hairstreak

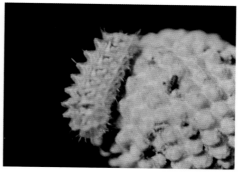

Ministrymon azia Gray Ministreak

Atlides halesus Great Purple Hairstreak

Fixsenia favonius Oak Hairstreak

Hairstreaks

Incisalia irus Frosted Elfin

Very small and sluglike; bluish green with short hairs. Page 89.
Eats the flower buds and young leaves of Sundial Lupine.

Mitoura grynea Juniper Hairstreak

Very small and sluglike; bright green with bold white markings. Page 91.
Eats the leaves of Red Cedar.

Mitoura hesseli Hessel's Hairstreak

Very small and sluglike; dark green with distinctive white markings. Page 91.
Eats the leaves of Atlantic White Cedar.

Incisalia niphon Eastern Pine Elfin

Very small and sluglike; bright green with white stripes. Page 90.
Eats the needles of Sand Pine.

Satyrium calanus Banded Hairstreak

Small and sluglike; color variable, green or brown with reddish brown on top of the thorax and posterior end. Page 87.
Eats the young leaves of hickories and sometimes Turkey Oak.

Satyrium kingi King's Hairstreak

Small and sluglike; bright green with faint yellowish markings. Page 88.
Eats the young leaves of Common Sweetleaf.

Incisalia irus Frosted Elfin

Mitoura grynea Juniper Hairstreak

Mitoura hesseli Hessel's Hairstreak

Incisalia niphon Eastern Pine Elfin

Satyrium calanus Banded Hairstreak

Satyrium kingi King's Hairstreak

Hairstreaks

Satyrium liparops Striped Hairstreak

Small and sluglike; green with faint markings. Page 88.
Eats the young leaves of Sparkleberry and hawthorns.

Incisalia henrici Henry's Elfin

Very small and sluglike; color variable, green or red with faint diagonal lines. Page 90.
Eats the young leaves of hollies and in the Panhandle also eats Redbud.

Chlorostrymon simaethis Silver-banded Hairstreak

Very small and sluglike; green with faint stripes, thick bodied, head brown. Page 86.
Eats the young seeds of balloonvines (heartseeds), sometimes tended by ants.

Parrhasius m-album White M Hairstreak

Small and sluglike; color variable, green or red with faint diagonal lines. Page 92.
Eats the young leaves of oaks.

Strymon melinus Gray Hairstreak

Small and sluglike; color variable, green or red with faint diagonal lines and somewhat bristly hairs. Page 92.
Eats the flower buds of milkpeas, ticktrefoils, partridge peas, fanpetals, and many other plants.

Strymon istapa Mallow Scrub-Hairstreak

Very small and sluglike; very similar to the Gray Hairstreak. Page 94.
Eats flower buds of fanpetals, Sleepy Morning, and Bay Cedar.

Satyrium liparops Striped Hairstreak

Incisalia henrici Henry's Elfin

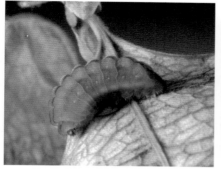

Chlorostrymon simaethis Silver-banded Hairstreak

Parrhasius m-album White M Hairstreak

Strymon melinus Gray Hairstreak

Strymon istapa Mallow Scrub-Hairstreak

Hairstreaks and Blues

Strymon martialis Martial Scrub-Hairstreak

Very small and sluglike; green with short hairs. Page 93.
Mostly eats the flower buds of Bay Cedar.

Strymon acis Bartram's Hairstreak

Very small and sluglike; pale green with short hairs. Page 93.
Eats the flower buds and young leaves of Pineland Croton.

Celastrina ladon 'Edwards' Spring Azure

Very small and sluglike; green mottled with purple and black, white chevrons on back. Page 99.
Host plant may be Flowering Dogwood, often tended by ants.

Celastrina neglecta 'Summer' Spring Azure

Very small and sluglike; chain of white chevrons on back. Page 99.
Eats the flower buds of many trees and shrubs, often tended by ants.

Hemiargus thomasi Miami Blue

Very small and sluglike; usually bright green or sometimes red with darker heart line on back, head black. Page 97.
Eats the young seeds of balloonvines (heartseeds) and Gray Nickerbean, sometimes tended by ants.

Hemiargus ammon Nickerbean Blue

Very small and sluglike; color variable, green or highly patterned with white chevrons on the back. Page 97.
Eats the flower buds of acacias.

Strymon martialis Martial Scrub-Hairstreak

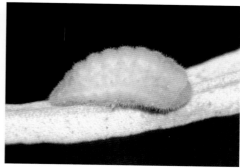

Strymon acis Bartram's Hairstreak

Celastrina ladon 'Edwards' Spring Azure

Celastrina neglecta 'Summer' Spring Azure

Hemiargus thomasi Miami Blue

Hemiargus ammon Nickerbean Blue

Blues, Metalmarks, and Snouts

Hemiargus ceraunus Ceraunus Blue

Very small and sluglike; color variable, green to red with white lines on the sides. Page 98.
Eats the flower buds of Alicia, indigos, and partridge peas.

Everes comyntas Eastern Tailed-Blue

Very small and sluglike; color variable, green to red. Page 98.
Eats the flower buds of clovers.

Brephidium isophthalma Eastern Pygmy-Blue

Very small and sluglike; bright green with faint markings. Page 96.
Eats glassworts, associated with ants.

Leptotes cassius Cassius Blue

Very small and sluglike; color variable, green with faint markings or highly patterned with white chevrons on the back. Page 96.
Eats the flower buds of Cape Leadwort and legumes such as False Tamarind, milkpeas, and others.

Calephelis virginiensis Little Metalmark

Very small and sluglike; pale green with two rows of yellowish green or reddish brown spots on the back, body has very long hairs at sides and down the back. Page 100.
Eats the undersides of the leaves of thistles, Vanillaleaf, and sometimes Hempvine.

Libytheana carinenta American Snout

Small size; with narrow yellow lines, small yellow spots, and a pair of small black spots on top of the thorax. Page 101.
Eats the leaves of hackberry.

Hemiargus ceraunus Ceraunus Blue

Everes comyntas Eastern Tailed-Blue

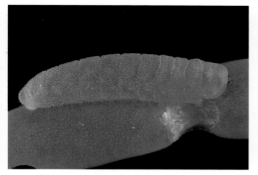

Brephidium isophthalma Eastern Pygmy-Blue

Leptotes cassius Cassius Blue

Calephelis virginiensis Little Metalmark

Libytheana carinenta American Snout

181

Heliconians and Admirals

Agraulis vanillae Gulf Fritillary

Medium size; orange with black spines. Page 102.
Eats the leaves of passionflowers and Pitted Stripeseed.

Dryas iulia Julia Heliconian

Medium size; black with white lines and spots, head orange with black spots. Page 102.
Eats the leaves of passionflowers.

Heliconius charithonia Zebra Heliconian

Medium size; white with black spines. Page 103.
Eats the leaves of passionflowers.

Euptoieta claudia Variegated Fritillary

Medium size; orange with white lines outlined in black. Page 103.
Eats the leaves of passionflowers, flaxes, and perhaps violets.

Basilarchia arthemis astyanax Red-spotted Purple

Medium size; top of thorax and beginning abdominal segments without small spines. Page 112.
Eats the leaves of Wild Cherry, Deerberry, and occasionally willows.

Basilarchia archippus Viceroy

Medium size; top of thorax and beginning abdominal segments with small spines. Page 113.
Eats the leaves of willows.

Agraulis vanillae Gulf Fritillary

Dryas iulia Julia Heliconian

Heliconius charitonius Zebra Heliconian

Euptoieta claudia Variegated Fritillary

Basilarchia arthemis astyanax Red-spotted Purple

Basilarchia archippus Viceroy

Admirals and Brushfoots

Eunica monima Dingy Purplewing

Small size; short spines on body, head without long horns. The younger caterpillars live and feed communally in a messy silken nest. Page 113. Eats the leaves of Gumbo-Limbo.

Eunica tatila Florida Purplewing

Medium size; body with stout spines, top of head with a pair of long horns, knobbed at the tips. Page 114. Eats the leaves of Crabwood.

Junonia coenia Common Buckeye

Medium size; legs orange or black, bases of lower spines orange, body striped and spotted with white. Page 109. Eats the leaves of false foxgloves, American Bluehearts, toadflaxes, blacksennas, plantains, and twinflowers.

Junonia evarete Mangrove Buckeye

Medium size; legs and bases of lower spines orange, body mostly black. Page 110. Eats the young leaves of Black Mangrove.

Junonia genoveva Tropical Buckeye

Medium size; legs and body black. Page 111. Eats the leaves of Blue Porterweed.

Anartia jatrophae White Peacock

Medium size; black with stout orange spines on the top of the abdomen, head with a pair of long, knobbed horns. Page 111. Eats the leaves of Herb-of-Grace and Fogfruit.

Eunica monima Dingy Purplewing

Eunica tatila Florida Purplewing

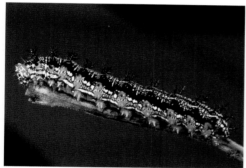

Junonia coenia Common Buckeye

Junonia evarete Mangrove Buckeye

Junonia genoveva Tropical Buckeye

Anartia jatrophae White Peacock

Brushfoots

Siproeta stelenes Malachite

Large size; similar to White Peacock, but spines longer and more slender. Page 112.
Eats the leaves and flower bracts of Green Shrimp Plant.

Chlosyne nycteis Silvery Checkerspot

Small size; head black, body black with a broad cream colored stripe on sides. The younger caterpillars live and feed communally in a silken nest. Page 104.
Eats the leaves of sunflowers.

Anthanassa texana seminole 'Seminole' Texan Crescent

Small size; head black with white patches, body black with pale mottling on the sides. The younger caterpillars live and feed communally in a silken nest. Page 104.
Eats the leaves of Looseflower Waterwillow.

Anthanassa frisia Cuban Crescent

Small size; first row of spines on top of the thorax orange. The younger caterpillars live and feed communally in a silken nest. Page 105.
Eats the leaves of foldwings.

Phyciodes phaon Phaon Crescent

Small size; body brown with broad paler stripes. The younger caterpillars live and feed communally in a silken nest. Page 105.
Eats the leaves of Fogfruit and sometimes Looseflower Waterwillow.

Phyciodes tharos Pearl Crescent

Small size; similar to the Phaon Crescent, but darker with less distinct stripes. Page 106.
Eats the leaves of asters.

Siproeta stelenes Malachite

Chlosyne nycteis Silvery Checkerspot

Anthanassa texana seminole 'Seminole' Texan Crescent

Anthanassa frisia Cuban Crescent

Phyciodes phaon Phaon Crescent

Phyciodes tharos Pearl Crescent

Brushfoots

Polygonia comma Eastern Comma

Medium size; black with cream colored spines. Lives in a leaf nest. Page 107.
Probably eats the leaves of nettles and elms.

Nymphalis antiopa Mourning Cloak

Medium size; black variegated with white and a row of reddish spots on the back. The younger caterpillars live and feed communally in a silken nest. Page 107.
Probably eats the leaves of willows, River Birch, and elms in Florida.

Polygonia interrogationis Question Mark

Medium size; with orange spines on back. Page 106.
Eats the leaves of hackberries and elms.

Vanessa virginiensis American Lady

Medium size; color variable, body typically banded with black and yellow, two rows of small white spots on back, spines black with orange bases. Lives in a nest of silk and flower parts. Page 108.
Eats the leaves of everlastings.

Vanessa cardui Painted Lady

Medium size; color variable, body typically banded with black and yellow, spines pale with oranges bases. Lives in a silken nest. Page 108.
May eat thistles in Florida.

Vanessa atalanta Red Admiral

Medium size; color variable, usually body black speckled with white, spines black with orange bases, a broken cream colored stripe on the sides. Lives in a leaf nest. Page 109.
Eats the leaves of False Nettle, Pellitory, and nettles.

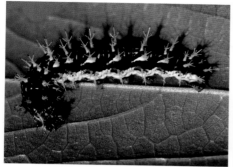

Polygonia comma Eastern Comma

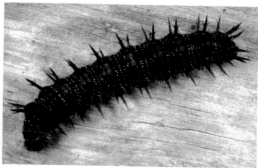

Nymphalis antiopa Mourning Cloak

Polygonia interrogationis Question Mark

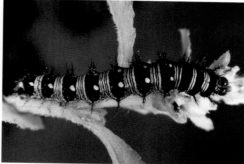

Vanessa virginiensis American Lady

Vanessa cardui Painted Lady

Vanessa atalanta Red Admiral

Leafwings, Emperors, Admirals, and Milkweed Butterflies

Anaea troglodyta floridalis Florida Leafwing

Medium size; head with a pebbly texture, a pale yellow stripe on sides of body. Page 115.
Eats the leaves of Pineland Croton.

Anaea andria Goatweed Leafwing

Medium size; body green to grayish green, sometimes with purplish blotches. Lives in a leaf nest. Page 115.
Eats the leaves of Silver Croton.

Asterocampa celtis Hackberry Emperor

Medium size; upper part of head blackish, body green with narrow yellow stripes and diagonal markings. Lives in a leaf nest. Page 116.
Eats the leaves of hackberries.

Asterocampa clyton Tawny Emperor

Medium size; only the branched spines on top of head black, body with broad yellow stripes. Lives in a leaf nest. Page 116.
Eats the leaves of hackberries.

Marpesia petreus Ruddy Daggerwing

Medium size; gaudy color pattern with a single row of long spines on the back, top of head with a pair of extremely long horns. Page 114.
Eats the young leaves of Strangler Fig and Wild Banyan Tree.

Danaus plexippus Monarch

Medium size; body with narrow black, yellow, and white bands, with two pairs of fleshy filaments. Page 121.
Eats the leaves and flowers of milkweeds.

Anaea troglodyta floridalis Florida Leafwing

Anaea andria Goatweed Leafwing

Asterocampa celtis Hackberry Emperor

Asterocampa clyton Tawny Emperor

Marpesia petreus Ruddy Daggerwing

Danaus plexippus Monarch

Milkweed Butterflies, Satyrs, and Wood-Nymphs

Danaus gilippus Queen

Medium size; body with wide black bands marked with yellow, three pairs of fleshy filaments. Page 121.
Eats the leaves and flowers of White Twinevine, Latexplant, swallow-worts, and milkweeds.

Danaus eresimus Soldier

Medium size; body with a broad white stripe on sides and three pairs of fleshy filaments. Page 122.
Eats the leaves and flowers of White Twinevine, Latexplant, and milkweeds.

Hermeuptychia sosybius Carolina Satyr

Small size; head with a pair of minute spines on top, body green with a very narrow yellow line interspersed with tiny white spots on the upper sides, posterior end with a pair of very short tails. Page 119.
Eats the leaves of grasses.

Neonympha areolata Georgia Satyr

Small size; head with a small pair of pink spines on top, body green with narrow yellow stripes, posterior end with a pair of short tails. Page 119.
Eats the leaves of grasses and sedges.

Megisto cymela Little Wood-Satyr

Small size; head with a small pair of spines on top, body brown, posterior end with a pair of short tails. Page 120.
Eats the leaves of grasses.

Cercyonis pegala Common Wood-Nymph

Medium size; head rounded, body green with narrow yellow stripes, posterior end with a pair of short pink tails. Page 120.
Eats the leaves of grasses.

Danaus gilippus Queen

Danaus eresimus Soldier

Hermeuptychia sosybius Carolina Satyr

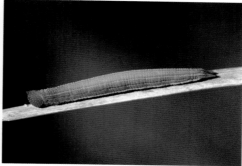

Neonympha areolata Georgia Satyr

Megisto cymela Little Wood-Satyr

Cercyonis pegala Common Wood-Nymph

Satyrs and Spread-winged Skippers

Enodia portlandia Southern Pearly-eye

Medium size; head with a pair of short spines on top, body green or brown, posterior end with a pair of short tails. Page 117.
Eats the leaves of Switchcane.

Satyrodes appalachia Appalachian Brown

Medium size; head with a pair of short spines on top, body green with narrow yellow stripes, posterior end with a pair of short tails. Page 118.
Eats the leaves of Narrowfruit Horned Beaksedge.

Cyllopsis gemma Gemmed Satyr

Small size; spines on top of head longer than width of head, body green or brown, posterior end with a pair of short tails. Page 118.
Eats the leaves of woodoats.

Achalarus lyciades Hoary Edge

Medium size; head dark, body light brown, very similar to the cloudy-wings, but with a few small spines toward the top of the head, and paler body color. Page 127.
Eats the leaves of pigeonwings.

Thorybes bathyllus Southern Cloudywing

Medium size; body brownish in color. Page 128.
Eats the leaves of ticktrefoils and Hairy Lespedeza.

Thorybes pylades Northern Cloudywing

Medium size; body pinkish brown in color. Page 128.
Eats the leaves of ticktrefoils and Florida Hoarypea.

Enodia portlandia *Southern Pearly-eye*

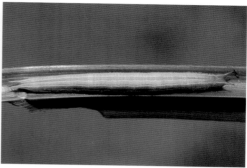
Satyrodes appalachia *Appalachian Brown*

Cyllopsis gemma *Gemmed Satyr*

Achalarus lyciades *Hoary Edge*

Thorybes bathyllus *Southern Cloudywing*

Thorybes pylades *Northern Cloudywing*

Spread-winged Skippers

Thorybes confusis Confused Cloudywing

Medium size; body pale brown. Page 129.
Eats the leaves of ticktrefoils.

Urbanus dorantes Dorantes Longtail

Medium size; body green or occasionally brown with a chain of yellow spots outlined with darker color on the sides. Page 126.
Eats the leaves of ticktrefoils.

Epargyreus zestos Zestos Skipper

Medium size; head dark brown with yellow eye patches, body bluish green. Page 124.
Eats the leaves of Florida Hammock Milkpea.

Epargyreus clarus Silver-spotted Skipper

Medium size; head reddish brown with yellow eye patches, body yellow with narrow black transverse stripes. Page 124.
Eats the leaves of indigobush, Groundnut, ticktrefoils, Black Locust, wisteria, and other legumes.

Urbanus proteus Long-tailed Skipper

Medium size; head brown with a black face and yellow eye patches, body speckled with black, a yellow and orange stripe on the sides. Page 125.
Eats the leaves of False Moneywort, butterfly peas, pigeonwings, ticktrefoils, milkpeas, cultivated beans, cowpeas, wisteria, and many other legumes.

Autochton cellus Golden Banded-Skipper

Medium size; head reddish brown with yellow eye patches, body nearly transparent with broad yellow stripes on the sides. Page 127.
Eats the leaves of Hogpeanut.

Thorybes confusis *Confused Cloudywing*

Urbanus dorantes *Dorantes Longtail*

Epargyreus zestos *Zestos Skipper*

Epargyreus clarus *Silver-spotted Skipper*

Urbanus proteus *Long-tailed Skipper*

Autochton cellus *Golden Banded-Skipper*

Spread-winged Skippers

Phocides pigmalion Mangrove Skipper

Medium size; head reddish brown with yellow eye patches, young caterpillars red with transverse yellow stripes, mature larvae white. Page 123.
Eats the leaves of Red Mangrove.

Polygonus leo Hammock Skipper

Medium size; head white with a black stripe around the margin and two black spots on upper face. Page 125.
Eats the leaves of Florida Fishpoison Tree.

Ephyriades brunneus Florida Duskywing

Small size; head black with orange patches. Page 130.
Eats the leaves of Long Key Locustberry.

Erynnis martialis Mottled Duskywing

Small size; head pebbly near the top. Page 132.
Eats the leaves of New Jersey Tea.

Erynnis juvenalis Juvenal's Duskywing

Small size; head pale brown with orange patches, body with a narrow yellow stripe on the sides. Page 131.
Eats the leaves of oaks.

Erynnis horatius Horace's Duskywing

Small size; similar to Juvenal's Duskywing, but without the yellow stripes on the body. Page 131.
Eats the leaves of oaks.

Phocides pigmalion *Mangrove Skipper*

Polygonus leo *Hammock Skipper*

Ephyriades brunneus *Florida Duskywing*

Erynnis martialis *Mottled Duskywing*

Erynnis juvenalis *Juvenal's Duskywing*

Erynnis horatius *Horace's Duskywing*

Spread-winged Skippers

Erynnis zarucco Zarucco Duskywing

Small size; body with cream colored line on sides interrupted with yellow spots. Page 133.
Eats the leaves of milkpeas, Bladderpod, and other legumes.

Erynnis baptisiae Wild Indigo Duskywing

Small size, very similar to the Zarucco Duskywing. Page 133.
Eats the leaves of wild indigos.

Erynnis brizo Sleepy Duskywing

Small size; head more rounded than other duskywings, body color green in summer becoming brown during the winter. Page 130.
Eats the leaves of scrub oaks.

Staphylus hayhurstii Hayhurst's Scallopwing

Small size; black head with feathery hairs, pale thoracic shield, body nearly transparent. Page 129.
Eats the leaves of Juba's Bush.

Pholisora catullus Common Sootywing

Small size; head black with feathery hairs, thoracic shield dark brown and white, body green frosted with white. Page 135.
Eats the leaves of Lamb'squarters.

Pyrgus albescens White Checkered-Skipper

Small size; very similar to other checkered-skippers, but body more frosted with white. Page 134.
Eats the leaves of fanpetals.

Erynnis zarucco *Zarucco Duskywing*

Erynnis baptisiae *Wild Indigo Duskywing*

Erynnis brizo *Sleepy Duskywing*

Staphylus hayhurstii *Hayhurst's Scallopwing*

Pholisora catullus *Common Sootywing*

Pyrgus albescens *White Checkered-Skipper*

201

Spread-winged Skippers and Grass-Skippers

Pyrgus communis Common Checkered-Skipper

Small size; head black with feathery hairs, body green with a yellowish caste, and indistinct dark lines. Page 134.
Eats the leaves of fanpetals.

Pyrgus oileus Tropical Checkered-Skipper

Small size; similar to other checkered-skippers, but prothoracic shield with three pale marks. Page 135.
Eats the leaves of fanpetals.

Cymaenes tripunctus Three-spotted Skipper

Small size; head white with a black line around the edge and through the middle of the face, body green frosted with white. Page 137.
Eats the leaves of grasses.

Lerema accius Clouded Skipper

Medium size; head white with a black line around the edge, three black lines on the face, and a short brown line at the top of the face, body green frosted with white. Page 137.
Eats numerous grasses with wide leaves.

Amblyscirtes hegon Pepper and Salt Skipper

Small size; head pale with brown stripes, two small points near the jaws, thoracic shield black, body thickly frosted with white. Page 153.
Probably eats the leaves of Fowl Mannagrass.

Amblyscirtes aesculapius Lace-winged Roadside-Skipper

Small size; head pale with black stripes, two small points near the jaws, thoracic shield narrow and black, body lightly frosted with white. Page 154.
Eats the leaves of Switchcane.

Pyrgus communis *Common Checkered-Skipper*

Pyrgus oileus *Tropical Checkered-Skipper*

Cymaenes tripunctus *Three-spotted Skipper*

Lerema accius *Clouded Skipper*

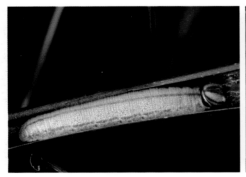

Amblyscirtes hegon *Pepper and Salt Skipper*

Amblyscirtes aesculapius *Lace-winged Roadside-Skipper*

Grass-Skippers

Amblyscirtes vialis Common Roadside-Skipper

Small size; head pale with brown stripes, two small points near the jaws, thoracic shield black. Page 154.
Eats the leaves of grasses.

Amblyscirtes alternata Dusky Roadside-Skipper

Small size; head pale with brown stripes, stripes on face interrupted, two small points near the jaws, thoracic shield narrow and black, body thickly frosted with white. Page 155.
Eats the leaves of Skeletongrass.

Nastra lherminier Swarthy Skipper

Small size; head pale with reddish brown stripes, thoracic shield indistinct, body green with yellow stripes. Page 136.
Eats the leaves of bluestems and other grasses.

Nastra neamathla Neamathla Skipper

Small size; very similar to the Swarthy Skipper, but the stripes on the head are slightly wider. Page 136.
Eats the leaves of bluestem and other grasses.

Atrytone arogos Arogos Skipper

Small size; head pale with narrow brown stripes, thoracic shield narrow and black, body color bluish white. Page 145.
Eats the leaves of Lopsided Indiangrass in peninsular Florida and Toothachegrass in the Panhandle

Ancyloxypha numitor Least Skipper

Small size; head with diffuse brown stripes on face, thoracic shield very narrow, white and black, body green with yellow mottling. Page 138.
Eats the leaves of Southern Cutgrass and Southern Wild Rice.

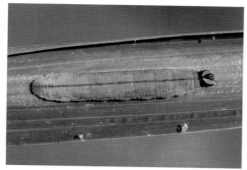
Amblyscirtes vialis *Common Roadside-Skipper*

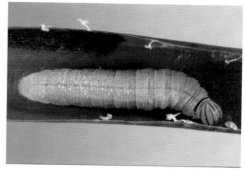
Amblyscirtes alternata *Dusky Roadside-Skipper*

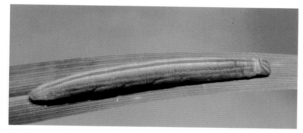
Nastra lherminier *Swarthy Skipper*

Nastra neamathla *Neamathla Skipper*

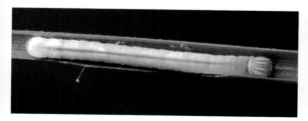
Atrytone arogos *Arogos Skipper*

Ancyloxypha numitor *Least Skipper*

Grass-Skippers

Amblyscirtes reversa Reversed Roadside-Skipper

Small size; triangular black patch on the face, with two points near the jaws, thoracic shield black, body color bluish white. Page 155.
Eats the leaves of Switchcane.

Anatrytone logan Delaware Skipper

Medium size; head pale with black stripes, a black thoracic shield, and two black chevrons on the posterior end of the abdomen, body color pale blue. Page 146.
Eats the leaves of Maidencane and other grasses.

Problema byssus Byssus Skipper

Medium size; head pale with black stripes, thoracic shield black and white, body color bluish white with a yellowish caste on the thorax and posterior end. Page 146.
Eats the leaves of Eastern Gamagrass, Sugarcane Plumegrass, and other grasses.

Lerodea eufala Eufala Skipper

Small size; head pale with brown markings, thoracic shield indistinct, body color green. Page 156.
Eats the leaves of weedy grasses.

Euphyes arpa Palmetto Skipper

Medium size; head with wide brown stripes and a black spot on the upper face, thoracic shield white and black, body bluish green frosted with white. Page 149.
Eats the leaves of Saw Palmetto.

Euphyes pilatka Palatka Skipper

Medium size; head with three black lines separated by white, thoracic shield with a narrow black line, body bluish green frosted with white. Page 149.
Eats the leaves of Sawgrass.

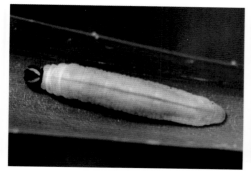

Amblyscirtes reversa Reversed Roadside-Skipper

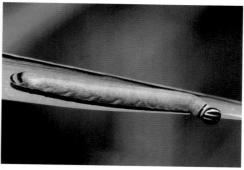

Anatrytone logan Delaware Skipper

Problema byssus Byssus Skipper

Lerodea eufala Eufala Skipper

Euphyes arpa Palmetto Skipper

Euphyes pilatka Palatka Skipper

Grass-Skippers

Euphyes dion Dion Skipper

Medium size; head with very wide brown stripes, thoracic shield narrowly black. Page 150.
Eats the leaves of sedges.

Euphyes dukesi Dukes' Skipper

Medium size; closely similar to the Dion Skipper, but brown stripes on face narrower. Page 151.
Eats the leaves of beaksedges.

Euphyes berryi Berry's Skipper

Medium size; closely resembling Dukes' Skipper, but brown line around margin of head slightly wider. Page 151.
Eats the leaves of sedges.

Euphyes vestris Dun Skipper

Medium size; similar to Berry's Skipper, but thoracic shield white and black, and a black crescent on the posterior end of the body. Page 151.
Eats the leaves of sedges.

Hylephila phyleus Fiery Skipper

Medium size; head shiny black with two short, faint pale stripes on upper face, body brownish with tiny dark spots. Page 139.
Eats the leaves of weedy grasses.

Atalopedes campestris Sachem

Medium size; head shiny black with two short brown stripes on upper face, body greenish brown. Page 145.
Eats the leaves of grasses.

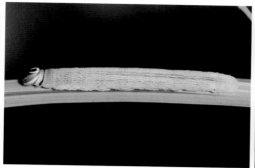

Euphyes dion Dion Skipper

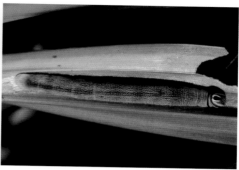

Euphyes dukesi Dukes' Skipper

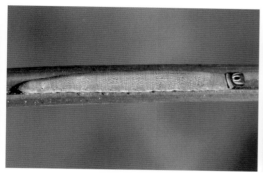

Euphyes berryi Berry's Skipper

Euphyes vestris Dun Skipper

Hylephila phyleus Fiery Skipper

Atalopedes campestris Sachem

Grass-Skippers

Hesperia attalus Dotted Skipper

Medium size; head shiny black with two short white stripes on upper face, body greenish brown. Page 140.
Eats the leaves of grasses.

Hesperia meskei Meske's Skipper

Medium size; head shiny black with two short white stripes on upper face, body brown. Page 140.
Eats the leaves of grasses.

Polites baracoa Baracoa Skipper

Small size; head brown with short white and black stripes on upper face, body brown with dark lines on the sides, posterior end with dark markings. Page 141.
Eats the leaves of grasses.

Polites vibex Whirlabout

Small size; head black with two short white lines on upper face, body green with small dark spots. Page 143.
Eats the leaves of many weedy grasses.

Polites themistocles Tawny-edged Skipper

Small size; head black, body brownish green with dark lines on the sides and tiny dark spots, posterior end with dark markings. Page 141.
Eats the leaves of grasses.

Polites origenes Crossline Skipper

Small size; head black, body brownish, posterior end with only a few small dark spots. Page 142.
Eats the leaves of grasses.

Hesperia attalus Dotted Skipper

Hesperia meskei Meske's Skipper

Polites baracoa Baracoa Skipper

Polites vibex Whirlabout

Polites themistocles Tawny-edged Skipper

Polites origenes Crossline Skipper

Grass-Skippers

Wallengrenia otho Southern Broken-Dash

Small size; head black, body brownish green with a pale orange stripe on the sides of the thorax. Page 143.
Eats the leaves of grasses.

Wallengrenia egeremet Northern Broken-Dash

Small size; head black, body brownish, the posterior end blackish. Page 144.
Eats the leaves of grasses.

Copaeodes minimus Southern Skipperling

Very small size; head green with two small points on top, body green with white frosting, posterior end pointed. Page 139.
Eats the leaves of Bermudagrass and other weedy grasses.

Panoquina panoquin Salt Marsh Skipper

Small size; head green with faint reddish lines, body with a narrow cream colored stripe on the sides. Page 157.
Eats the leaves of Coral Dropseed and Seashore Dropseed.

Panoquina panoquinoides Obscure Skipper

Small size; head green with faint reddish lines, body with faint lines. Page 158.
Eats the leaves of Saltgrass and Saltmarsh Cordgrass.

Panoquina ocola Ocola Skipper

Medium size; head green, body green with a yellowish caste. Page 158.
Eats the leaves of wetland grasses.

Wallengrenia otho Southern Broken-Dash

Wallengrenia egeremet Northern Broken-Dash

Copaeodes minimus Southern Skipperling

Panoquina panoquin Salt Marsh Skipper

Panoquina panoquinoides Obscure Skipper

Panoquina ocola Ocola Skipper

Grass-Skippers

Poanes aaroni Aaron's Skipper

Medium size; head light brown with three black lines. Page 147.
Eats the leaves of Maidencane and other grasses.

Poanes viator Broad-winged Skipper

Medium size; head light brown with a black line and two black spots.
Page 148.
Eats the leaves of Southern Wild Rice and Wild Rice.

Poanes zabulon Zabulon Skipper

Small size; head dark brown, body with faint stripes. Page 147.
Eats the leaves of grasses.

Poanes yehl Yehl Skipper

Medium size; head black, body with faint stripes. Page 148.
Eats the leaves of grasses.

Pompeius verna Little Glassywing

Small size; head very shiny black. Page 144.
Eats the leaves of grasses.

Atrytonopsis hianna Dusted Skipper

Medium size; dark brown head, narrow black thoracic shield, pinkish
body with long hairs. Page 152.
Eats the leaves of Lopsided Indiangrass.

Poanes aaroni Aaron's Skipper

Poanes viator Broad-winged Skipper

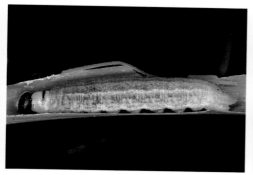

Poanes zabulon Zabulon Skipper

Poanes yehl Yehl Skipper

Pompeius verna Little Glassywing

Atrytonopsis hianna Dusted Skipper

Grass-Skippers and Giant-Skippers

Oligoria maculata Twin-spot Skipper

Medium size; brown head, black thoracic shield, pinkish body with short hairs. Page 156.
Eats the leaves of bluestem grasses and Lopsided Indiangrass.

Calpodes ethlius Brazilian Skipper

Large size; head brown with a black spot on face, transparent skin. Page 157.
Eats the leaves of cannas and Alligatorflag.

Asbolis capucinus Monk Skipper

Large size; orange head, posterior end of body edged with black. Page 152.
Eats the leaves of Coconut Palm and other palms.

Megathymus yuccae Yucca Giant-Skipper

Large size and thick body; head reddish brown. Makes a tent in center of host rosette. Page 159.
Bores into yucca stems and roots.

Megathymus cofaqui Cofaqui Giant-Skipper

Large size and thick body; head blackish. Constructs a tent at base of plant just before pupation. Page 160.
Bores into yucca stems and roots.

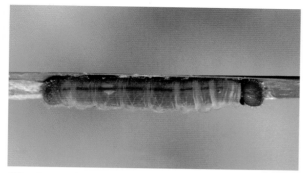

Oligoria maculata Twin-spot Skipper

Calpodes ethlius Brazilian Skipper

Asbolis capucinus Monk Skipper

Megathymus yuccae Yucca Giant-Skipper

Megathymus cofaqui Cofaqui Giant-Skipper

Gymnosperms (Cone-bearing Plants)
Cupressaceae (Cedar family)

Chamaecyparis thyoides
Atlantic White Cedar

Description: Evergreen tree to about 50' tall, with tiny scalelike leaves, deeply furrowed bark, and the branchlets arranged in a plane. The fruit is a small dry cone that releases winged seeds.
Habitat: Wetlands. Margins of blackwater streams and occasionally spring runs.
Distribution: Florida Panhandle and Ocala National Forest.
Notes: Uncommon and local. Propagated from seeds and cuttings.
Caterpillars: Hessel's Hairstreak (*Mitoura hesseli*).

Juniperus virginiana (formerly *Juniperus silicicola*)
Red Cedar

Description: Evergreen tree to about 50' tall, with small scalelike leaves; juvenile foliage is prickly to the touch, mature foliage is smooth. The fruit is a chalky or bluish berrylike cone that is eaten and dispersed by birds.
Habitat: Uplands and wetlands. Beaches, hammocks, disturbed sites, and margins of salt marshes.
Distribution: Mostly northern and central Florida.
Notes: Common. Propagated from seeds and cuttings.
Caterpillars: Juniper Hairstreak (*Mitoura grynea*).

Pinaceae (Pine family)

Pinus clausa

Sand Pine

Description: Small to medium tree typically less than 50' tall, often somewhat leaning, with short twisted needles in bundles of three, usually found in dense stands. Cones small, firmly held to the branches, and usually requiring fire to open.
Habitat: Uplands. Scrubs and an invader in sandhills.
Distribution: Coastal areas as well as interior sand ridges throughout the state.
Notes: Locally common. Propagated from seeds. This pine is fire-dependent. Wildfire in sand pine scrub is uncommon and devastating, killing most of the trees. The intense heat also melts the resin on the outside of the cones, allowing the seeds to be released.
Caterpillars: Eastern Pine Elfin (*Incisalia niphon*).

Zamiaceae (Zamia family)

Zamia pumila

Coontie, Florida Arrowroot

Description: Perennial, evergreen herb from 2' to 4' tall with stiff, fernlike leaves and a stout underground stem. Plants either male or female. Produces reddish brown cones near the ground, female cones larger and thicker than the males. Seeds large with a hard coat within a fleshy, bright orange covering.
Habitat: Uplands. Sandhills, dry hammocks, and pine rocklands.
Distribution: Peninsular Florida.
Notes: Uncommon in the wild, but widely used in landscaping. Propagated from seeds. All parts of the plant are extremely poisonous if ingested. Once harvested for the fine starch stored in the stems, rendered edible only by grinding the stems and washing the red toxin away with water.
Caterpillars: Atala (*Eumaeus atala*).

Monocotyledons
(Plants with One Seed Leaf)

Agavaceae (Agave family)

Yucca aloifolia

Spanish Bayonet

Description: Perennial evergreen herb to 10' tall with thick stems bearing stiff, daggerlike leaves edged with tiny teeth and tipped with a sharp spine. Forms clumps via underground stems. Flowers large, waxy, white, downward pointing, in dense clusters on short stalks produced from the tips of the stems. Blooms sporadically in spring and summer.
Habitat: Uplands. Beaches and gardens.
Distribution: Exotic plant from Mexico and the West Indies now widely naturalized throughout the state.
Notes: Common. Propagated from stem cuttings.
Caterpillars: Yucca Giant-Skipper (*Megathymus yuccae*) and Cofaqui Giant-Skipper (*Megathymus cofaqui*).

Yucca filamentosa

Adam's Needle

Description: Perennial evergreen herb with rosettes of stiff straplike leaves to 2' tall from thick underground stems. Leaves with threadlike fibers dangling from the margins and a short spine at the tip. Flowers large, waxy, white, downward pointing, in dense clusters on long stalks to 8' tall. Blooms sporadically in spring and early summer.
Habitat: Uplands. Sandhills and dry hammocks and pinelands.
Distribution: Northern and central Florida.
Notes: Common. *Yucca flaccida* from central Florida is similar, but the leaves are leathery instead of stiff.
Caterpillars: Yucca Giant-Skipper (*Megathymus yuccae*) and Cofaqui Giant-Skipper (*Megathymus cofaqui*).

Arecaceae (Palm family)

Cocos nucifera
Coconut Palm

Description: Large tree typically to 30' tall with pinnately compound leaves to 8' long. Dense clusters of small white flowers on short stalks. Large green, yellow, or brown edible fruit.
Habitat: Uplands. Beaches, shorelines, and gardens.
Distribution: Exotic tree from the Old World tropics grown in coastal areas of central and southern Florida.
Notes: Common. Propagated from seeds.
Caterpillars: Monk Skipper (*Asbolis capucinus*).

Sabal palmetto
Cabbage Palm

Description: Large tree up to 40' tall with fanlike leaves bearing a central fold, on long petioles without teeth. Small white flowers in wispy clusters on flower stalks as long as or longer than the leaves. Blooms from spring through summer.
Habitat: Uplands and wetlands. Swamps, hammocks, flatwoods, and disturbed sites.
Distribution: Mostly peninsular Florida.
Notes: Abundant. Propagated from seeds. The state tree of Florida. As the older leaves are shed, the petiole breaks off at the base leaving the "boot." Eventually the boots are shed as well, exposing the rough trunk. The small black fruits are eaten by birds.
Caterpillars: Monk Skipper (*Asbolis capucinus*).

Serenoa repens

Saw Palmetto

Description: Shrubby palm with flat fanlike leaves and usually a prostrate trunk rooting along the ground. Petioles edged with small teeth. Small white flowers with a coconut fragrance in dense clusters on stalks shorter than the leaves. Foul-tasting black berries produced in late summer and fall. Blooms in April and May.
Habitat: Uplands. Prairies, flatwoods, hammocks, sandhills, and scrubs.
Distribution: Coastal areas of the panhandle and throughout the peninsula.
Notes: Abundant. Propagated from seeds. The flowers are attractive to a wide variety of beetles, flies, bees, wasps, moths, and butterflies, especially hairstreaks. The green berries are harvested in large quantities, processed, and sold as a prostate cancer preventative.
Caterpillars: Palmetto Skipper (*Euphyes arpa*) and Monk Skipper (*Asbolis capucinus*).

Cannaceae (Canna family)

Canna flaccida

Bandana-of-the-Everglades, Yellow Canna

Description: Perennial herb up to 4' tall with smooth, lance-shaped leaves. Forms patches via rhizomes. Large yellow flowers produced in clusters at the tips of the flower stalks followed by dry brown pods bearing round, hard, black seeds. Blooms from spring through fall.
Habitat: Wetlands. Wet flatwoods, wet prairies, shallow marshes, and ditches.
Distribution: Throughout the state.
Notes: Locally common. Propagated from seeds and root divisions. Many ornamental hybrids of tropical species with red or green leaves and various flower colors are widely grown in Florida gardens.
Caterpillars: Brazilian Skipper (*Calpodes ethlius*).

Cyperaceae (Sedge family)

Sedges can be identified by their three-angled stems. The flowers and fruit are enclosed under papery bracts and are called spikelets. The seeds are nutlets.

Carex glaucescens
Clustered Sedge

Description: Perennial clumping sedge with coarse bluish leaves to about 3' tall. Spikelets pointed and arranged in clusters dangling from the tips of the flower stalks. Nutlets with a tubercle at the tip and enclosed in an inflated sack. Produces seeds from summer through fall.
Habitat: Wetlands. Margins of swamps, seeps, and bogs.
Distribution: Northern and central Florida.
Notes: Common. Propagated from root divisions and seeds.
Caterpillars: Dion Skipper (*Euphyes dion*).

Carex lupuliformis
False Hop Sedge

Description: Perennial clumping sedge with shiny yellowish green leaves to about 3' tall. Spikelets pointed and arranged in dense erect clusters at the tips of the flower stalks. Nutlets with a tubercle at the tip and enclosed in an inflated sack. Produces seeds from summer through fall.
Habitat: Wetlands. Swamps and wet hammocks.
Distribution: Northern and central Florida.
Notes: Common. Propagated from root divisions and seeds.
Caterpillars: Dukes' Skipper (*Euphyes dukesi*).

Cladium jamaicense

Jamaica Swamp Sawgrass

Description: Large perennial sedge up to 8' tall with tough coarse leaves. Forms dense patches via underground runners. Small teeth on the midrib and leaf margins easily cut clothing and exposed skin. Spikelets small, brown, and numerous, in clusters on branches at the tips of the flower stalks. Produces seeds from summer through fall.
Habitat: Wetlands. Marshes, wet prairies, wet flatwoods, and ditches.
Distribution: Throughout the state.
Notes: Locally abundant. Propagated from root divisions and seeds.
Caterpillars: Palatka Skipper (*Euphyes pilatka*).

Rhynchospora inundata

Narrowfruit Horned Beaksedge

Description: Coarse, perennial sedge with shiny leaves to about 4' tall. Forms patches via underground runners. Nutlets with several long bristles at the base and a tubercle to about ½" long at the tip. Produces seeds from spring through fall.
Habitat: Wetlands. Swamps, wet flatwoods, and ditches.
Distribution: Throughout the state.
Notes: Common. Propagated from root divisions and seeds. This is one of the larger species of beaksedges in Florida. Millet Beaksedge (*Rhynchospora miliacea*) is also eaten by the larvae of Dukes' Skipper.
Caterpillars: Appalachian Brown (*Satyrodes appalachia*) and Dukes' Skipper (*Euphyes dukesi*).

Scirpus cyperinus

Woolgrass

Description: Perennial clump-forming sedge to about 5' tall with broad leaves. Spikelets brown, ovoid, with long bristles attached to the base, numerous on drooping branches clustered near the tips of the flower stalks.
Habitat: Wetlands. Swamps, wet flatwoods, and ditches.
Distribution: Northern and central Florida.
Notes: Common. Propagated from root divisions and seeds.
Caterpillars: Dion Skipper (*Euphyes dion*).

Marantaceae (Arrowroot family)

Thalia geniculata

Alligatorflag, Fireflag

Description: Perennial herb to 8' tall with large, smooth, lance-shaped leaves on long petioles. Forms clumps via rhizomes. Flowers purple, in drooping clusters on zigzag branches at the tips of the flower stalks. Blooms in summer and fall.
Habitat: Wetlands. Marshes, swamps, and ditches.
Distribution: Mostly in central and southern Florida.
Notes: Common. Propagated from root divisions and seeds.
Caterpillars: Brazilian Skipper (*Calpodes ethlius*).

Poaceae (Grass family)

Unlike sedges, grasses have round stems, but similar to sedges have the flowers and seeds enclosed by several papery bracts; these are called spikelets. Some grasses have bristlelike structures called awns on the tips of one or more of the bracts or groups of bristles at the base of the spikelets. Key characteristics for identifying grasses include the shape and arrangement of the spikelets and branches of the flower stalks, their habit (clumping vs. creeping), size, and presence of hairs or underground stems.

Andropogon virginicus

Broomsedge Bluestem

Description: Perennial bunchgrass with green or chalky stems and leaves. The bases of the leaves are in one plane. The erect flower stalks range from 2' to 4' tall. Spikelets fuzzy with a short awn, arranged in paired groups at the tips of the flower stalk branches. Produces seeds in late summer and fall.
Habitat: Uplands and wetlands. Sandhills, flatwoods, wet prairies, margins of swamps, roadsides, and disturbed areas.
Distribution: Throughout the state.
Notes: Common. Propagated from root divisions and seeds.
Caterpillars: Common Wood-Nymph (*Cercyonis pegala*), Swarthy Skipper (*Nastra lherminier*), Neamathla Skipper (*Nastra neamathla*), Crossline Skipper (*Polites origenes*), Delaware Skipper (*Anatrytone logan*), and Twin-spot Skipper (*Oligoria maculata*).

Arundinaria gigantea

Switchcane

Description: Woody perennial grass with hollow stems from 3' to 8' tall, the wide leaves to about 6" long arising both along the stem and from short branches, with long hairs at the base of the petiole. Forms dense thickets called canebrakes via underground runners. Large dangling spikelets widely spaced on stalks from the tips of the stems and upper branches. Produces seeds only rarely, usually after a fire. This is our only native bamboo.

Habitat: Wetlands. Seepage slopes in flatwoods and at the edges of hammocks, along blackwater streams, and margins of swamps.

Distribution: Northern and central Florida.

Notes: Locally abundant. Propagated from root divisions.

Caterpillars: Southern Pearly-eye (*Enodia portlandia*), Delaware Skipper (*Anatrytone logan*), Lace-winged Skipper (*Amblyscirtes aesculapias*), Reversed Roadside-Skipper (*Amblyscirtes reversa*), and possibly Yehl Skipper (*Poanes yehl*).

Chasmanthium laxum

Slender Woodoats

Description: Perennial bunchgrass to about 1.5' tall with long leaves. The arching flower stalks have very short branches, the flat spikelets arranged in groups of 4 or 5 together on a short stalk. Produces seeds from spring through fall.

Habitat: Uplands and wetlands. Wet to moist hammocks and margins of swamps.

Distribution: Northern and central Florida.

Notes: Common. Propagated from root divisions and seeds. Several related species, including Indian Woodoats or River Oats (*Chasmanthium latifolium*), Shiny Woodoats (*Chasmanthium nitidum*), and Birdbill Woodoats (*Chasmanthium ornithorhynchum*), occur in northern Florida and may also be eaten by butterfly caterpillars.

Caterpillars: Gemmed Satyr (*Cyllopsis gemma*), Clouded Skipper (*Lerema accius*), Byssus Skipper (*Problema byssus*), and possibly Zabulon Skipper (*Poanes zabulon*) and Yehl Skipper (*Poanes yehl*).

Cynodon dactylon
Bermudagrass

Description: Perennial, fine-textured grass to about 8" tall with narrow leaves in one plane from thin erect stalks. Stems also running along the surface and belowground. Flower stalk with branches arranged like spokes of a wheel. Spikelets small, in two rows on one side of the branches. Produces seeds throughout the year.
Habitat: Uplands. Roadsides and weedy disturbed sites.
Distribution: Native to Africa, but widely naturalized throughout the state.
Notes: Abundant. Propagated from seeds and root divisions. Cultivated as turf grass and for pastures, but very weedy.
Caterpillars: Southern Skipperling (*Copaeodes minimus*), and Fiery Skipper (*Hylephila phyleus*).

Dichanthelium aciculare
(formerly *Panicum aciculare*)
Needleleaf Witchgrass

Description: Perennial bunchgrass less than 6" tall with narrow leaves. Flower stalk with short branches, the spikelets small, rounded, and few in number. Produces seeds from spring through fall.
Habitat: Uplands. Scrubs, sandhills, and dry pinelands.
Distribution: Throughout the state.
Notes: Common. Propagated from seeds and root divisions.
Caterpillars: Tawny-edged Skipper (*Polites themistocles*).

Distichlis spicata

Saltgrass

Description: Perennial grass with short flat leaves arranged oppositely in one plane on stalks from 6" to 1.5' tall. Flower stalk with flat spikelets in groups of six to fifteen attached by a short stalk and arranged in a dense cluster at the tip of the plant. Produces seeds throughout the year.
Habitat: Wetlands. Salt marshes and edges of mangrove swamps.
Distribution: Coastal areas throughout the state.
Notes: Common. Propagated from root divisions and seeds.
Caterpillars: Salt Marsh Skipper (*Panoquina panoquin*) and probably Obscure Skipper (*Panoquina panoquinoides*).

Leersia hexandra

Southern Cutgrass

Description: Sprawling perennial grass to about 1' tall. Forms dense patches via underground runners. Leaves rough to the touch and with tiny teeth on the margins that can cut the skin. Spikelets flattened with short hairs arranged in small groups on drooping branches near the tips of the flower stalk.
Habitat: Wetlands. Freshwater marshes, pond and lake margins, ditches.
Distribution: Throughout the state.
Notes: Common. Propagated from root divisions and seeds.
Caterpillars: Least Skipper (*Ancyloxypha numitor*) and Ocola Skipper (*Panquina ocola*).

Panicum hemitomon

Maidencane

Description: Erect or floating perennial grass with smooth, broad leaves on slender stems to about 4' tall. Leaf sheaths with short hairs. Forms dense patches via underground stems. Flower stalk with short branches tightly bunched together near the tip, the spikelets small and pointed. Produces seeds sporadically from spring through fall.

Habitat: Wetlands and uplands. Margins of lakes, freshwater marshes, flatwoods, wet prairies, and ditches.

Distribution: Throughout the state.

Notes: Abundant. Propagated from root divisions and seeds.

Caterpillars: Clouded Skipper (*Lerema accius*), Delaware Skipper (*Anatrytone logan*), and Aaron's Skipper (*Poanes aaroni*).

Panicum maximum

Guineagrass

Description: Large, perennial, clumping grass with broad leaves. Flower stalk open with numerous branches near the tip. The spikelets small and pointed. Produces seeds all year.

Habitat: Uplands. Roadsides, margins of hammocks, agricultural fields, and other weedy disturbed sites.

Distribution: Originally from Africa, now naturalized throughout the state.

Notes: Abundant. Weedy and not recommended for propagation.

Caterpillars: Clouded Skipper (*Lerema accius*).

Panicum rigidulum
Redtop Panicum

Description: Coarse perennial grass to about 1.5' tall, forming small clumps. The leaves with or without short hairs and often reddish in color. The spikelets are small and pointed, densely arranged along the branches of the flower stalk. Produces seeds in summer and fall.

Habitat: Wetlands. Swamps, wet hammocks, and ditches.

Distribution: Throughout the state.

Notes: Common. Propagated from root divisions and seeds.

Caterpillars: Clouded Skipper (*Lerema accius*) and Delaware Skipper (*Anatrytone logan*).

Saccharum giganteum (formerly *Erianthus giganteus*)
Sugarcane Plumegrass

Description: Large perennial grass with long, wide leaves to about 3' tall arising from a basal clump. The flower stalks to 8' tall with numerous branches clustered together near the tip. The spikelets fuzzy with a short awn, reddish at first, changing to white at maturity. Produces seeds in late summer and fall.

Habitat: Wetlands. Margins of swamps, freshwater marshes, wet flatwoods, and ditches.

Distribution: Throughout the state.

Notes: Common. Propagated from root divisions and seeds. The related Sugarcane (*Saccharum officinarum*) is grown on plantations in southern Florida and on a small scale in gardens throughout the state. It is also eaten by skipper caterpillars.

Caterpillars: Clouded Skipper (*Lerema accius*), Delaware Skipper (*Anatrytone logan*), and Byssus Skipper (*Problema byssus*).

Sorghastrum secundum
Lopsided Indiangrass

Description: Perennial bunchgrass from 1' to 3' tall with wide, smooth leaves. Flower stalks to about 4' tall. Spikelets with a long awn, dangle from one side of the flower stalk near the tip. Produces seeds in late summer and fall.
Habitat: Uplands. Sandhills, prairies, and dry pinelands.
Distribution: Northern, central, and southern Florida.
Notes: Common. Propagated from root divisions and seeds. A beautiful grass for the garden.
Caterpillars: Swarthy Skipper (*Nastra lherminier*), Delaware Skipper (*Anatrytone logan*), Arogos Skipper (*Atrytone arogos*), Dusted Skipper (*Atrytonopsis hianna*), Eufala Skipper (*Lerodea eufala*), and Twin-spot Skipper (*Oligoria maculata*).

Spartina alterniflora
Saltmarsh Cordgrass, Smooth Cordgrass

Description: Perennial erect grass from 1' to 4' tall with wide smooth leaves arranged alternately on stems arising in clumps from underground runners. Flower stalk with several widely spaced branches near the tip. Spikelets arranged in two rows on the lower sides of the branches. Produces seeds in summer and fall.
Habitat: Wetlands. Salt marshes and the margins of brackish streams and waterways.
Distribution: Coastal areas of northern, central, and southern Florida.
Notes: Abundant. Propagated from root divisions and seeds.
Caterpillars: Salt Marsh Skipper (*Panoquina panoquin*).

Sporobolus virginicus
Seashore Dropseed

Description: Perennial grass to about 1' tall with flat leaves arranged in one plane and underground runners, forming small clumps. Flower stalk to 2' tall with numerous small spikelets attached by short stalks in a dense cluster at the tip. Produces seeds throughout the year.

Habitat: Wetlands. Salt marshes and the margins of mangrove swamps.

Distribution: Coastal areas of northern, central, and southern Florida.

Notes: Common. Propagated from root divisions and seeds. Coral Dropseed (*Sporobolus domingensis*), found in the Keys and southern Florida, is also eaten by skippers.

Caterpillars: Obscure Skipper (*Panoquina panoquinoides*) and probably Salt Marsh Skipper (*Panoquina panoquin*).

Stenotaphrum secundatum
St. Augustinegrass

Description: Trailing perennial grass with opposite leaves to about 1' tall, rooting along the stem. Flower stalk to about 8" long without branches, thick, with the spikelets appressed on one side. Produces seeds throughout the year.

Habitat: Margins of swamps, hydric hammocks, and yards.

Distribution: Throughout the state.

Notes: Abundant. One of the most commonly used lawn grasses in Florida. Widely available at garden centers.

Caterpillars: Carolina Satyr (*Hermeuptychia sosybius*), Clouded Skipper (*Lerema accius*), Fiery Skipper (*Hylephila phyleus*), and Whirlabout (*Polites vibex*).

Tripsacum dactyloides

Eastern Gamagrass, Fakahatcheegrass

Description: Large perennial clump-forming grass to about 4' tall with wide leaves and short rhizomes. Tiny teeth on the margins of the leaves can cause razorlike cuts to clothing and skin. Flower stalk to about 6' tall, with three to five erect branches clustered near the tip. Female spikelets large and appressed to the lower half of the branches, smaller male spikelets on the outer half of the branches and breaking off after the pollen has been released. Produces seeds from spring through fall.

Habitat: Uplands and wetlands. Wet flatwoods and the margins of streams, canals, freshwater marshes, swamps, and hammocks.

Distribution: Northern, central, and southern Florida.

Notes: Common. Propagated from root divisions and seeds. Can become weedy.

Caterpillars: Three-spotted Skipper (*Cymaenes tripunctus*), Clouded Skipper (*Lerema accius*), and Byssus Skipper (*Problema byssus*).

Zizaniopsis miliacea

Southern Wild Rice, Giant Cutgrass

Description: Large perennial grass to about 6' tall. Forms dense patches via underground runners. Tiny teeth on the margins of the leaves can cause razorlike cuts to clothing and skin. Flower stalk with numerous drooping branches. Female spikelets on short stalks attached to the outer half of the branches, male spikelets toward the branch bases. Produces seeds in spring and summer.

Habitat: Wetlands. Swamps and the margins of rivers, streams, and lakes.

Distribution: Northern, central, and southern Florida.

Notes: Uncommon. Propagated from root divisions and seeds. Can become weedy in small ponds or waterways.

Caterpillars: Clouded Skipper (*Lerema accius*), Least Skipper (*Ancyloxypha numitor*), and Broad-winged Skipper (*Poanes viator*).

Smilacaceae (Smilax family)

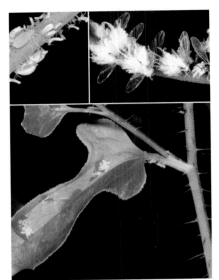

Smilax tamnoides
Bristly Greenbrier

Description: Perennial, evergreen vine with short tendrils from the leaf axils and numerous sharp, black spines on the lower stems. Leaves leathery, to about 4" long, pointed at the tip, the base squarish or heart-shaped. Flowers greenish in small clusters on a short stalk from the leaf axils. Fruit small, shiny black with a large seed. Blooms in spring.

Habitat: Uplands and wetlands. Dry to wet hammocks and margins of swamps.

Distribution: Mostly northern and central Florida.

Notes: Common. Host for Woolly Maple Aphid. Earleaf Greenbrier (*Smilax auriculata*), Saw Greenbrier (*Smilax bona-nox*), and Cat Greenbrier (*Smilax glauca*) also support the aphid and butterfly.

Caterpillars: Harvester (*Feniseca tarquinius*) is carnivorous on the Woolly Maple Aphid.

Neoprociphilus aceris
Woolly Maple Aphid (inset)

Description: Relatively large, oblong aphids, the body about 1/8" long. The internal tissues are reddish, but outer body appears purplish and is covered by a powdery, white wax. The aphids occur in dense colonies on greenbrier stems and the undersides of leaves. The winged forms bear a fluffy coat of wax filaments.

Dicotyledons
(Plants with Two Seed Leaves)

Acanthaceae (Acanthus family)

Blechum pyramidatum
Browne's Blechum, Green Shrimp Plant

Description: Perennial, sparsely hairy herb with erect, easily breakable stems and underground runners. Grows to 2' tall. Leaves opposite, lance shaped, without teeth. Flowers tubular, whitish, produced within large green bracts in compact heads at the tips of the stems. Blooms all year.
Habitat: Uplands. Edges of hammocks and shady disturbed sites.
Distribution: Native to tropical America. Naturalized in central and southern Florida.
Notes: Locally common. Very weedy, not recommended for cultivation.
Caterpillars: Malachite (*Siproeta stelenes*).

Dicliptera sexangularis
Sixangle Foldwing

Description: Short-lived perennial herb with erect, easily breakable stems to 3' tall. Leaves opposite, lance shaped, without teeth. Flowers tubular, bright red, produced at the tips of the stems. Blooms all year.
Habitat: Uplands. Beach dunes, edges of tropical hammocks, and disturbed sites.
Distribution: Coastal areas of central and southern Florida, occasionally inland.
Notes: Locally common. Very weedy, not recommended for cultivation.
Caterpillars: Cuban Crescent (*Anthanassa frisia*).

Dyschoriste oblongifolia
Oblongleaf Twinflower

Description: Perennial herb with erect stems to 8" tall with underground runners. Leaves opposite, oblong, with indistinct petioles and wavy margins. Flowers tubular, lavender with dark purple spots in throat, produced singly in leaf axils, but the pair at each node bloom simultaneously. Blooms from spring through fall.
Habitat: Uplands. Sandhills and dry pinelands.
Distribution: Throughout Florida. Usually occurs in scattered patches.
Notes: Common. Propagated from root divisions. Prefers dry, sandy soil. A nice, low maintenance perennial for gardens. The similar Swamp Twinflower (*Dyschoriste humistrata*) has smaller flowers, grows at the edges of swamps, and is also eaten by the Common Buckeye.
Caterpillars: Common Buckeye (*Junonia coenia*).

Justicia ovata
Looseflower Waterwillow

Description: Perennial herb with erect stems to 1.5' tall and underground runners. Leaves opposite, lance shaped, without teeth, to 4" long. Small orchidlike white to pale purple flowers in a short spike at the tips of the stems. Blooms from spring through summer.
Habitat: Wetlands. Swamps and the margins of rivers and streams.
Distribution: Throughout the state.
Notes: Locally common. Propagated from root divisions. Needs wet to moist soil.
Caterpillars: 'Seminole' Texan Crescent (*Anthanassa texana seminole*).

Amaranthaceae (Amaranth family)

Chenopodium album
Lamb'squarters

Description: Erect, branching annual herb to about 5' tall. Leaves alternate, to 3" long on long petioles, whitish below, older leaves turning reddish, lance shaped to squarish, the margins irregularly toothed or lobed. Tiny greenish white flowers in dense clusters at the tips of the branches. Blooms from spring through summer.
Habitat: Uplands. Cultivated fields and disturbed sites.
Distribution: Native to Eurasia, but naturalized in northern and central Florida.
Notes: Locally common. Propagated from seeds, but very weedy.
Caterpillars: Common Sootywing (*Pholisora catullus*).

Iresine diffusa
Juba's Bush

Description: Perennial herb with erect, easily breakable stems to 4' tall. Leaves lance shaped, opposite, without teeth, petioles indistinct, to about 3" long. Small greenish white flowers in clusters at tips of the stems. Blooms late summer and fall.
Habitat: Uplands. Edges of hammocks and roadsides.
Distribution: Throughout the state.
Notes: Common. Propagated from seeds, cuttings, and root divisions.
Caterpillars: Hayhurst's Scallopwing (*Staphylus hayhurstii*).

Sarcocornia perennis (formerly *Salicornia perennis*)

Perennial Glasswort, Virginia Glasswort

Description: Trailing, branching perennial with succulent stems to about 1' tall. Leaves tiny and scalelike. Flowers minute and inconspicuous, sparsely produced on short stalks at the tips of the stems. Blooms during summer and fall.
Habitat: Wetlands. Salt marshes and the edges of mangrove swamps.
Distribution: Coastal areas and occasionally inland around salt springs.
Notes: Locally abundant. Propagated from root divisions.
Caterpillars: Eastern Pygmy-Blue (*Brephidium isophthalma*).

Anacardiaceae (Cashew family)

Schinus terebinthifolius

Brazilian Pepper

Description: Shrub or small tree to 25' tall. Leaves glossy, compound with seven to nine lance-shaped leaflets, small teeth on the margins, new growth reddish. The leaves smell of turpentine when crushed and the sap gives people a poison-ivylike rash. Small white flowers in dense clusters at tips of the stems followed by small bright red berries that are eaten by birds. Blooms spring and summer.
Habitat: Uplands and moist disturbed sites. Readily invades pine flatwoods and other natural communities.
Distribution: Central and southern Florida. Native to South America.
Notes: Abundant. One of the worst invasive exotic plants in Florida; not recommended for cultivation.
Caterpillars: Fulvous Hairstreak (*Electrostrymon angelia*) and Red-banded Hairstreak (*Calycopis cecrops*).

Annonaceae (Custard-Apple family)

Asimina angustifolia
Slimleaf Pawpaw

Description: Deciduous shrub to about 4' tall
with a long tap root. Leaves very long and narrow
to oblong, without teeth, pungent smelling when
crushed. Large white flowers with a purple center
produced in late spring and early summer. The
fleshy oblong fruit is green at first, becoming
black at maturity in summer.
Habitat: Uplands. Sandhills and dry pinelands.
Distribution: Northern and central Florida.
Notes: Common. Propagated from seeds. Plants
dug from the wild do not survive well.
Caterpillars: Zebra Swallowtail (*Eurytides
marcellus*).

Asimina incana
Woolly Pawpaw

Description: Deciduous shrub to 4' tall with a
very long tap root. Leaves lance shaped, without
teeth, covered with short silvery hairs when
young, pungent smelling when crushed. Large
white flowers produced before or with the new
leaves in spring. Fruits produced sparingly in
summer.
Habitat: Uplands. Sandhills and scrubs.
Distribution: Northern and central Florida.
Notes: Common. Propagated from seeds. Slow
growing, but a very nice shrub for the garden.
Caterpillars: Zebra Swallowtail (*Eurytides
marcellus*).

Asimina obovata
Bigflower Pawpaw

Description: Deciduous shrub to 10' tall with a deep tap root. Leaves bright green, widest beyond the middle, without teeth, sparse reddish brown hairs on the young stems and undersides of leaves, pungent smelling when crushed. Large white flowers produced after the leaves are fully expanded in late spring and early summer. Fruits produced sparingly in summer.
Habitat: Uplands. Scrubs.
Distribution: Mostly central Florida.
Notes: Locally common. Propagated from seeds. One of our prettiest pawpaws.
Caterpillars: Zebra Swallowtail (*Eurytides marcellus*).

Asimina pygmaea
Dwarf Pawpaw

Description: Deciduous shrub from 1' to 3' tall with a long tap root. Leaves narrow, to about 4" long, pungent smelling when crushed. Small maroon flowers produced from late spring to early summer and occasionally in the fall. Fruits produced sparingly in summer.
Habitat: Uplands. Pine flatwoods and sandhills.
Distribution: Northern and central Florida.
Notes: Common. Propagated from seeds.
Caterpillars: Zebra Swallowtail (*Eurytides marcellus*).

Asimina reticulata

Netted Pawpaw, Flatwoods Pawpaw

Description: Semideciduous shrub to about 4' tall with a deep tap root. Leaves lance shaped with a bluish tinge, pungent smelling when crushed. Flowers large, white with a maroon center, produced in spring. Fruits produced sparingly in summer.
Habitat: Uplands. Dry pinelands and scrubs.
Distribution: Central Florida and southward along the coasts to Miami and Naples.
Notes: Common. Propagated from seeds.
Caterpillars: Zebra Swallowtail (*Eurytides marcellus*).

Apiaceae (Carrot family)

Cicuta maculata

Spotted Water Hemlock

Description: Large perennial herb having a loose rosette of compound leaves. Leaves pinnately or bipinnately compound, up to 7" long, aromatic when crushed. The leaflets lanceolate with small teeth on the margins. Small white flowers in large flat clusters borne at the tips of branching stalks reaching to about 5' tall. Blooms in summer and fall.
Habitat: Wetlands. Marshes, ditches, and the margins of lakes, swamps, and sluggish streams.
Distribution: Throughout the state.
Notes: Common. May occur as scattered individuals or in large patches. Propagated from seeds. All parts of this plant are deadly poisonous if ingested, and bruised leaves may produce a rash on exposed skin.
Caterpillars: Black Swallowtail (*Papilio polyxenes*).

Foeniculum vulgare
Sweet Fennel

Description: Perennial herb producing a compact rosette of compound leaves. Leaves very finely divided (threadlike) to 12" long, aromatic when crushed. Small yellow flowers borne in large flat clusters at the tips of stalks reaching to 5' or more tall.
Habitat: Gardens.
Distribution: Cultivated herb from Europe. Grown throughout the state.
Notes: Frequently grown in gardens. Propagated from seeds.
Caterpillars: Black Swallowtail (*Papilio polyxenes*).

Oxypolis filiformis
Water Dropwort, Water Cowbane

Description: Slender perennial herb, with leaves reduced to only the petioles. Leaves to 6" long, with cross membranes, aromatic when crushed. Small white flowers borne in flat clusters at the tips of branching stalks growing to 4' or more tall. Blooms late summer and fall.
Habitat: Wetlands. Wet flatwoods and prairies, seepage slopes, and ditches.
Distribution: Throughout the state.
Notes: Common. Propagated from seeds. All parts of this plant are poisonous if ingested, and the bruised leaves may produce a rash on exposed skin.
Caterpillars: Black Swallowtail (*Papilio polyxenes*).

Ptilimnium capillaceum
Mock Bishopsweed

Description: Annual herb to about 1.5' tall with finely divided leaves and small white flowers. Leaves alternate and threadlike. Flowers tiny, arranged in small, flat-topped clusters at the tips of the stems, with a characteristic ring of threadlike bracts where the flower stalks branch from the stem. Blooms from spring through fall.
Habitat: Wetlands. Wet weedy areas, pastures, shallow marshes, wet prairies, and margins of ditches, rivers, ponds, lakes, and swamps.
Distribution: Throughout the state.
Notes: Common. Propagated from seeds.
Caterpillars: Black Swallowtail (*Papilio polyxenes*).

Spermolepis divaricata
Roughfruit Scaleseed

Description: Annual herb to about 1.5' tall with finely divided leaves and small white flowers. Leaves alternate and threadlike. Flowers tiny, arranged in small flat clusters without bracts at the tips of the stems. Blooms in spring.
Habitat: Uplands. Roadsides and weedy disturbed areas.
Distribution: Northern and central Florida.
Notes: Common. Propagated from seeds.
Caterpillars: Black Swallowtail (*Papilio polyxenes*).

Apocynaceae (Dogbane family)

Asclepias curassavica
Scarlet Milkweed

Description: Erect perennial herb to about 5' tall. Aboveground portions evergreen. Leaves opposite, narrowly lance shaped to about 3" long. Flowers red with a yellow center or all yellow. Blooms throughout the year.
Habitat: Uplands. Gardens, pastures, and roadsides.
Distribution: Native to tropical America. Naturalized in southern and central Florida, but can be grown throughout the state.
Notes: Common. Propagated from cuttings and seed. Many insects, including butterflies, visit the flowers for nectar.
Caterpillars: Monarch (*Danaus plexippus*), Queen (*Danaus gilippus*), and Soldier (*Danaus eresimus*).

Asclepias humistrata
Sandhill Milkweed, Pinewoods Milkweed

Description: Trailing perennial herb less than 1' tall. Aboveground portions deciduous. Leaves opposite, grayish green with pink veins, broadly lance shaped to oval, up to 5" long. Flowers pale pink. Blooms in spring and summer.
Habitat: Uplands. Sandhills and dry pinelands.
Distribution: Northern and central Florida.
Notes: Locally common. Propagated from seed. The flowers are attractive to many butterflies and other insects.
Caterpillars: Monarch (*Danaus plexippus*) and Queen (*Danaus gilippus*).

Asclepias incarnata
Pink Swamp Milkweed

Description: Erect short-lived herb from 3' to 5' tall. Aboveground portions deciduous. Leaves opposite, narrowly lance shaped to about 3" long. Flowers pink or occasionally white. Blooms spring through fall.
Habitat: Wetlands. Swamps and freshwater marshes.
Distribution: Peninsular Florida.
Notes: Uncommon. Propagated from seed. The flowers are visited by butterflies and other insects for nectar.
Caterpillars: Monarch (*Danaus plexippus*) and Queen (*Danaus gilippus*).

Asclepias perennis
White Swamp Milkweed

Description: Erect perennial herb to about 2' tall. Aboveground portions evergreen. Leaves opposite, narrowly lance shaped to about 3" long. Flowers white, often with a pinkish tinge. Blooms spring through fall.
Habitat: Wetlands. Swamps.
Distribution: Northern and central Florida.
Notes: Common. Propagated from cuttings and seed. Butterflies and other insects are attracted to the flowers.
Caterpillars: Monarch (*Danaus plexippus*) and Queen (*Danaus gilippus*).

Calotropis gigantea
Giant Milkweed

Description: Perennial herb to 6' tall with large leaves and clusters of large pale purple flowers. Leaves opposite, to about 8" long, smooth, without stalks. Flowers large, 5 petals, arranged in small clusters on long stalks. Blooms most of the year.
Habitat: Uplands. Gardens.
Distribution: Native to Africa. Cultivated as a garden ornamental in central and southern Florida.
Notes: Uncommon. Propagated from cuttings and seeds.
Caterpillars: Monarch (*Danaus plexippus*) and Queen (*Danaus gilippus*).

Cynanchum angustifolium
Gulf Coast Swallowwort

Description: Perennial evergreen vine with opposite leaves and milky sap. Leaves narrow to about 1.5" long. Flowers white, borne in small clusters from the leaf axils. Blooms from spring through fall.
Habitat: Uplands. Margins of coastal hammocks and salt marshes.
Distribution: Coastal areas throughout Florida.
Notes: Locally common. Propagated from seeds, cuttings, and layering of vines. Leafless Swallowwort (*Cynanchum scoparium*) occurs in hammocks mostly in Peninsular Florida.
Caterpillars: Queen (*Danaus gilippus*) and Soldier (*Danaus eresimus*).

Matelea floridana

Florida Milkvine

Description: Perennial vine having green trailing or climbing stems, opposite leaves, and milky sap. Leaves broadly lance shaped to about 3" long. Flowers maroon, borne in small clusters from the leaf axils. Blooms in summer and fall.
Habitat: Uplands. Hammocks and sandhills.
Distribution: Peninsular Florida.
Notes: Uncommon. Propagated from seeds.
Caterpillars: Queen (*Danaus gilippus*).

Morrenia odorata

Latexplant

Description: Evergreen vine having green strongly climbing stems, opposite leaves, and milky sap. Leaves broadly lance shaped to about 3" long. Flowers greenish white, borne in large clusters from the leaf axils. Fruit a large, woody follicle that splits open on one side to release the seeds. Blooms throughout the year.
Habitat: Wetlands and uplands. Freshwater marshes, margins of salt marshes, rivers, and canals, as well as ditch banks, citrus groves, and disturbed areas.
Distribution: Native to South America. Naturalized in southern and central Florida.
Notes: Locally common. Very weedy, not recommended for cultivation.
Caterpillars: Queen (*Danaus gilippus*), Soldier (*Danaus eresimus*), and occasionally Monarch (*Danaus plexippus*).

Sarcostemma clausum

White Twinevine

Description: Evergreen vine having green prostrate or climbing stems, opposite leaves, and milky sap. Leaves broadly lance shaped to about 3" long. Flowers white, borne in large clusters from the leaf axils. Blooms throughout the year.
Habitat: Wetlands and uplands. Freshwater marshes, margins of salt marshes, rivers, and canals, as well as ditch banks and disturbed areas.
Distribution: Southern and central Florida.
Notes: Common. Propagated from seeds, cuttings, and layering of vines. Does well in hanging baskets if kept moist.
Caterpillars: Queen (*Danaus gilippus*), Soldier (*Danaus eresimus*), and occasionally Monarch (*Danaus plexippus*).

Aquifoliaceae (Holly family)

Ilex cassine

Dahoon

Description: Evergreen, broadleaved tree to 40' tall with smooth bark. Leaves alternate, leathery with small spines, especially at the tip, to about 3" long. Inconspicuous greenish flowers borne in small clusters from the leaf axils, followed by bright red berries on female trees in the fall. Blooms in spring.
Habitat: Wetlands. Shallow swamps and wet flatwoods.
Distribution: Throughout the state.
Notes: Common. Propagated from cuttings or seeds. Individual trees are either male or female. In order to grow a female individual that produces the handsome red berries, cuttings must be made from known female plants.
Caterpillars: Henry's Elfin (*Incisalia henrici*).

Aristolochiaceae (Birthwort family)

Aristolochia gigantea
Giant Dutchman's-Pipe

Description: Perennial vine with heart-shaped leaves and large flowers. Leaves alternate, with a strong, acrid smell when crushed. Flowers to about 5" long, with a point on top and divided into two lobes below, maroon reticulated with white. Blooms most of the year.
Habitat: Uplands. Gardens.
Distribution: Native to tropical America. Cultivated as a garden ornamental in central and southern Florida.
Notes: Uncommon. Propagated from seeds, layering of stems, or with difficulty from cuttings. The flowers of the Brazilian form of Giant Dutchman's-Pipe have very long lobes.
Caterpillars: Polydamas Swallowtail (*Battus polydamas*).

Aristolochia grandiflora
Largeflower Dutchman's-Pipe

Description: Perennial vine with heart-shaped leaves and very large white and maroon flowers. Leaves alternate, pointed at the tip, to about 8" long, with a strong, acrid smell when crushed. Flowers to about 12" long, notched above and with a skinny twisted tail below, white with reticulated maroon lines. Blooms most of the year.
Habitat: Uplands. Gardens.
Distribution: Native to tropical America. Cultivated as a garden ornamental in central and southern Florida.
Notes: Uncommon. Propagated from seeds, layering of stems, or with difficulty from cuttings.
Caterpillars: Polydamas Swallowtail (*Battus polydamas*).

Aristolochia littoralis (formerly Aristolochia elegans)

Calico Flower, Elegant Dutchman's-Pipe

Description: Perennial vine with rounded, heart-shaped leaves and large flowers. Leaves alternate with a strong, acrid smell when crushed. Flowers rounded on top and shallowly notched below, reticulated with maroon, to about 3" long. Blooms most of the year.

Habitat: Gardens.

Distribution: Native to tropical America. Cultivated throughout the state, but may be top-killed by freezes in northern Florida.

Notes: Common. Propagated from seeds, layering of stems, or with difficulty from cuttings.

Caterpillars: Pipevine Swallowtail (*Battus philenor*) and Polydamas Swallowtail (*Battus polydamas*).

Aristolochia tomentosa

Woolly Dutchman's-Pipe

Description: Perennial vine with heart-shaped leaves and small flowers. Leaves alternate, pointed at tip, with short hairs beneath. Flowers only about 1" long, with three yellowish lobes and a dark center, covered with short hairs. Blooms in summer and fall.

Habitat: Uplands. Hammocks.

Distribution: Panhandle region, but can be grown in northern and central Florida gardens.

Notes: Uncommon. Propagated from seeds, layering of stems, or root divisions.

Caterpillars: Pipevine Swallowtail (*Battus philenor*) and Polydamas Swallowtail (*Battus polydamas*).

Aristolochia ringens
Gaping Dutchman's-Pipe

Description: Large perennial vine with heart-shaped leaves and pelican-shaped flowers. Leaves alternate, acrid smelling when crushed. Flowers white and reddish brown. Blooms throughout the year.
Habitat: Gardens.
Distribution: Native to South America. Cultivated in central and southern Florida.
Notes: Uncommon. Propagated from seeds, layering of stems, or with difficulty from cuttings.
Caterpillars: Polydamas Swallowtail (*Battus polydamas*).

Aristolochia serpentaria (formerly Aristolochia hastata)
Virginia Snakeroot

Description: Perennial herb 6" to 12" tall. Leaves heart shaped or linear in moist to dry areas. Flowers inconspicuous, on short stalks near the ground. Flowers in summer and fall.
Habitat: Uplands. Moist hammocks to dry sandhills.
Distribution: Northern and central Florida.
Notes: Common. Propagated from seeds or root divisions.
Caterpillars: Pipevine Swallowtail (*Battus philenor*).

Bidens alba

Spanish Needles, Beggarticks

Description: Perennial herb up to 5' tall with squarish stems and white and yellow flowers. Leaves compound, to 5" long, with three lance-shaped leaflets having small teeth on the margins. Flowers in compact heads, ray flowers white, disk flowers yellow in clusters at the tips of the stems. Blooms throughout the year, especially summer and fall.
Habitat: Uplands. Roadsides, weed lots, and other disturbed sites.
Distribution: Throughout the state.
Notes: Abundant. Very weedy, not recommended for cultivation. Many butterflies and other insects are attracted to the flowers.
Caterpillars: Dainty Sulphur (*Nathalis iole*).

Cirsium horridulum

Yellow Thistle, Purple Thistle

Description: Short-lived perennial with spiny leaves and large flowers. Leaves to 1' long, dark green above with dense white hairs below and bearing sharp spines on the margins. Flowers in compact heads, color varies from white to pink or purple. Blooms mostly in late spring and sparsely in the fall.
Habitat: Uplands. Pinelands, pastures, roadsides, and disturbed sites.
Distribution: Throughout the state.
Notes: Common. Propagated from seeds. The flowers are very attractive to butterflies and other insects.
Caterpillars: Little Metalmark (*Calephelis virginiensis*).

Gamochaeta falcata (formerly *Gnaphalium falcatum*)

Narrowleaf Purple Everlasting

Description: Annual herb up to 1' tall with narrow leaves. Undersides of leaves and stems with dense silvery hairs. Whitish flowers in compact heads at the tips of the stems. Blooms in spring and early summer.
Habitat: Uplands. Weedy disturbed sites.
Distribution: Throughout the state, but less abundant in southern Florida.
Notes: Common. Propagated from seeds.
Caterpillars: American Lady (*Vanessa virginiensis*).

Gamochaeta pensylvanica (formerly *Gnaphalium pensylvanicum*)

Pennsylvania Everlasting

Description: Annual herb up to about 1' tall. Leaves widest near the tip, with cobwebby hairs, especially on the lower sides. Whitish flowers in compact heads at the tips of the stems. Blooms in spring and early summer.
Habitat: Uplands. Weedy disturbed sites.
Distribution: Throughout the state.
Notes: Common. Propagated from seeds.
Caterpillars: American Lady (*Vanessa virginiensis*).

Pseudognaphalium obtusifolium
(formerly *Gnaphalium obtusifolium*)

Sweet Everlasting

Description: Annual herb up to 2.5' tall. Leaves dark green above, white below. Whitish flowers in small, compact heads in clusters at the tips of the stems. Leaves and flowers with a sweet-smelling fragrance. Blooms late summer and fall.
Habitat: Uplands. Flatwoods and dry pinelands.
Distribution: Throughout the state, but less frequent in southern Florida.
Notes: Common. Propagated from seeds.
Caterpillars: American Lady (*Vanessa virginiensis*).

Symphyotrichum dumosum
(formerly *Aster dumosus*)

Rice Button Aster

Description: Perennial herb up to 4' tall with underground runners. Belowground portions of stems purplish. Basal leaves up to 3" long, widest near tip, stem leaves linear. Flowers in compact heads, ray flowers pale purple, disk flowers yellow, in clusters at the tips of stems. Blooms late summer and fall.
Habitat: Uplands. Roadsides, weed lots, and other disturbed sites.
Distribution: Throughout the state.
Notes: Common. Propagated from root divisions or seeds, but very weedy in the garden. Other asters that may potentially be eaten by Pearl Crescent caterpillars include Elliott's Aster (*Symphyotrichum elliottii*), Walter's Aster (*Symphyotrichum walteri*), Climbing Aster (*Symphyotrichum carolinianus*), and Eastern Silver Aster (*Symphyotrichum concolor*).
Caterpillars: Pearl Crescent (*Phyciodes tharos*).

Avicenniaceae (Black Mangrove family)

Avicennia germinans

Black Mangrove

Description: Shrub or small tree with black bark, roots with pencil-like pneumatophores arising vertically from the soil. Young twigs and stems squarish. Leaves green above, whitish below, without teeth. Seeds large, beanlike. Flowers whitish in small clusters at the tips of the branches. Blooms in fall.
Habitat: Wetlands. Salt marshes and mangrove swamps.
Distribution: Grows along the coast from about Cedar Key and St. Augustine southward.
Notes: Abundant. Propagated from seeds. The flowers are attractive to butterflies and other insects.
Caterpillars: Mangrove Buckeye (*Junonia evarete*).

Bataceae (Saltwort family)

Batis maritima

Saltwort

Description: Perennial herb to 1.5' tall with trailing succulent stems. Leaves succulent, to about 1" long, yellowish green, opposite, without stalks, salty tasting. Tiny whitish green flowers in short clusters. Blooms March through October.
Habitat: Wetlands. Salt marshes and edges of mangrove swamps.
Distribution: Coastal areas.
Notes: Common. Propagated from root divisions.
Caterpillars: Great Southern White (*Ascia monuste*) and probably Eastern Pygmy-Blue (*Brephidium isophthalma*).

Betulaceae (Birch family)

Alnus serrulata

Hazel Alder

Description: Small deciduous tree to about 20' tall. Leaves alternate, with short petioles and wavy margins, to about 4" long. Fruits conelike.
Habitat: Wetlands. Margins of streams and rivers.
Distribution: Northern Florida.
Notes: Locally common. Host for Woolly Alder Aphid. Propagated from seeds.
Caterpillars: The Harvester (*Feniseca tarquinius*) is carnivorous on the Woolly Alder Aphid.

Prociphilus tesselatus (formerly *Paraprociphilus tesselatus*)

Woolly Alder Aphid (inset)

Description: Relatively large plump aphids, the body to about 1/8" long. The outer body is grayish and covered by a white wax. The wax is also secreted as long filaments that give the aphids a woolly coat. The aphids occur in dense colonies on Hazel Alder branches.

Brassicaceae (Mustard family)

Brassica nigra

Abyssinian Mustard, Black Mustard

Description: Erect annual herb to 3' tall with yellow flowers. Leaves alternate to 6" long, divided into three to seven lobes, with sparse hairs. Flowers with four petals, about 0.5" wide, arranged on long branching stalks. Blooms in spring and early summer.
Habitat: Uplands. Roadsides, agricultural fields, weedlots, and disturbed sites.
Distribution: Native to Eurasia. Naturalized in northern and central Florida.
Notes: Locally common. Propagated from seeds. There are two similar plants in northern Florida that are eaten by the Cabbage White. India Mustard (*Brassica juncea*) lacks hairs on the stems and leaves, and the flowers of Wild Radish (*Raphanus raphanistrum*) are white or pale purple.
Caterpillars: Cabbage White (*Pieris rapae*).

Capparis flexuosa

Limber Caper, Bayleaf Capertree

Description: Shrub to about 15' tall, young stems with short reddish hairs. Leaves shiny above, alternate, oblong, blunt or with a small notch at tip. Flowers with short white, yellow, or pinkish petals and long stamens, in small clusters at the tips of the branches, fragrant, opening at night. Blooms in spring and summer.
Habitat: Uplands. Tropical hardwood hammocks.
Distribution: Southern Florida northward along the coasts to Merritt Island and Tampa Bay.
Notes: Locally common in the Keys. Propagated from seeds. A nice ornamental for the tropical garden.
Caterpillars: Florida White (*Appias drusilla*) and occasionally Great Southern White (*Ascia monuste*).

Cardamine bulbosa

Bulbous Bittercress

Description: Perennial herb to 1.5' tall with a rosette of leaves from which the flower stalk emerges. Leaves alternate to 2" long, with teeth on the margins. Small white flowers with four petals arranged in clusters at the tips of the stalks. Blooms in spring.
Habitat: Wetlands. Swamps along streams, spring runs, and rivers.
Distribution: Northern and central Florida.
Notes: Local and uncommon. Propagated from seeds.
Caterpillars: Falcate Orangetip (*Paramidea midea*).

Lepidium virginicum
Virginia Pepperweed

Description: Annual herb to 1.5' tall with a rosette of leaves from which the flower stalk
emerges. Leaves alternate, narrow with teeth on
the margins. Tiny white flowers with four petals
arranged in clusters at the tips of the stalks.
Blooms in spring and early summer.
Habitat: Uplands. Roadsides, citrus groves,
weedlots, and disturbed sites.
Distribution: Throughout the state.
Notes: Common to abundant. Propagated from
seeds, but very weedy.
Caterpillars: Checkered White (*Pontia protodice*),
Great Southern White (*Ascia monuste*), and occasionally Cabbage White (*Pieris rapae*).

Burseraceae (Gumbo-Limbo family)

Bursera simaruba
Gumbo-Limbo

Description: Tree to 50' tall with smooth, reddish
bark peeling in thin sheets. Leaves alternate,
compound, resinous, with lance-shaped leaflets.
Young growth is orange in color. Small white
flowers arranged in clusters at the tips of the
branches. Blooms in winter and spring.
Habitat: Uplands. Tropical hardwood hammocks.
Distribution: Southern Florida northward along
the coasts to Merritt Island and Tampa Bay.
Notes: Common. Propagated from cuttings and
seeds. This beautiful tree is often used in landscaping.
Caterpillars: Dingy Purplewing (*Eunica
monima*).

Celtidaceae (Hackberry family)

Celtis laevigata
Sugarberry, Hackberry

Description: Deciduous tree to about 60' tall
with broad leaves, corky growths on the bark,
and small orange-red fruit. Leaves alternate, lance
shaped, to about 3.5" long, the bases
nonsymmetrical, with long tapering tips, short
petioles, and margins with or without small
teeth. The young leaves are arranged in one
plane. Flowers tiny, greenish, from the leaf axils
in spring. Fruit on long stalks with one round
seed surrounding a thin sweet pulp and wrapped
in a papery coat.
Habitat: Uplands. Hammocks and shrubby disturbed sites.
Distribution: Northern, central, and southern
Florida.
Notes: Locally common. Propagated from seeds.
Often grows along fences where the birds deposit
the seeds. The closely related Hackberry (*Celtis
occidentalis*) is a smaller tree with wider leaves
that grows in the Panhandle area.
Caterpillars: American Snout (*Libytheana
carinenta*), Question Mark (*Polygonia
interrogationis*), Hackberry Emperor
(*Asterocampa celtis*), and Tawny Emperor
(*Asterocampa clyton*).

Trema micranthum
Nettletree

Description: Deciduous tree typically to about
25' tall with broad rough leaves arranged in one
plane and small orange fruit. Leaves alternate,
lance shaped, to about 3" long, hairy with a tapering tip, small teeth on the margins, and short
petioles. Flowers small, whitish, in the leaf axils.
Small round orange fruit on short stalks.
Habitat: Uplands. Margins of hammocks and
disturbed areas.
Distribution: Southern Florida.
Notes: Common. Propagated from seeds. Weedy
tree that colonizes forest edges.
Caterpillars: Martial Scrub-Hairstreak (*Strymon
martialis*).

Ericaceae (Heath family)

Oxydendrum arboreum

Sourwood

Description: Deciduous tree to about 30' tall with clusters of small bell-shaped flowers. Leaves alternate to about 6" long, with very small teeth on the margins, turning bright orange or red in the fall. Flowers white, evenly distributed along stalks at the tips of the branches. Blooms in May and June.
Habitat: Uplands. Sandhills, hammocks, and dry pinelands.
Distribution: Panhandle.
Notes: Locally common. Propagated from cuttings and seeds.
Caterpillars: 'Summer' Spring Azure (*Celastrina neglecta*).

Vaccinium arboreum

Sparkleberry

Description: Shrub or small tree to about 15' tall, often with multiple stems, mostly evergreen, with smooth to flaking reddish bark. Leaves alternate, round to oblong, to about 1.5" long, margins entire or with small teeth, dark green above. Flowers white, bell shaped, drooping, less than 1/4" long, in clusters from second year growth. Blooms in April and early May. Fruit shiny, black, somewhat dry, but well liked by birds.
Habitat: Uplands. Sandhills, hammocks and dry pinelands.
Distribution: Northern and central Florida.
Notes: Common. Propagated from cuttings and seeds. The flowers are attractive to butterflies and other insects.
Caterpillars: Striped Hairstreak (*Satyrium liparops*).

Vaccinium stamineum
Deerberry

Description: Deciduous shrub to about 6' tall with multiple stems. Leaves alternate, lance shaped, whitish below, without teeth on the margins. Flowers white, bell shaped, drooping, less than 1/4" long, produced from the leaf axils. Blooms in April and May. Fruit with a whitish bloom, green at first, turning blackish when mature, sour tasting.
Habitat: Uplands. Sandhills, dry hammocks, and flatwoods.
Distribution: Northern and central Florida.
Notes: Common. Propagated from cuttings and seeds.
Caterpillars: Red-spotted Purple (*Basilarchia arthemis astyanax*).

Euphorbiaceae (Spurge family)

Croton argyranthemus
Silver Croton, Healing Croton

Description: Perennial, erect herb to about 1' tall with brown stems. Leaves alternate, narrow, to about 2" long, green above, silvery or rusty brown below, with short petioles. Small white flowers in spikes at the tips of the branches. Blooms from spring through fall.
Habitat: Uplands. Sandhills and dry pinelands.
Distribution: Northern and central Florida.
Notes: Common. Propagated from seeds.
Caterpillars: Goatweed Leafwing (*Anaea andria*).

Croton linearis

Pineland Croton, Wild Croton, Granny-Bush

Description: Evergreen, branching shrub from 1'
to 3' tall. Leaves alternate, linear to 3" long, dark
green above, white below, with short petioles.
Small white flowers in spikes at the tips of the
branches. Blooms from spring through fall.
Habitat: Uplands. Tropical pinelands and
sandhills.
Distribution: Lower Keys and southeastern Florida.
Notes: Locally common on Big Pine Key. Propagated from seeds.
Caterpillars: Bartram's Scrub-Hairstreak
(*Strymon acis*) and Florida Leafwing (*Anaea
troglodyta floridalis*).

Drypetes lateriflora

Guiana Plum

Description: Tropical tree to 40' tall with shiny
leaves and smooth whitish bark. Leaves alternate,
to about 5" long, lance shaped, abruptly forming
a point at the tip. Flowers small, white, in small
clusters from the leaf axils. Blooms in spring and
summer.
Habitat: Uplands. Tropical hardwood hammocks.
Distribution: Found along the Atlantic coast
from Merritt Island southward into the Keys.
Notes: Common only on the southern peninsula
and the Florida Keys. Propagated from seeds.
The Florida White also uses Milkbark (*Drypetes
diversifolia*), a rare tree found in southern Miami-Dade County and the Florida Keys.
Caterpillars: Florida White (*Appias drusilla*).

Gymnanthes lucida
(formerly *Ateramnus lucidus*)
Crabwood, Oysterwood

Description: Evergreen shrub or small tree to about 25' tall. Leaves alternate, leathery, widest at middle, with wavy margins or indistinct teeth. Young leaves are orange in color. Flowers yellowish green on short spikes. Blooms in summer.
Habitat: Uplands. Tropical hardwood hammocks.
Distribution: Keys and southeastern mainland.
Notes: Common in the Upper Florida Keys. Propagated from seeds.
Caterpillars: Florida Purplewing (*Eunica tatila*).

Fabaceae (Pea family)

Acacia pinetorum
Pineland Acacia

Description: Shrub or small tree to about 15' tall with long thorns and zigzag branches. Leaves alternate, bipinnately compound, the leaflets less than 1/8" long, nine to fifteen pairs per pinna. Flowers yellow, in tight clusters on long stalks. Blooms in spring and summer.
Habitat: Uplands. Margins of coastal hammocks, dry pinelands, and disturbed sites.
Distribution: Southern peninsula and west coast to just north of Tampa.
Notes: Local and uncommon. Propagated from seeds. Sweet Acacia (*Acacia farnesiana*) is similar, but the leaflets are larger, and with ten to twenty-five pairs per pinna.
Caterpillars: Nickerbean Blue (*Hemiargus ammon*).

Aeschynomene americana
Shyleaf

Description: Annual herb to 5' tall. Leaves alternate, pinnately compound, about 2.5" long with numerous small leaflets. Flowers small, pale yellow, pealike on long stalks. Fruit similar to ticktrefoils, but without the hooked hairs. Blooms in summer and fall.
Habitat: Edges of wetlands. Margins of ditches, ponds, lakes, and moist disturbed sites.
Distribution: Throughout the state.
Notes: Common. Propagated from seeds. Sticky Jointvetch (*Aeschynomene viscidula*) is a low-growing relative found in dry pinelands and sandhills that is also eaten by the Barred Yellow.
Caterpillars: Barred Yellow (*Eurema daira*).

Amorpha fruticosa
Bastard Indigobush, False Indigobush

Description: Deciduous shrub to about 10' tall. Leaves alternate, pinnately compound to about 6" long, with a pungent odor when crushed. Small purple flowers with yellow anthers in dense clusters at the tips of the branches. Blooms in spring and summer.
Habitat: Wetlands and uplands. Margins of rivers, swamps, and wet hammocks and occasionally in sandhills.
Distribution: Throughout the state.
Notes: Common. Propagated from seeds. Lusterspike Indigobush (*Amorpha herbacea*) is a similar species found in dry pinelands in northern and central Florida and as a rare variety in the pine rocklands of Miami-Dade County.
Caterpillars: Southern Dogface (*Zerene cesonia*) and Silver-spotted Skipper (*Epargyreus clarus*).

Amphicarpaea bracteata
American Hogpeanut

Description: Twining herbaceous vine with sparse short hairs. Leaves alternate to about 2.5" long with three broad leaflets. Flowers pale purple in small clusters on stalks from the leaf axils. Blooms in summer and fall.
Habitat: Uplands. Hammocks.
Distribution: Northern and central Florida.
Notes: Uncommon. Propagated from seeds.
Caterpillars: Silver-spotted Skipper (*Epargyreus clarus*) and Golden Banded-Skipper (*Autochton cellus*).

Apios americana
Groundnut

Description: Twining herbaceous vine with compound leaves. Leaves alternate to about 4" long with five to seven lance-shaped leaflets. Flowers lavender and dark purple in small clusters from the leaf axils. Blooms in summer and fall.
Habitat: Edges of wetlands. Wet hammocks and margins of streams and lakes.
Distribution: Northern and central Florida.
Notes: Common. Propagated from seeds.
Caterpillars: Silver-spotted Skipper (*Epargyreus clarus*).

Baptisia alba
White Wild Indigo

Description: Deciduous perennial herb to about 4' tall with smooth leaves and stems. Leaves alternate to about 2" long with three leaflets. Flowers white, pealike, arranged on a long spike. Fruit a hard, inflated, oblong pod, dry and black at maturity. Blooms in spring and early summer.
Habitat: Uplands. Dry pinelands and margins of hammocks.
Distribution: Northern and central Florida.
Notes: Locally common. Propagated from seeds.
Caterpillars: Wild Indigo Duskywing (*Erynnis baptisiae*).

Caesalpinia bonduc
Gray Nicker

Description: Vigorous perennial vine or sprawling shrub with short recurved spines on the leaves and stems, forming dense thickets on the ground or over other shrubs and trees. Leaves opposite, bipinnately compound, more than 1' long. Flowers yellow in short spikes from the leaf axils. Fruit a spiny flat pod, brown at maturity and bearing a few gray, rounded seeds about 3/4" in diameter. Blooms throughout the year.
Habitat: Uplands. Beaches and edges of hammocks.
Distribution: Coastal areas of central and southern Florida.
Notes: Common. Propagated from seeds.
Caterpillars: Miami Blue (*Hemiargus thomasi*), Martial Scrub-Hairstreak (*Stryman martialis*), Ceraunus Blue (*Hemiargus ceraunus*), Nicker-bean Blue (*Hemiargus drumon*).

Centrosema virginianum

Spurred Butterfly Pea

Description: Twining herbaceous perennial vine with compound leaves and large flowers. Leaves with three usually narrow lance-shaped leaflets having greenish undersides. Flowers pealike with a large purple lower petal, a white patch with a few purple lines in the throat, the side petals tightly enclosing the upper petal. Fruit a flat brown pod. Blooms in summer and fall.
Habitat: Uplands. Sandhills, dry pinelands, and the margins of hammocks.
Distribution: Mostly in northern and central Florida, occasionally in the southern part of the state. Similar to Atlantic Pigeonwings (*Clitoria mariana*).
Notes: Common. Propagated from seeds.
Caterpillars: Long-tailed Skipper (*Urbanus proteus*).

Cercis canadensis

Eastern Redbud

Description: Deciduous tree to about 20' tall with heart-shaped leaves and pealike flowers. Leaves alternate, the margins without teeth; long petioles. Flowers pink, in small clusters from the trunk and older branches before the leaves are produced. Fruit flat brown pods to about 4" long. Blooms in spring.
Habitat: Uplands. Hammocks and gardens.
Distribution: Northern Florida.
Notes: Common. Propagated from seeds. Often used in landscaping.
Caterpillars: Henry's Elfin (*Incisalia henrici*).

Chamaecrista fasciculata (formerly *Cassia fasciculata*)

Partridge Pea

Description: Annual herb usually from 1' to 3' tall with large yellow flowers. Leaves alternate, to about 3" long, pinnately compound with numerous small leaflets, nectar gland near base of petiole wider than long. Flowers 1/2" or more wide, yellow, solitary or in small groups from the leaf axils. Fruit a flat dry pod, about 2" long, that bursts open at maturity to disperse the seeds. Blooms in summer and fall.
Habitat: Uplands. Dry pinelands, margins of hammocks, coastal dunes, open disturbed sites.
Distribution: Throughout the state.
Notes: Abundant. Propagated from seeds.
Caterpillars: Cloudless Sulphur (*Phoebis sennae*), Gray Hairstreak (*Strymon melinus*), and Ceraunus Blue (*Hemiargus ceraunus*).

Chamaecrista nictitans (formerly *Cassia nictitans*)

Sensitive Pea

Description: Annual herb to about 2' tall with small yellow flowers. Leaves alternate to about 2" long, pinnately compound with numerous small leaflets, nectar gland near base of petiole longer than wide. Leaflets slowly folding closed when touched. Flowers less than 1/2" wide. Fruit a dry brown pod. Blooms in summer and fall.
Habitat: Uplands. Sandhills, dry pinelands, and disturbed sites.
Distribution: Throughout the state.
Notes: Common. Propagated from seeds. Similar to Partridge Pea, but the flowers are smaller and the nectar gland on the leaves narrower.
Caterpillars: Cloudless Sulphur (*Phoebis sennae*), Gray Hairstreak (*Strymon melinus*), and Ceraunus Blue (*Hemiargus ceraunus*).

Chapmannia floridana
Alicia

Description: Perennial herb to 3' tall having glandular hairs on the stem, small compound leaves, and yellow flowers. Leaves alternate to 2" long with three to seven narrowly lance-shaped leaflets. Flowers clustered at the tip of a tall spike, opening in morning and withering by afternoon. Blooms from spring through fall.
Habitat: Uplands. Sandhills and scrubs.
Distribution: Northern and central peninsula.
Notes: Common. Propagated from seeds.
Caterpillars: Ceraunus Blue (*Hemiargus ceraunus*).

Clitoria mariana
Atlantic Pigeonwings

Description: Perennial vine having an erect to trailing stem, bluish green leaves, and large flowers. Leaves alternate with three broad lance-shaped leaflets having whitish undersides. Flowers pale lavender with darker lines in the throat, the short side petals spreading. Fruit a dry flat pod to 2" long. Blooms from spring through summer.
Habitat: Uplands. Sandhills, scrubs, dry pinelands, margins of hammocks.
Distribution: Throughout the state.
Notes: Common. Propagated from seeds. Spurred Butterfly Pea (*Centrosema virginianum*) is similar, but has narrower leaflets and the side petals are not spreading.
Caterpillars: Long-tailed Skipper (*Urbanus proteus*), Hoary Edge (*Achalarus lyciades*), and Southern Cloudywing (*Thorybes bathyllus*).

Dalbergia ecastaphyllum

Coinvine

Description: Evergreen sprawling shrub with somewhat leathery leaves and clusters of white flowers from the leaf axils. Leaves alternate, having a single leaflet 3" to 6" long, glossy, without teeth. Fruit flat, coinlike pods in small bunches in the leaf axils. Blooms in spring and summer.
Habitat: Uplands. Beach dunes, margins of hammocks, disturbed sites.
Distribution: Coastal areas of central and southern Florida.
Notes: Locally common. Propagated from seeds and root sprouts.
Caterpillars: Statira Sulphur (*Aphrissa statira*), and occasionally Gray Scrub-Hairstreak (*Strymon melinus*).

Dalea feayi

Feay's Prairieclover

Description: Semiwoody perennial, herb with branching stems to 2' tall, short compound leaves, and heads of lavender flowers. Leaves alternate to 2" long with five to nine narrow leaflets. Flowers small, in dense clusters at the tips of the branches. Blooms from spring through fall.
Habitat: Uplands. Scrubs, sandhills, and dry pinelands.
Distribution: Throughout the state, except the western Panhandle.
Notes: Locally common. Propagated from seeds.
Caterpillars: Southern Dogface (*Zerene cesonia*).

Dalea pinnata
Summer Farewell

Description: Perennial semiwoody herb to 3' tall
with erect branches, short compound leaves, and
heads of white flowers. Leaves alternate to 1.5"
long with numerous narrow leaflets. Flowers
small, in dense clusters at the tips of the
branches. Blooms in late summer and fall.
Habitat: Uplands. Sandhills.
Distribution: Northern, central, and southern
Florida.
Notes: Locally common. Propagated from seeds.
Caterpillars: Southern Dogface (*Zerene cesonia*).

Desmodium incanum

Creeping Ticktrefoil

Description: Perennial herb to about 1' tall with
underground stems, rough textured leaves, and
seedpods that stick to clothing. Leaves alternate,
hairy, with three broadly lance-shaped leaves.
Flowers pink, pealike, on short spikes. Fruit long
flat pods that break into segments and densely
covered with hooked hairs. Blooms from spring
through fall.
Habitat: Uplands. Margins of hammocks, dis-
turbed sites.
Distribution: Northern, central, and southern
Florida.
Notes: Common. Very weedy, not recommended
for cultivation.
Caterpillars: Gray Hairstreak (*Strymon melinus*),
Long-tailed Skipper (*Urbanus proteus*), Dorantes
Longtail (*Urbanus dorantes*), and Hoary Edge
(*Achalarus lyciades*).

Desmodium tortuosum

Dixie Ticktrefoil, Florida Beggarweed

Description: Annual herb to 5' or more tall with erect stems, leaves often spotted with red, and seed pods having rounded segments that easily stick to clothing. Leaves alternate, hairy, with three broad lance-shaped leaves. Flowers pink, pealike, widely spaced on long spikes. Blooms throughout the year.

Habitat: Uplands. Roadsides and disturbed areas.

Distribution: Native to Central and South America. Naturalized throughout the state.

Notes: Common. Very weedy, not recommended for cultivation.

Caterpillars: Silver-spotted Skipper (*Epargyreus clarus*), Long-tailed Skipper (*Urbanus proteus*), and Dorantes Longtail (*Urbanus dorantes*).

Galactia elliottii

Elliott's Milkpea

Description: Perennial herbaceous vine with dark green compound leaves and white pealike flowers. Leaves alternate, to 8" long with five to nine oval leaflets. Flowers in small clusters at the tips of long stalks from the leaf axils. Fruit a flat hairy pod to 2" long. Blooms from spring through fall.

Habitat: Uplands. Scrubs, sandhills, and dry pinelands.

Distribution: Throughout the state, except the Keys and western Panhandle.

Notes: Common. Propagated from seeds.

Caterpillars: Zarucco Duskywing (*Erynnis zarucco*).

Galactia striata
Florida Hammock Milkpea

Description: Perennial herbaceous vine with tri-foliate leaves and small pink flowers. Leaves alternate, three broadly lance-shaped leaflets. Flowers pealike on short spikes from the leaf axils. Fruit dry, flat pods. Blooms throughout the year.
Habitat: Uplands. Tropical hammocks and pinelands.
Distribution: Coastal areas of southern Florida.
Notes: Common in the Florida Keys. Propagated from seeds.
Caterpillars: Zestos Skipper (*Epargyreus zestos*).

Galactia volubilis
Downy Milkpea

Description: Herbaceous perennial vine with tri-foliate leaves and small pink flowers on long spikes. Leaves alternate, three lance-shaped leaflets. Flowers pealike, well spaced on long stalks from the leaf axils. Fruit flat, dry pods. Blooms from spring through fall.
Habitat: Uplands. Sandhills, dry pinelands, and margins of hammocks.
Distribution: Northern, central, and southern Florida.
Notes: Common. Propagated from seeds. The Eastern Milkpea (*Galactia regularis*) is similar, but the flower stalks are shorter.
Caterpillars: Cassius Blue (*Leptotes cassius*), Silver-spotted Skipper (*Epargyreus clarus*), Long-tailed Skipper (*Urbanus proteus*), and Zarucco Duskywing (*Erynnis zarucco*).

Indigofera caroliniana
Carolina Indigo

Description: Perennial herb to 6' tall with compound leaves and small pink flowers. Leaves to 6" long with nine to fifteen small oval leaflets, the stem and leaves deciduous. Flowers pealike, in long spikes from the leaf axils. Fruit short, rounded, downward-pointing pods containing few seeds. Blooms from spring through fall.
Habitat: Uplands. Sandhills and scrubs.
Distribution: Mostly northern and central Florida.
Notes: Common. Propagated from seeds.
Caterpillars: Ceraunus Blue (*Hemiargus ceraunus*) and Zarucco Duskywing (*Erynnis zarucco*).

Indigofera spicata
Trailing Indigo

Description: Trailing perennial herb with short compound leaves and dense clusters of small pink flowers. Leaves to 4" long with five to nine small oval leaflets. Flowers pealike, in short erect clusters. Fruit hairy, round in cross section, downward-pointing pods.
Habitat: Uplands. Weedy lawns, roadsides, and disturbed areas.
Distribution: Native to Africa. Naturalized in most of Florida, except the western Panhandle.
Notes: Common. Propagated from seeds.
Caterpillars: Ceraunus Blue (*Hemiargus ceraunus*) and Zarucco Duskywing (*Erynnis zarucco*).

Lespedeza hirta
Hairy Lespedeza

Description: Perennial herb to 4' tall with erect stems, short compound leaves, and small purplish flowers in dense clusters at the tips of the stalks. Leaves alternate, with three lance-shaped leaflets to about 2" long. Flowers pealike, in compact heads. Blooms in fall.
Habitat: Uplands. Sandhills and dry pinelands.
Distribution: Northern and central Florida.
Notes: Common. Propagated from seeds.
Caterpillars: Gray Hairstreak (*Strymon melinus*) and Southern Cloudywing (*Thorybes bathyllus*).

Leucaena leucocephala
White Leadtree

Description: Evergreen tree to 30' tall with compound leaves and large heads of tiny white flowers. Leaves alternate, to 12" long, with small, narrow leaflets and a strong odor. Flowers in dense round heads on long stalks. Fruits long flat pods in dense downward-pointing clusters. Blooms throughout the year.
Habitat: Uplands. Weedy disturbed sites and roadsides.
Distribution: Native to the Caribbean region. Naturalized in central and southern Florida.
Notes: Common in the Florida Keys. Very weedy, not recommended for cultivation.
Caterpillars: Gray Ministreak (*Ministrymon azia*).

Lupinus perennis
Sundial Lupine

Description: Perennial herb to about 8" tall with underground runners, compound leaves, and spikes of pealike flowers. Leaves with numerous narrow leaflets arranged like the spokes of a wheel on long petioles. Flowers blue or occasionally white. Fruit a hairy pod that bursts open at maturity, scattering the seeds. Blooms in spring.
Habitat: Uplands. Sandhills.
Distribution: Northern Florida.
Notes: Rare. Propagated from seeds.
Caterpillars: Frosted Elfin (*Incisalia irus*).

Lysiloma latisiliquum
False Tamarind

Description: Deciduous tree to 60' tall with finely divided compound leaves and heads of small white flowers. Leaves to 5" long, with numerous narrow leaflets. The shed leaves give a spicy fragrance to the air around the trees. Flowers in dense clusters at the tips of long stalks. Fruit a long, flat, downward-pointing pod. Blooms from spring through fall.
Habitat: Uplands. Tropical hammocks.
Distribution: Southern Florida.
Notes: Common. Propagated from seeds. The flowers are attractive to butterflies and other insects.
Caterpillars: Large Orange Sulphur (*Phoebis agarithe*), Mimosa Yellow (*Eurema nise*), and Cassius Blue (*Leptotes cassius*).

Medicago lupulina

Black Medick

Description: Annual herb to 10" tall with cloverlike leaves and small heads of yellow flowers. Leaves alternate, with three oblong leaflets bearing small teeth on the margins. Flowers tiny, in round clusters at the tips of long stalks from the leaf axils. Blooms in spring and early summer.
Habitat: Uplands. Roadsides, unkempt lawns, and weedy, disturbed areas.
Distribution: Native to Europe. Naturalized in northern and central Florida
Notes: Abundant. Propagated from seeds.
Caterpillars: Orange Sulphur (*Colias eurytheme*).

Melilotus albus

White Sweetclover

Description: Branching annual herb to 4' tall with compound leaves and small white flowers. Leaves alternate, with three lance-shaped or oblong leaflets. Flowers white, in long spikes at the tips of the branches. Fruit a short pod bearing a few seeds. Blooms mostly in late spring and early summer.
Habitat: Uplands. Roadsides and weedy, disturbed areas.
Distribution: Native to Europe. Naturalized in northern and central Florida.
Notes: Common. Propagated from seeds. The flowers are attractive to butterflies, especially hairstreaks.
Caterpillars: Orange Sulphur (*Colias eurytheme*).

Mimosa strigillosa
Powderpuff
Description: Perennial prostrate plant to 8" tall with underground stems, finely divided compound leaves, the leaflets folding closed when touched, and heads of pink flowers on long stalks. Leaves alternate with numerous narrow leaflets, deciduous. Blooms from spring through fall.
Habitat: Uplands. Disturbed sites.
Distribution: Northern and central Florida.
Notes: Uncommon. Propagated from seeds and root divisions. A very nice ground cover for the garden.
Caterpillars: Little Yellow (*Eurema lisa*).

Piscidia piscipula
Florida Fishpoison Tree, Jamaican Dogwood
Description: Deciduous tree to 40' tall with coarse compound leaves and dense clusters of purple pealike flowers. Leaves alternate, with seven to nine large oval leaflets, thick and leathery. Flowers in clusters from the leaf axils. Fruit an angled pod. Blooms in spring and early summer.
Habitat: Uplands. Tropical hammocks.
Distribution: Southern Florida and northward along the coast to Tampa Bay and Merritt Island.
Notes: Common. Propagated from seeds. The flowers are attractive to adult butterflies and other insects.
Caterpillars: Fulvous Hairstreak (*Electrostrymon angelia*) and Hammock Skipper (*Polygonus leo*).

Pithecellobium keyense
Florida Keys Blackbead

Description: Tropical tree to about 25' tall with compound leaves and short spines on the branches. Leaves alternate, usually bearing two leaflets with a short spine at the tip. Flowers pinkish white with numerous stamens, petals absent, arranged in small, dense clusters at the tip of a long stalk. Blooms in fall, winter, and spring.
Habitat: Uplands. Tropical hardwood hammocks.
Distribution: Coastal areas of southeastern Florida and the Keys.
Notes: Common. Propagated from seeds. Catclaw Blackbead (*Pithecellobium unguis-cati*), found along the Gulf Coast from Tampa into the Keys, is also eaten by butterfly caterpillars.
Caterpillars: Large Orange Sulphur (*Phoebis agarithe*) and Cassius Blue (*Leptotes cassius*).

Robinia pseudoacacia
Black Locust

Description: Deciduous tree to about 50' tall with compound leaves, spines on the branches, and small white flowers. Leaves alternate, pinnately compound, to 8" or more long, bearing seven to nineteen small oblong leaflets. Flowers pealike, in dense hanging clusters from the leaf axils. Blooms in spring.
Habitat: Uplands. Gardens.
Distribution: Native to the eastern and midwestern United States north of Florida.
Notes: Uncommon. Propagated from seeds. A fast-growing shade tree used in the northern part of the state.
Caterpillars: Silver-spotted Skipper (*Epargyreus clarus*).

Senna alata (formerly *Cassia alata*)
Candlestick Plant

Description: Perennial shrub to 20' with coarse compound leaves and waxy flowers in erect, compact spikes. Leaves alternate to 20" long with seven to nine oblong leaflets, without nectar glands on the petiole. Flowers bright yellow, in candlelike spikes. Fruit a four-angled pod. Blooms all year.
Habitat: Gardens.
Distribution: Central and southern Florida. Native to Central and South America.
Notes: Common. Propagated from seeds. Easy to grow. Some of the exotic sennas, especially Valamuerto (*Senna pendula*), have become invasive weeds in central and southern Florida.
Caterpillars: Cloudless Sulphur (*Phoebis sennae*) and Orange-barred Sulphur (*Phoebis philea*).

Senna mexicana var *chapmanii* (formerly *Cassia bahamensis*)
Chapman's Wild Sensitive Plant

Description: Perennial, branching shrub to 5' tall with short compound leaves having a nectar gland between the first pair of leaflets, and bright yellow flowers. Leaves alternate, to 6" long, with five to seven lance-shaped leaflets. Flowers with five petals, in clusters at the tips of the branches. Fruit a flat pod. Blooms throughout the year.
Habitat: Uplands. Tropical pinelands and margins of hammocks.
Distribution: Southern Florida.
Notes: Uncommon. Propagated from seeds.
Caterpillars: Cloudless Sulphur (*Phoebis sennae*), Orange-barred Sulphur (*Phoebis philea*), and Sleepy Orange (*Eurema nicippe*).

Senna obtusifolia (formerly *Cassia obtusifolia*)

Coffeeweed, Sicklepod

Description: Annual herb to 5' tall with short compound leaves bearing a nectar gland between the first pair of leaflets, yellow flowers, and long sickle-shaped pods. Leaves alternate, to 6" long, with six oval leaflets, widest beyond the middle. Flowers with five petals in pairs from the leaf axils. Fruit a long, round, downward-curving pod.
Habitat: Uplands. Roadsides, agricultural fields, and weedy, disturbed areas.
Distribution: Native to Central and South America. Naturalized throughout the state.
Notes: Abundant. Propagated from seeds.
Caterpillars: Cloudless Sulphur (*Phoebis sennae*) and Sleepy Orange (*Eurema nicippe*).

Senna occidentalis (formerly *Cassia occidentalis*)

Septicweed

Description: Annual herb to 5' tall with compound leaves bearing a nectar gland at the base of the petiole, yellow flowers, and flat pods. Leaves alternate, to 8" long, with six to twelve lance-shaped leaflets. Flowers with five petals in pairs from the leaf axils. Fruit a flat, upward-curving pod containing numerous seeds.
Habitat: Uplands. Roadsides, agricultural fields, and weedy, disturbed areas.
Distribution: Native to Central and South America. Naturalized throughout the state.
Notes: Common. Propagated from seeds.
Caterpillars: Cloudless Sulphur (*Phoebis sennae*) and Sleepy Orange (*Eurema nicippe*).

Sesbania vesicaria

Bladderpod

Description: Perennial herb, to 10' tall with compound leaves having numerous leaflets and small pealike flowers on long stalks. Leaves to 10" long with many narrow leaflets. Flowers yellow or reddish in small clusters on drooping stalks from the leaf axils. Fruit a flattened pod containing one or two seeds. Blooms in spring through fall.
Habitat: Wetlands. Ditches, lake margins, and wet disturbed areas.
Distribution: Mostly northern and central Florida.
Notes: Common. Propagated from seeds. Two other related species are eaten by butterfly caterpillars. Danglepod (*Sesbania herbacea*) is similar, but has long sickle-shaped pods containing numerous seeds. Rattlebox (*Sesbania punicea*) is an exotic shrub from South America with large orange flowers and angled pods.
Caterpillars: Zarucco Duskywing (*Erynnis zarucco*).

Stylosanthes biflora

Sidebeak Pencilflower

Description: Wispy perennial herb with hairy stems, small leaves, and yellow pealike flowers. Leaves alternate, small with three narrow leaflets. Flowers in small clusters from the tips of the stems. Blooms in summer and fall.
Habitat: Uplands. Sandhills and dry pinelands.
Distribution: Mostly northern and central Florida.
Notes: Common. Propagated from seeds.
Caterpillars: Barred Yellow (*Eurema daira*).

Stylosanthes hamata

Cheesytoes

Description: Mounding perennial herb with small leaves and tiny yellow flowers. Leaves alternate, about 1/2" long with three narrow leaflets. Small pealike flowers from the tips of the stems. Blooms all year.
Habitat: Uplands. Weedy disturbed sites.
Distribution: Southern Florida.
Notes: Common. Propagated from seeds.
Caterpillars: Barred Yellow (*Eurema daira*).

Tephrosia florida

Florida Hoarypea

Description: Perennial herb with prostrate stems, compound leaves, and reddish pealike flowers on long upright stalks. Leaves alternate, erect, with three to nineteen small oblong leaflets. Flowers in small clusters at the tips of the long stalks, white at first but quickly changing to red. Fruit long, flat pods. Blooms in spring, summer, and fall.
Habitat: Uplands. Sandhills and dry pinelands.
Distribution: Mostly northern and central Florida.
Notes: Common. Propagated from seeds.
Caterpillars: Northern Cloudywing (*Thorybes pylades*).

Trifolium repens

White Clover

Description: Perennial herb with creeping stems on or below the ground, small leaves resembling shamrocks, and heads of white flowers. Leaves divided into three small leaflets, often having white chevron markings. Flowers small, white, in dense clusters at the tips of long stalks. Blooms all year.

Habitat: Uplands. Lawns, pastures, and road-sides.

Distribution: Throughout the state.

Notes: Common. Propagated from seeds and root divisions.

Caterpillars: Orange Sulphur (*Colias eurytheme*) and occasionally the Southern Dogface (*Zerene cesonia*).

Vigna luteola

Hairypod Cowpea

Description: Perennial vine with compound leaves and yellow, pealike flowers. Leaves with three leaflets, broadly lance-shaped, sparsely hairy. Flowers in small clusters at the tips of long stalks. Fruit a beanlike pod. Blooms throughout the year.

Habitat: Uplands and wetlands. Disturbed sites and margins of ditches and ponds.

Distribution: Throughout the state.

Notes: Common. Propagated from seeds.

Caterpillars: Gray Hairstreak (*Strymon melinus*), Cassius Blue (*Leptotes cassius*), Ceraunus Blue (*Hemiargus ceraunus*), and Long-tailed Skipper (*Urbanus proteus*).

Fagaceae (Beech family)

Quercus laevis
Turkey Oak

Description: Deciduous tree to 30' or more tall with large, deeply lobed leaves and rough, dark bark. Leaves alternate, turning reddish in the fall. Flowers inconspicuous, in drooping catkins. Acorns large, about equal in length and width, light brown. Blooms in spring.
Habitat: Uplands. Sandhills and dry pinelands.
Distribution: Mostly northern and central Florida.
Notes: Common. Propagated from seeds. A nice, drought resistant tree.
Caterpillars: Banded Hairstreak (*Satyrium calanus*), Sleepy Duskywing (*Erynnis brizo*), Juvenal's Duskywing (*Erynnis juvenalis*), and Horace's Duskywing (*Erynnis horatius*).

Quercus laurifolia
Laurel Oak

Description: Briefly deciduous tree to 60' or more tall with simple leaves, and smooth to scaly grayish bark. Leaves alternate, deeply lobed on young trees, narrowly lance-shaped on mature trees, usually shed in the spring. Flowers inconspicuous. Acorns small, squat, dark brown. Blooms in spring.
Habitat: Uplands and wetlands. Hydric to xeric hammocks.
Distribution: Throughout the state.
Notes: Abundant. Propagated from seeds. Laurel Oak is a fast-growing shade tree, often used in landscaping.
Caterpillars: Horace's Duskywing (*Erynnis horatius*) and probably White M Hairstreak (*Parrhasius m-album*).

Quercus myrtifolia
Myrtle Oak

Description: Evergreen tree typically 5' to 15' tall with small oval leaves. Leaves alternate, leathery, without teeth on the margins. Flowers inconspicuous. Acorns small, squat, dark brown. Blooms in the spring.
Habitat: Uplands. Scrubs, sandhills, and dry pinelands.
Distribution: Throughout the state.
Notes: Locally common. Propagated from seeds.
Caterpillars: Sleepy Duskywing (*Erynnis brizo*), Horace's Duskywing (*Erynnis horatius*), and probably Juvenal's Duskywing (*Erynnis juvenalis*).

Quercus nigra
Water Oak

Description: Briefly deciduous tree to 60' or more tall, the leaves widest at the tips. Leaves alternate, deeply lobed on young trees, to spoon shaped on mature trees. Flowers inconspicuous. Acorns small, squat, dark brown. Blooms in the spring.
Habitat: Uplands and wetlands. Moist to wet hammocks.
Distribution: Mostly northern and central Florida.
Notes: Abundant. Propagated from seeds. Water Oak is a fast-growing shade tree.
Caterpillars: Horace's Duskywing (*Erynnis horatius*).

Quercus stellata
Post Oak

Description: Deciduous tree usually less than 20'
tall with deeply lobed leaves and rough, scaly
bark. Leaves alternate, to about 4" long, widest
beyond the middle. Flowers inconspicuous.
Acorns small, squat, dark brown.
Habitat: Uplands. Sandhills and dry pinelands.
Distribution: Mostly northern Florida.
Notes: Locally common. Propagated from seeds.
Caterpillars: White M Hairstreak (*Parrhasius m-
album*).

Quercus virginiana
Virginia Live Oak

Description: Evergreen tree to 60' or more tall
with small tough leaves, thick drooping branches,
and dark, rough bark. Leaves alternate, of variable shape on young trees, mostly simple and
widest beyond the middle on mature trees, dark
green above, pale below, usually shed over a brief
period in the spring. Flowers inconspicuous.
Acorns much longer than wide, dark brown.
Blooms in spring.
Habitat: Uplands and wetlands. Moist to wet
hammocks.
Distribution: Throughout the state.
Notes: Common. Propagated from seeds. Live
Oak is a beautiful and majestic tree, characteristic
of the south. The closely similar Sand Live Oak
(*Quercus geminata*) occurs in scrubs and
sandhills throughout the state and is also eaten
by butterfly caterpillars.
Caterpillars: Horace's Duskywing (*Erynnis
horatius*) and White M Hairstreak (*Parrhasius m-
album*).

Juglandaceae (Walnut family)

Carya glabra
Pignut Hickory

Description: Deciduous tree to 60' or more tall with compound leaves that are aromatic when crushed. Leaves alternate, 6" or more in length, with seven to nine lance-shaped leaflets having small teeth on the margins, turning bright yellow in the fall. Flowers inconspicuous. Fruit large, the green husk breaking away in segments to reveal a single hard nut.
Habitat: Uplands. Dry to mesic hammocks.
Distribution: Northern and central Florida.
Notes: Common. Propagated from seeds. Several other common hickories are also used by butterflies. Scrub Hickory (*Carya floridana*) is very similar to Pignut Hickory, but is smaller and occurs only in central Florida. Mockernut Hickory (*Carya alba*) has larger leaves with short hairs on the undersides and is found in northern and central Florida.
Caterpillars: Banded Hairstreak (*Satyrium calanus*).

Lauraceae (Laurel family)

Persea borbonia
Red Bay

Description: Evergreen tree to 40' or more tall with simple leaves that are aromatic when crushed and often with whitish, globular galls. Leaves alternate, lance shaped, without teeth on the margins, having short petioles, dark green above, whitish below. Flowers inconspicuous. Fruit bluish black, fleshy with a large seed. Blooms in late spring.
Habitat: Uplands. Hammocks.
Distribution: Throughout the state.
Notes: Common. Propagated from seeds. Two other similar bays occur in Florida: Silk Bay (*Persea borbonia* var. *humilis*) grows in scrubs, and the leaves are rusty or brownish below, Swamp Bay (*Persea palustris*) occurs in wetlands and has short hairs along the midrib below. The fruit are eaten by birds.
Caterpillars: Spicebush Swallowtail (*Pterourus troilus*) and Palamedes Swallowtail (*Pterourus palamedes*).

Sassafras albidum

Sassafras

Description: Deciduous tree typically from 10' to 25' tall, the young branches green, the leaves either simple, mittenlike, or bearing two lobes. Leaves with short petioles, alternate, aromatic when crushed, without teeth on the margins, turn red in the fall. Flowers small, yellow, in clusters from the leaf axils. Fruit fleshy with a large seed, bluish black. Blooms in spring.
Habitat: Uplands. Sandhills, hammocks, and fencerows.
Distribution: Northern and central Florida.
Notes: Common in northern Florida. Propagated from seeds. The fruit are eaten by birds.
Caterpillars: Spicebush Swallowtail (*Pterourus troilus*).

Magnoliaceae (Magnolia family)

Liriodendron tulipifera

Tuliptree, Yellow Poplar

Description: Deciduous tree to 60' or more tall having dark, furrowed bark. Leaves alternate, aromatic when crushed, with a wide base and a flat to concave tip, long petiole, and whitish undersides. Flowers yellow, tuliplike, fragrant, produced singly at the tips of the branches. The fleshy red fruit burst from pockets in the thick receptacle. Blooms in spring.
Habitat: Uplands. Hammocks.
Distribution: Northern and central Florida.
Notes: Common in the Panhandle area. Propagated from seeds.
Caterpillars: Eastern Tiger Swallowtail (*Pterourus glaucus*).

Magnolia virginiana
Sweetbay

Description: Deciduous or semi-evergreen tree to 60' or more tall with large leaves, green above and silvery white below. Leaves alternate, lance shaped, aromatic when crushed. Flowers white, fragrant, produced singly at the tips of the branches. The fleshy red fruit burst from pockets in the thick receptacle. Blooms in spring and summer.
Habitat: Wetlands. Bayheads, swamps, seeps, hydric hammocks, and flatwoods.
Distribution: Throughout the state.
Notes: Common. Propagated from seeds.
Caterpillars: Eastern Tiger Swallowtail (*Pterourus glaucus*).

Malpighiaceae (Barbados Cherry family)

Byrsonima lucida
Long Key Locustberry

Description: Evergreen, branching shrub from 3' to 6' tall with small, leathery leaves and clusters of showy flowers. Leaves opposite, simple, oblong, widest beyond the middle, with very short petioles that clasp the stem. Flowers white, aging to pink or red, in clusters at the tips of the branches, four petals, the petals linear toward the base and wide at the tip. Blooms throughout the year.
Habitat: Uplands. Pine rocklands and margins of tropical hammocks.
Distribution: Highly localized in the Keys and southeastern mainland.
Notes: Common on Big Pine Key. Propagated from seeds. Adult butterflies are attracted to the flowers.
Caterpillars: Florida Duskywing (*Ephyriades brunneus*).

Malvaceae (Mallow family)

Sida acuta
Common Fanpetals, Common Wireweed

Description: Perennial, semiwoody herb with branching stems, typically to about 2' tall, bearing small yellow or cream colored flowers. Leaves alternate, lance shaped with small teeth on the margins and very short petioles. Flowers with five lobes, on very short stalks, born singly from the leaf axils. Fruit a dry capsule containing many seeds. Blooms throughout the year.
Habitat: Uplands. Roadsides, vacant lots, and weedy disturbed areas.
Distribution: Mostly peninsular Florida.
Notes: Abundant. Very weedy, not recommended for cultivation.
Caterpillars: Gray Hairstreak (*Strymon melinus*), Mallow Scrub-Hairstreak (*Strymon istapa*), Common Checkered-Skipper (*Pyrgus communis*), White Checkered-Skipper (*Pyrgus albescens*), and Tropical Checkered-Skipper (*Pyrgus oileus*).

Sida rhombifolia
Cuban Jute, Indian Hemp

Description: Annual, semiwoody herb with branching stems to about 3' with small leaves and yellow flowers. Leaves alternate, oblong with tiny teeth on the margins and long petioles. Flowers on long stalks from the leaf axils. Fruit a dry capsule containing many seeds. Blooms throughout the year.
Habitat: Uplands. Weedy sites.
Distribution: Throughout the state.
Notes: Abundant. Very weedy, not recommended for cultivation. Similar to Common Fanpetals, but has long flower stalks.
Caterpillars: Gray Hairstreak (*Strymon melinus*), Mallow Scrub-Hairstreak (*Strymon istapa*), Common Checkered-Skipper (*Pyrgus communis*), White Checkered-Skipper (*Pyrgus albescens*), and Tropical Checkered-Skipper (*Pyrgus oileus*).

Waltheria indica
Sleepy Morning

Description: Herb to about 4' tall with erect stems. Leaves alternate, oblong with wavy margins. Flowers yellow, in dense clusters from the leaf axils. Blooms all year. Similar in appearance to *Sida* species.
Habitat: Uplands. Disturbed areas near hammocks and pinelands, as well as weedlots.
Distribution: Uplands. Central and southern Florida.
Notes: Common. Propagated from seeds.
Caterpillars: Mallow Scrub-Hairstreak (*Strymon istapa*).

Moraceae (Mulberry family)

Ficus aurea
Strangler Fig, Golden Fig

Description: Evergreen tree to 60' or more tall with milky sap, leathery leaves, aerial roots, and small fleshy fruit. Leaves alternate, smooth, lance shaped with short petioles, no teeth on margins. Flowers encapsulated inside the fleshy receptacle and pollinated by tiny wasps. Fruit small, dark brown, without stalks.
Habitat: Uplands. Tropical hammocks and swamps.
Distribution: Central and southern Florida.
Notes: Common. Propagated from cuttings and seeds. This interesting tree is not recommended for small gardens, since the roots may invade and damage septic systems, walkways, driveways, foundations, or walls. The fruit are relished by wildlife, especially birds.
Caterpillars: Ruddy Daggerwing (*Marpesia petreus*).

Ficus citrifolia

Wild Banyan Tree, Short-leaved Fig

Description: Tropical tree to 50' tall with milky
sap and shiny leaves. Leaves alternate, to about 4"
long, lance shaped, on long stalks. Fruit on tips of
long stalks.
Habitat: Uplands. Tropical hardwood hammocks.
Distribution: Mostly coastal areas of southern
Florida and the Keys.
Notes: Uncommon. Propagated from cuttings.
Caterpillars: Ruddy Daggerwing (*Marpesia
petreus*).

Myricaceae (Bayberry family)

Myrica cerifera

Wax Myrtle, Southern Bayberry

Description: Evergreen shrub or small tree to
about 30' tall with aromatic leaves, and often
sprouting from the roots to form thickets. Leaves
alternate, narrowly lance shaped, with irregular
teeth on the margins, fragrant when crushed.
Flowers tiny, in short spikes from the leaf axils.
Clusters of small waxy fruit produced only on female plants in fall. Blooms in spring.
Habitat: Uplands and wetlands. Flatwoods, wet
prairies, edges of marshes, swamps, and hammocks.
Distribution: Throughout the state.
Notes: Abundant. Propagated from cuttings,
seeds, and root divisions. This plant is often used
for hedges in Florida gardens. A low, creeping
form (*Myrica cerifera* var. *pumila*) occurs in
sandhills and dry prairies.
Caterpillars: Red-banded Hairstreak (*Calycopis
cecrops*).

Oleaceae (Olive family)

Fraxinus pennsylvanica

Green Ash

Description: Deciduous tree to 40' or more tall with compound leaves, the trunk having a swollen base. Leaves opposite, with about seven lance-shaped leaflets with tiny teeth on the margins, the foliage turning brilliant yellow in the fall. Flowers small, greenish, in clusters from the leaf axils. The winged fruit are narrow and pointed. Blooms in spring.
Habitat: Wetlands. Swamps bordering rivers and lakes.
Distribution: Northern and central Florida.
Notes: Abundant. Propagated from seeds. This fast-growing shade tree is frequently used in landscaping in northern Florida. Other similar species include White Ash (*Fraxinus americana*), a larger tree having whitish undersides to the leaves, found in rich upland forests, and Carolina Ash (*Fraxinus caroliniana*), which is similar to Green Ash but the wings on the fruit are much larger.
Caterpillars: Eastern Tiger Swallowtail (*Pterourus glaucus*).

Orobanchaceae (Broomrape family)

Agalinis fasciculata

Beach False Foxglove

Description: Annual herb with erect stems to 4' tall, finely divided leaves, and showy tubular flowers. Leaves opposite, rough textured, and linear. Flowers with five lobes, purple with a yellow throat, hairy. Fruit a dry capsule. Blooms in late summer and fall.
Habitat: Uplands and wetlands. Pine flatwoods and wet prairies.
Distribution: Throughout the state, except extreme southern Florida.
Notes: Locally common. Propagated from seeds, but this plant is semiparasitic on the roots of other plants and difficult to grow in gardens. Several similar species of *Agalinis* occur in Florida.
Caterpillars: Common Buckeye (*Junonia coenia*).

Seymeria cassioides

Yaupon Blacksenna

Description: Annual herb with branching, erect stems to 2' tall, short narrow leaves, and small yellow flowers. Leaves opposite, divided into linear segments. Flowers with five lobes, solitary on stalks from the leaf axils. Blooms in late summer and fall.

Habitat: Uplands. Scrubs, sandhills, and dry pinelands.

Distribution: Northern and central Florida.

Notes: Locally common. Propagated from seeds, but semiparasitic on the roots of other plants and difficult to grow in gardens. Piedmont Blacksenna (*Seymeria pectinata*) is similar, but has lance-shaped leaves, hairy stems, and larger flowers.

Caterpillars: Common Buckeye (*Junonia coenia*).

Passifloraceae (Passionflower family)

Passiflora incarnata

Purple Passionflower, Maypop

Description: Deciduous perennial herbaceous vine with leathery leaves, tendrils, and large purplish flowers. Leaves alternate, three lobed, having small teeth on the margins and long petioles bearing two tiny nectar glands. Flowers about 2.5" wide, bearing five petals and five petal-like sepals. Fruit large, containing numerous seeds, each enclosed by a juicy sac, edible when fully ripe. Blooms from spring through fall.

Habitat: Uplands. Sandhills and dry weedy areas.

Distribution: Mostly northern and central Florida.

Notes: Common. Propagated from root divisions and seeds. This plant spreads by underground stems, but may be grown in pots to help keep the plant contained. The similar Incense Passionflower (*Passiflora 'Incense'*), a hybrid between *P. incarnata* and a Mexican species, has five-lobed leaves.

Caterpillars: Gulf Fritillary (*Agraulis vanillae*) and Zebra Heliconian (*Heliconius charitonius*).

Passiflora lutea
Yellow Passionflower

Description: Deciduous perennial vine with broad leaves, tendrils, and small yellowish flowers. Leaves alternate, with three rounded lobes, often with silvery markings above, the petioles without nectar glands. Flowers about ½" wide, cream colored. Fruit a small black berry. Spreads by underground stems. Blooms from spring through summer.
Habitat: Uplands. Hammocks.
Distribution: Northern and central Florida.
Notes: Common. Propagated from root divisions and seeds.
Caterpillars: Gulf Fritillary (*Agraulis vanillae*) and Zebra Heliconian (*Heliconius charitonius*).

Passiflora suberosa
Corkystem Passionflower

Description: Perennial herbaceous vine with corky lower stems, tendrils, and small yellowish flowers. Leaves of various shapes, usually trilobed in northern Florida and lance shaped in central and southern regions, the margins without teeth, petioles with nectar glands, evergreen. Fruit a small purple or black berry. Spreads by underground stems. Blooms throughout the year.
Habitat: Uplands. Hammocks and weedy areas.
Distribution: Peninsular Florida.
Notes: Common. Propagated from root divisions and seeds.
Caterpillars: Gulf Fritillary (*Agraulis vanillae*), Julia Heliconian (*Dryas iulia*), and Zebra Heliconian (*Heliconius charitonius*).

Picramniaceae (Bitterbush family)

Alvaradoa amorphoides
Mexican Alvaradoa

Description: Evergreen shrub or small tree typically to about 15' tall with compound leaves bearing numerous small leaflets. Leaves alternate, pinnately compound, bearing small oval, leathery leaflets, somewhat similar to Wild Tamarind foliage. Flowers small, densely arranged on long drooping stalks from the tips of the branches. Blooms in fall and winter.
Habitat: Uplands. Tropical hardwood hammocks.
Distribution: Limited to a few small parks around Homestead, Miami-Dade County.
Notes: Rare. Propagated from seeds.
Caterpillars: Dina Yellow (*Eurema dina*).

Picramnia pentandra
Florida Bitterbush

Description: Evergreen shrub usually to about 10' tall with compound leaves. Leaves alternate, 8" or more long with five to nine shiny lance-shaped leaflets. Flowers tiny, greenish, in small clusters on drooping stalks. Individual plants either male or female. Fruit fleshy, turns black at maturity. Blooms throughout the year, especially summer.
Habitat: Uplands. Tropical hardwood hammocks.
Distribution: Limited to a few parks in coastal Miami-Dade County.
Notes: Very rare. Propagated from seeds.
Caterpillars: Dina Yellow (*Eurema dina*).

Plumbaginaceae (Leadwort family)

Plumbago auriculata
Cape Leadwort

Description: Evergreen shrub to about 5' tall with small leaves and clusters of bright blue flowers. Leaves alternate, to about 2" long, widest beyond the middle. Flowers tubular, in short spikes at the tips of the branches. Fruit oblong, with stalked glands. Blooms throughout the year.
Habitat: Gardens and roadside plantings.
Distribution: Originally from southern Africa. Grown throughout the state, but top-killed by freezing temperatures in northern Florida.
Notes: Common. Propagated from cuttings. This ornamental shrub is widely grown in Florida gardens.
Caterpillars: Cassius Blue (*Leptotes cassius*).

Rhamnaceae (Buckthorn family)

Ceanothus americanus
New Jersey Tea

Description: Deciduous branching shrub to about 4' tall with leaves having three main veins arising from near the base of the blade. Leaves alternate, broadly lance shaped, with tiny teeth on the margins. Flowers small, white, in dense clusters at the tips of long stalks. Blooms in early summer.
Habitat: Uplands. Sandhills and dry pinelands.
Distribution: Mostly northern Florida.
Notes: Uncommon. Propagated from seeds. The flowers are attractive to adult butterflies and other insects.
Caterpillars: Gray Scrub-Hairstreak (*Strymon melinus*) and Mottled Duskywing (*Erynnis martialis*).

Rhizophoraceae (Red Mangrove family)

Rhizophora mangle
Red Mangrove

Description: Evergreen tropical tree to about 20' with large leathery leaves and abundant branching prop roots. Leaves opposite, broadly lance shaped with a short petiole. Flowers small, with four yellow petals, in clusters from the leaf axils. Fruit brown, germinating on the tree, a green cigar-shaped seedling to 8" long, growing while still attached and dropping into the sea when mature. Blooms throughout the year.
Habitat: Coastal wetlands. Salt marshes and mangrove swamps.
Distribution: Coastal areas of central and southern Florida.
Notes: Abundant. Propagated from the elongate seedlings that float on the water and are pushed by waves onto mudflats where they root.
Caterpillars: Mangrove Skipper (*Phocides pigmalion*).

Rosaceae (Rose family)

Prunus serotina
Black Cherry

Description: Deciduous tree to 40' or more tall with scaly bark, simple leaves, and small, fleshy fruit. Leaves alternate, broadly lance shaped, with a short often reddish petiole bearing two small glands, small teeth on the margins, cherrylike smell when crushed. Flowers small, with five white petals, in long clusters from near the tips of the branches. Fruit black, fleshy, containing a single hard seed. Blooms in spring.
Habitat: Uplands. Hammocks, abandoned fields, and fence rows.
Distribution: Northern and central Florida.
Notes: Abundant. Propagated from seeds. The flowers are very attractive to adult butterflies and other insects.
Caterpillars: Eastern Tiger Swallowtail (*Pterourus glaucus*) and Red-Spotted Purple (*Basilarchia arthemis astyanax*).

Rutaceae (Citrus family)

Amyris elemifera
Sea Torchwood

Description: Evergreen shrub or small tree from 6' to 25' tall with compound leaves. Leaves opposite, with three lance-shaped, leathery leaflets having somewhat long stalks, dotted with small glands, fragrant when crushed, reddish when young. Flowers small, white, in clusters at the tips of the branches. Fruit dark purple with a single large seed. Blooms throughout the year.

Habitat: Uplands. Tropical hammocks.

Distribution: The Keys and Atlantic coast north to Merritt Island.

Notes: Local and uncommon. Propagated from seeds. The fruit are attractive to birds. Balsam Torchwood (*Amyris balsamifera*) is similar but has up to five leaflets and is found only in a few places in the Upper Keys and southeastern mainland.

Caterpillars: Schaus' Swallowtail (*Heraclides aristodemus*), Bahamian Swallowtail (*Heraclides andraemon*), and occasionally Giant Swallowtail (*Heraclides cresphontes*).

Citrus reticulata
Tangerine

Description: Evergreen trees usually from 10' to 25' tall, often with long spines and large fleshy yellow or orange fruit. Leaves broadly lance shaped, without teeth on the margins, dotted with oil glands, having short petioles (winged in some species), fragrant when crushed. Flowers small, white with five petals, very fragrant. Blooms in spring.
Habitat: Uplands. Hammocks, gardens, and groves.
Distribution: Originally from tropical Asia. Grown throughout peninsular Florida.
Notes: Common. Propagated by grafting for fruit production. Plants grown from seed are often very spiny and take years to initiate flowering. Other types of citrus are commonly grown in Florida: *Citrus aurantifolia* (Key Lime), *Citrus limon* (Lemon), *Citrus sinensis* (Sweet Orange), and the hybrid *Citrus* x *paradisi* (Grapefruit). Sour Orange (*Citrus aurantium*), a very sour and bitter tasting fruit, was widely used as rootstock for grafting and is now naturalized throughout peninsular Florida.
Caterpillars: Giant Swallowtail (*Heraclides cresphontes*) and occasionally Bahamian Swallowtail (*Heraclides andraemon*).

Ptelea trifoliata
Common Hoptree, Wafer Ash

Description: Deciduous shrub or small tree usually from 6' to 15' tall with compound leaves. Leaves with three lance-shaped leaflets, margins without teeth, fragrant when crushed. Flowers small, greenish white, having three to four petals, fragrant, produced in clusters from the tips of the branches. Fruit coinlike and papery. Blooms in spring.
Habitat: Uplands. Hammocks.
Distribution: Northern and central Florida.
Notes: Uncommon and local. Propagated from seeds.
Caterpillars: Giant Swallowtail (*Heraclides cresphontes*).

Ruta graveolens
Rue

Description: Perennial herb with fernlike bluish green foliage, aromatic when crushed. Leaves compound with small rounded leaflets, to about 5" long. Flowers small, yellow, borne in clusters at the tips of stalks up to 3' tall. Blooms in summer and fall.
Habitat: Gardens.
Distribution: Cultivated herb from Europe. Grown throughout the state.
Notes: Common. Propagated from seeds.
Caterpillars: Black Swallowtail (*Papilio polyxenes*) and Giant Swallowtail (*Heraclides cresphontes*).

Zanthoxylum clava-herculis
Hercules-club, Toothache Tree

Description: Deciduous tree usually 15' to 25' tall with shiny dark green leaves and large recurved spines on the trunk. Leaves pinnately compound with seven to nine lance-shaped leaflets and small spines below, highly aromatic when crushed and causing numbing of the tongue if chewed, young leaves and petioles reddish in color. Flowers small, white, in dense clusters at the tips of the branches. Fruit small and round, a dry husk covering a shiny black seed. Blooms in spring.
Habitat: Uplands. Sandhills, dry hammocks, and fencerows.
Distribution: Throughout the state.
Notes: Locally common. Propagated from seeds. Related species found in Florida include the extremely rare Biscayne Pricklyash (*Zanthoxylum coriaceum*) and Yellowwood (*Z. flavum*) that occur at only a few sites in the Keys and on the southeastern coast. Common Pricklyash (*Zanthoxylum americanum*) is an uncommon tree in the Panhandle.
Caterpillars: Giant Swallowtail (*Heraclides cresphontes*).

Zanthoxylum fagara
Wild Lime, Lime Pricklyash

Description: Evergreen tree typically 10' to 30'
tall with spines like cats' claws on the leaves and
branches. Leaves with a winged petiole, often
yellowish green, compound with seven to nine
small rounded leaflets, aromatic when crushed.
Flowers small, yellowish white, in clusters at the
tips of the branches. Fruit small and round, a
dry husk covering a shiny black seed. Blooms
throughout the year.
Habitat: Uplands. Hammocks.
Distribution: Central and southern Florida.
Notes: Common. Propagated from seeds and cuttings.
Caterpillars: Bahamian Swallowtail (*Heraclides
andraemon*) and Giant Swallowtail (*Heraclides
cresphontes*).

Salicaceae (Willow family)

Salix caroliniana
Carolina Willow, Coastalplain Willow

Description: Deciduous shrub or small tree typically from 10' to 30' tall. Leaves alternate, long
and narrow with very fine teeth along the margins, whitish below, young growth often reddish
in color. Flowers in single sex clusters from the
leaf axils. Blooms in spring.
Habitat: Wetlands. Swamps, marshes, ditches,
and wet disturbed sites.
Distribution: Throughout the state.
Notes: Abundant. Propagated from cuttings and
seeds. The flowers are attractive to adult
butterflies and other insects. Black Willow (*Salix
nigra*) is similar, but grows to be a large tree and
the leaves are green beneath. Black Willow is usually found along streams and rivers in northern
Florida. Weeping Willow (*Salix babylonica*) is a
large tree from China that is often planted in
northern Florida gardens. The branches are limber and hang downward.
Caterpillars: Viceroy (*Basilarchia archippus*)
and occasionally Red-spotted Purple (*Basilarchia
arthemis astyanax*).

Sapindaceae (Soapberry family)

Cardiospermum corindum
Balloonvine, Heartseed

Description: Perennial herbaceous vine with tendrils, compound leaves, and inflated fruit. Leaves alternate, with three leaflets having large teeth on the margins. Flowers small and white, in clusters from the leaf axils. Fruit three parted, soft and rubbery when green, papery, brittle, and brown when mature; divided inside by a thin papery membrane. Seeds hard and black at maturity with a white heart-shaped scar less than half the width of the seed. Blooms throughout the year.
Habitat: Uplands. Edges of tropical hammocks and weedy disturbed sites.
Distribution: Florida Keys and southern Florida.
Notes: Uncommon. Propagated from seeds.
Caterpillars: Silver-banded Hairstreak (*Chlorostrymon simaethus*), Miami Blue (*Hemiargus thomasi*), and occasionally Gray Hairstreak (*Strymon melinus*).

Surianaceae (Bay Cedar family)

Suriana maritima
Bay Cedar

Description: Evergreen shrub to about 8' tall with somewhat succulent leaves. Leaves alternate, short, linear, without teeth, clustered near the tips of the branches, aromatic when crushed. Flowers yellow, on long stalks, in small groups at the ends of the branches. Blooms throughout the year.
Habitat: Uplands. Beaches and edges of salt marshes.
Distribution: Coastal areas of central and southern Florida.
Notes: Uncommon. Propagated from seeds.
Caterpillars: Martial Scrub-Hairstreak (*Strymon martialis*) and Mallow Scrub-Hairstreak (*Strymon istapa*).

Symplocaceae (Sweetleaf family)

Symplocos tinctoria
Common Sweetleaf, Horse Sugar

Description: Deciduous to semi-evergreen shrub typically from 4' to 10' tall with small greenish fruit. Leaves alternate, lance shaped to oblong, leathery, usually without teeth on the margins. Flowers, yellow, in clusters from the older twigs in spring.
Habitat: Uplands. Sandhills and hammocks.
Distribution: Mostly northern Florida.
Notes: Locally common. Propagated from seeds.
Caterpillars: King's Hairstreak (*Satyrium kingi*).

Ulmaceae (Elm family)

Ulmus alata
Winged Elm or Cork Elm

Description: Deciduous tree typically to 30' or more tall with relatively small leaves, deeply furrowed bark, and corky growths on the branches. Leaves alternate, about 2.5" long, somewhat narrow, with doubly serrate margins and very short petioles. Flowers tiny, greenish, in small clusters. Fruit small, disk shaped, and papery. Blooms in early spring.
Habitat: Uplands and wetlands. Wet to moist hammocks.
Distribution: Northern and central Florida.
Notes: Common. Propagated from seeds.
Caterpillars: Question Mark (*Polygonia interrogationis*).

Ulmus americana
American Elm

Description: Deciduous tree to about 60' tall with broad leaves and a fluted trunk near the ground. Leaves alternate, to about 4.5" long, broadly lance shaped, the bases nonsymmetrical, with short petioles. Flowers small, in long catkins. Fruit small, disk shaped, and papery. Blooms in early spring.
Habitat: Uplands and wetlands. Wet to moist hammocks.
Distribution: Northern and central Florida.
Notes: Common. Propagated from seeds.
Caterpillars: Question Mark (*Polygonia interrogationis*).

Urticaceae (Nettle family)

Boehmeria cylindrica
False Nettle, Bog Hemp

Description: Perennial herb with erect stems to 4' tall, broad leaves, and tiny whitish flowers. Leaves opposite, to 6" long, three main veins, long often reddish petioles, coarse nonstinging hairs, and teeth on the margins. Flowers in erect clusters on stalks arising from the leaf axils. Blooms in summer and fall.
Habitat: Wetlands. Swamps, freshwater marshes, and hydric hammocks.
Distribution: Throughout Florida.
Notes: Common. Propagated from root divisions and seeds.
Caterpillars: Red Admiral (*Vanessa atalanta*).

Parietaria floridana

Florida Pellitory

Description: Annual often prostrate herb with
succulent stems and inconspicuous flowers.
Leaves alternate, to about 1" long, oval to lance
shaped, with long petioles. Flowers tiny, greenish,
in small clusters on short stalks from the leaf axils. Blooms in spring.
Habitat: Uplands. Moist hammocks and shady
disturbed areas.
Distribution: Peninsular Florida.
Notes: Abundant. A weedy plant frequently
present in gardens.
Caterpillars: Red Admiral (*Vanessa atalanta*).

Urtica chamaedryoides

Heartleaf Nettle

Description: Annual herb with erect stems, broad
leaves, and stinging hairs. Leaves opposite,
broadly lance shaped, to about 3" long, with teeth
on the margins. Flowers small, white, in dense
globular clusters on short stalks from the leaf axils. Blooms from spring through summer.
Habitat: Uplands. Hammocks.
Distribution: Northern and central Florida.
Notes: Uncommon. Propagated from seeds.
Burning Nettle (*Urtica urens*) is a weedy perennial nettle from Europe that has become naturalized in northern and central Florida. This plant
has stinging hairs and spreads by underground
runners.
Caterpillars: Red Admiral (*Vanessa atalanta*).

Verbenaceae (Vervain family)

Phyla nodiflora
Turkey Tangle Fogfruit, Capeweed, Matchheads, Carpetweed

Description: Perennial herb with trailing, often purplish stems, small leaves, and small pinkish white flowers. Leaves opposite, oval to oblong, to about 3/4" long, with small teeth on the margins. Flowers tubular, in dense heads at the tips of erect stalks. Blooms all year.
Habitat: Uplands and wetlands. Roadsides, pastures, and disturbed sites.
Distribution: Throughout the state.
Notes: Abundant. Propagated from stem cuttings.
Caterpillars: Phaon Crescent (*Phyciodes phaon*) and White Peacock (*Anartia jatrophae*).

Stachytarpheta jamaicensis
Blue Porterweed

Description: Perennial herb with trailing stems, broad leaves, and small blue flowers. Leaves opposite, lance shaped, to about 3.5" long, with small teeth on the margins. Flowers light blue, tubular, without stalks on a rattail-like spike, only a few flowers opening per day, starting at the base of the stalk. Blooms throughout the year.
Habitat: Uplands. Open disturbed sites.
Distribution: Southern and coastal central Florida.
Notes: Common. Propagated from cuttings and seeds.
Caterpillars: Tropical Buckeye (*Junonia genoveva*).

Veronicaceae (Speedwell family)

Bacopa monnieri
Herb-of-Grace, Waterhyssop

Description: Mat-forming perennial herb with succulent leaves and stems and pale blue flowers. Leaves opposite, oval to oblong, without teeth on the margins. Flowers small, with five lobes, arranged singly on long stalks. Blooms throughout the year.
Habitat: Wetlands. Wet flatwoods, lawns and margins of ditches and ponds.
Distribution: Mostly peninsular Florida.
Notes: Common. Propagated from stem cuttings and seeds. Adult butterflies are attracted to the flowers. Easy to cultivate in hanging baskets or as a ground cover.
Caterpillars: White Peacock (*Anartia jatrophae*).

Linaria canadensis
Canada Toadflax

Description: Annual herb with a basal rosette of leaves followed by slender flower stalks to 2' tall bearing small blue and white flowers. Leaves linear, opposite to alternate. Flowers resemble snapdragons, with a long backward-pointing spur in clusters at the tips of the flower stalks. Fruit a dry capsule containing many seeds. Blooms in spring.
Habitat: Uplands. Roadsides, weedy lawns, and disturbed sites.
Distribution: Throughout the state.
Notes: Common. Propagated from seeds. Apalachicola Toadflax (*Linaria floridana*) is similar, but the flowers have shorter spurs.
Caterpillars: Common Buckeye (*Junonia coenia*).

Viscaceae (Mistletoe family)

Phoradendron leucarpum

Oak Mistletoe

Description: Parasitic evergreen plant that forms clusters of foliage on the branches of hardwood trees. Leaves opposite, leathery, oval to oblong, to about 2.5" long. Flowers tiny, in small clusters on branching flower stalks at the tips of the stems. Fruit a white round berry eaten and dispersed by birds.
Habitat: Uplands and wetlands. Hammocks and swamps.
Distribution: Mostly northern and central Florida.
Notes: Common. Not easily propagated.
Caterpillars: Great Purple Hairstreak (*Atlides halesus*).

Zygophyllaceae (Caltrop family)

Guajacum sanctum

Holywood Lignumvitae

Description: Tropical tree to 25' tall with dense resinous wood, compound leaves, and blue flowers. Leaves opposite, pinnately compound, to about 2" long, with three to four pairs of asymmetrically shaped leaflets bearing a small spine at the tips. Flowers with five petals, in small clusters. Fruit an orange capsule that splits open revealing the bright red seeds. Blooms throughout the year.
Habitat: Uplands. Tropical hardwood hammocks and gardens.
Distribution: Coastal areas of Miami-Dade County and the Upper Keys.
Notes: Uncommon. Propagated from seeds.
Caterpillars: Possibly the Lyside Sulphur (*Kricogonia lyside*).

Checklist of Butterflies
That Breed in Florida

Swallowtails (family Papilionidae)

—— *Battus philenor* (Pipevine Swallowtail)
—— *Battus polydamas* (Polydamas Swallowtail)
—— *Eurytides marcellus* (Zebra Swallowtail)
—— *Heraclides andraemon* (Bahamian Swallowtail)
—— *Heraclides aristodemus* (Schaus' Swallowtail)
—— *Heraclides cresphontes* (Giant Swallowtail)
—— *Papilio polyxenes* (Black Swallowtail)
—— *Pterourus glaucus* (Eastern Tiger Swallowtail)
—— *Pterourus palamedes* (Palamedes Swallowtail)
—— *Pterourus troilus* (Spicebush Swallowtail)

Whites, Orangetips, and Sulphurs (family Pieridae)

Whites (subfamily Pierinae)

—— *Appias drusilla* (Florida White)
—— *Ascia monuste* (Great Southern White)
—— *Pieris rapae* (Cabbage White)
—— *Pontia protodice* (Checkered White)

Orangetips (subfamily Anthocharinae)

—— *Paramidea midea* (Falcate Orangetip)

Sulphurs (subfamily Coliadinae)

—— *Aphrissa statira* (Statira Sulphur)
—— *Colias eurytheme* (Orange Sulphur)

—— *Eurema daira* (Barred Yellow)
—— *Eurema dina* (Dina Yellow)
—— *Eurema lisa* (Little Yellow)
—— *Eurema nicippe* (Sleepy Orange)
—— *Eurema nise* (Mimosa Yellow)
—— *Kricogonia lyside* (Lyside Sulphur) (possibly breeding)
—— *Nathalis iole* (Dainty Sulphur)
—— *Phoebis agarithe* (Large Orange Sulphur)
—— *Phoebis philea* (Orange-barred Sulphur)
—— *Phoebis sennae* (Cloudless Sulphur)
—— *Zerene cesonia* (Southern Dogface)

Harvesters, Hairstreaks, and Blues (family Lycaenidae)

Harvesters (subfamily Miletinae)

—— *Feniseca tarquinius* (Harvester)

Hairstreaks (subfamily Theclinae)

—— *Atlides halesus* (Great Purple Hairstreak)
—— *Calycopis cecrops* (Red-banded Hairstreak)
—— *Chlorostrymon maesites* (Amethyst Hairstreak)
—— *Chlorostrymon simaethis* (Silver-banded Hairstreak)
—— *Electrostrymon angelia* (Fulvous Hairstreak)
—— *Eumaeus atala* (Atala)
—— *Fixsenia favonius* (Oak Hairstreak)
—— *Harkenclenus titus* (Coral Hairstreak)
—— *Incisalia henrici* (Henry's Elfin)
—— *Incisalia irus* (Frosted Elfin)
—— *Incisalia niphon* (Eastern Pine Elfin)
—— *Ministrymon azia* (Gray Ministreak)
—— *Mitoura grynea* (Juniper Hairstreak)
—— *Mitoura hesseli* (Hessel's Hairstreak)
—— *Parrhasius m-album* (White M Hairstreak)
—— *Satyrium calanus* (Banded Hairstreak)
—— *Satyrium kingi* (King's Hairstreak)
—— *Satyrium liparops* (Striped Hairstreak)
—— *Strymon acis* (Bartram's Hairstreak)
—— *Strymon istapa* (Mallow Scrub-Hairstreak)

—— *Strymon martialis* (Martial Scrub-Hairstreak)
—— *Strymon melinus* (Gray Hairstreak)

Blues (subfamily Polyommatinae)

—— *Brephidium isophthalma* (Eastern Pygmy-Blue)
—— *Celastrina ladon* ('Edwards' Spring Azure)
—— *Celastrina neglecta* ('Summer' Spring Azure)
—— *Everes comyntas* (Eastern Tailed-Blue)
—— *Hemiargus ammon* (Nickerbean Blue)
—— *Hemiargus ceraunus* (Ceraunus Blue)
—— *Hemiargus thomasi* (Miami Blue)
—— *Leptotes cassius* (Cassius Blue)

Metalmarks (family Riodinidae)

—— *Calephelis virginiensis* (Little Metalmark)

Brushfooted Butterflies (family Nymphalidae)

Snout Butterflies (subfamily Libytheinae)

—— *Libytheana carinenta* (American Snout)

Heliconians (subfamily Heliconiinae)

—— *Agraulis vanillae* (Gulf Fritillary)
—— *Dryas iulia* (Julia Heliconian)
—— *Heliconius charithonia* (Zebra Heliconian)

Brushfoots (subfamily Nymphalinae)

—— *Anartia jatrophae* (White Peacock)
—— *Anthanassa frisia* (Cuban Crescent)
—— *Anthanassa texana seminole* ('Seminole' Texan Crescent)
—— *Chlosyne nycteis* (Silvery Checkerspot)
—— *Euptoieta claudia* (Variegated Fritillary)
—— *Junonia coenia* (Common Buckeye)
—— *Junonia evarete* (Mangrove Buckeye)
—— *Junonia genoveva* (Tropical Buckeye)
—— *Nymphalis antiopa* (Mourning Cloak)

—— *Phyciodes phaon* (Phaon Crescent)
—— *Phyciodes tharos* (Pearl Crescent)
—— *Polygonia comma* (Eastern Comma)
—— *Polygonia interrogationis* (Question Mark)
—— *Siproeta stelenes* (Malachite)
—— *Vanessa atalanta* (Red Admiral)
—— *Vanessa cardui* (Painted Lady)
—— *Vanessa virginiensis* (American Lady)

Admirals (subfamily Limenitidinae)

—— *Basilarchia archippus* (Viceroy)
—— *Basilarchia arthemis astyanax* (Red-spotted Purple)
—— *Eunica monima* (Dingy Purplewing)
—— *Eunica tatila* (Florida Purplewing)
—— *Marpesia petreus* (Ruddy Daggerwing)

Leafwing Butterflies (subfamily Charaxinae)

—— *Anaea andria* (Goatweed Leafwing)
—— *Anaea troglodyta floridalis* (Florida Leafwing)

Emperors (subfamily Apaturinae)

—— *Asterocampa celtis* (Hackberry Emperor)
—— *Asterocampa clyton* (Tawny Emperor)

Milkweed Butterflies (subfamily Danainae)

—— *Danaus eresimus* (Soldier)
—— *Danaus gilippus* (Queen)
—— *Danaus plexippus* (Monarch)

Satyrs and Wood-Nymphs (subfamily Satyrinae)

—— *Cercyonis pegala* (Common Wood-Nymph)
—— *Cyllopsis gemma* (Gemmed Satyr)
—— *Enodia portlandia* (Southern Pearly-eye)
—— *Hermeuptychia sosybius* (Carolina Satyr)
—— *Megisto cymela* (Little Wood-Satyr)
—— *Neonympha areolata* (Georgia Satyr)
—— *Satyrodes appalachia* (Appalachian Brown)

Skippers (family Hesperiidae)

Spread-winged Skippers (subfamily Pyrginae)

—— *Achalarus lyciades* (Hoary Edge)
—— *Autochton cellus* (Golden Banded-Skipper)
—— *Epargyreus clarus* (Silver-spotted Skipper)
—— *Epargyreus zestos* (Zestos Skipper)
—— *Ephyriades brunneus* (Florida Duskywing)
—— *Erynnis baptisiae* (Wild Indigo Duskywing)
—— *Erynnis brizo* (Sleepy Duskywing)
—— *Erynnis horatius* (Horace's Duskywing)
—— *Erynnis juvenalis* (Juvenal's Duskywing)
—— *Erynnis martialis* (Mottled Duskywing)
—— *Erynnis zarucco* (Zarucco Duskywing)
—— *Phocides pigmalion* (Mangrove Skipper)
—— *Pholisora catullus* (Common Sootywing)
—— *Polygonus leo* (Hammock Skipper)
—— *Pyrgus albescens* (White Checkered-Skipper)
—— *Pyrgus communis* (Common Checkered-Skipper)
—— *Pyrgus oileus* (Tropical Checkered-Skipper)
—— *Staphylus hayhurstii* (Hayhurst's Scallopwing)
—— *Thorybes bathyllus* (Southern Cloudywing)
—— *Thorybes confusis* (Confused Cloudywing)
—— *Thorybes pylades* (Northern Cloudywing)
—— *Urbanus dorantes* (Dorantes Longtail)
—— *Urbanus proteus* (Long-tailed Skipper)

Grass-Skippers (subfamily Hesperiinae)

—— *Amblyscirtes aesculapius* (Lace-winged Roadside-Skipper)
—— *Amblyscirtes alternata* (Dusky Roadside-Skipper)
—— *Amblyscirtes hegon* (Pepper and Salt Skipper)
—— *Amblyscirtes reversa* (Reversed Roadside-Skipper)
—— *Amblyscirtes vialis* (Common Roadside-Skipper)
—— *Anatrytone logan* (Delaware Skipper)
—— *Ancyloxypha numitor* (Least Skipper)
—— *Asbolis capucinus* (Monk Skipper)
—— *Atalopedes campestris* (Sachem)
—— *Atrytone arogos* (Arogos Skipper)

—— *Atrytonopsis hianna loammi* (Dusted Skipper)
—— *Calpodes ethlius* (Brazilian Skipper)
—— *Copaeodes minimus* (Southern Skipperling)
—— *Cymaenes tripunctus* (Three-spotted Skipper)
—— *Euphyes arpa* (Palmetto Skipper)
—— *Euphyes berryi* (Berry's Skipper)
—— *Euphyes dion* (Dion Skipper)
—— *Euphyes dukesi* (Dukes' Skipper)
—— *Euphyes pilatka* (Palatka Skipper)
—— *Euphyes vestris* (Dun Skipper)
—— *Hesperia attalus* (Dotted Skipper)
—— *Hesperia meskei* (Meske's Skipper)
—— *Hylephila phyleus* (Fiery Skipper)
—— *Lerema accius* (Clouded Skipper)
—— *Lerodea eufala* (Eufala Skipper)
—— *Nastra lherminier* (Swarthy Skipper)
—— *Nastra neamathla* (Neamathla Skipper)
—— *Oligoria maculata* (Twin-spot Skipper)
—— *Panoquina ocola* (Ocola Skipper)
—— *Panoquina panoquin* (Salt Marsh Skipper)
—— *Panoquina panoquinoides* (Obscure Skipper)
—— *Poanes aaroni* (Aaron's Skipper)
—— *Poanes viator* (Broad-winged Skipper)
—— *Poanes yehl* (Yehl Skipper)
—— *Poanes zabulon* (Zabulon Skipper)
—— *Polites baracoa* (Baracoa Skipper)
—— *Polites origenes* (Crossline Skipper)
—— *Polites themistocles* (Tawny-edged Skipper)
—— *Polites vibex* (Whirlabout)
—— *Pompeius verna* (Little Glassywing)
—— *Problema byssus* (Byssus Skipper)
—— *Wallengrenia egeremet* (Northern Broken-Dash)
—— *Wallengrenia otho* (Southern Broken-Dash)

Giant-Skippers (subfamily Megathymidae)

—— *Megathymus cofaqui* (Cofaqui Giant-Skipper)
—— *Megathymus yuccae* (Yucca Giant-Skipper)

References

Butterfly Guides

Allen, T. J. 1997. *The Butterflies of West Virginia and Their Caterpillars*. Pittsburgh: University of Pittsburgh Press. 388 pp.

Brock, J. P., and K. Kaufman. 2003. *Butterflies of North America*. Kaufman Focus Guides. New York: Houghton Mifflin. 383 pp.

Calhoun, J. V. 1997. Updated list of the butterflies and skippers of Florida (Lepidoptera: Papilionoidea and Hesperioidea). *Holarctic Lepidoptera* 4(2): 39–50.

Daniels, J. C. 2003. *Butterflies of Florida Field Guide*. Cambridge, Minn.: Adventure Publications. 256 pp.

———. 2000. *Your Florida Guide to Butterfly Gardening: A Guide for the Deep South*. Gainesville: University Press of Florida. 112 pp.

Emmel, T. C. 1997. *Florida's Fabulous Butterflies*. Tampa: World Publications. 96 pp.

Gerberg, E. J., and R. H. Arnett, Jr. 1989. *Florida Butterflies*. Baltimore: Natural Science Publications. 90 pp.

Glassberg, J., M. C. Minno, and J. V. Calhoun. 2000. *Butterflies Through Binoculars: Florida*. New York: Oxford University Press. 242 pp.

Harris, L., Jr. 1972. *Butterflies of Georgia*. Norman: University of Oklahoma Press. 326 pp.

Kimball, C. P. 1965. *The Lepidoptera of Florida: An Annotated Checklist*. Gainesville: Florida Department of Agriculture, Division of Plant Industry. 363 pp.

Minno, M. C., and T. C. Emmel. 1993. *Butterflies of the Florida Keys*. Gainesville, Fla.: Scientific Publishers. 168 pp.

Minno, M. C., and M. Minno. 1999. *Florida Butterfly Gardening: A Complete Guide to Attracting, Identifying, and Enjoying Butterflies of the Lower South*. Gainesville: University Press of Florida. 210 pp.

Mitchell, R. T., and H. S. Zim. 1964. *Butterflies and Moths: A Guide to the More Common American Species*. New York: Golden Press. 160 pp.

Opler, P. A., and G. O. Krizek. 1984. *Butterflies East of the Great Plains: An Illustrated Natural History*. Baltimore: Johns Hopkins University Press. 294 pp.

Opler, P. A., and V. Malikul. 1992. *A Field Guide to Eastern Butterflies*. Boston: Houghton Mifflin. 396 pp.

Putnam, P., and M. Putnam. 1997. *North America's Favorite Butterflies: A Pictorial Guide*. Minocqua, Wis.: Willow Creek Press. 136 pp.

Pyle, R. M. 1984. *The Audubon Society Handbook for Butterfly Watchers*. New York: Scribners. 274 pp.

Scott, J. A. 1986. *The Butterflies of North America.* Stanford: Stanford University Press. 583 pp.

Stehr, F. W. 1987. *Immature Insects.* Dubuque: Kendall/Hunt Publishing. 754 pp.

Stiling, P. D. 1989. *Florida's Butterflies and Other Insects.* Sarasota: Pineapple Press. 95 pp.

Trass, P. F. 2000. *Gardening for Florida's Butterflies.* St. Petersburg, Fla.: Great Outdoors Publishing. 136 pp.

Wright, A. B. 1998. *Peterson First Guide to Caterpillars of North America.* Boston: Houghton Mifflin. 128 pp.

Plant Guides

Bell, C. R., and B. J. Taylor. 1982. *Florida Wild Flowers and Roadside Plants.* Chapel Hill: Laurel Hill Press. 308 pp.

Clewell, A. F. 1985. *Guide to the Vascular Plants of the Florida Panhandle.* Gainesville: University Presses of Florida. 605 pp.

Haehle, R. G., and J. Brookwell. 1999. *Native Florida Plants: Low-Maintenance Landscaping and Gardening.* Houston: Gulf Publishing. 360 pp.

Hall, D. W. 1993. *Illustrated Plants of Florida and the Coastal Plain.* Gainesville, Fla.: Maupin House. 431 pp.

Hammer, R. L. 2002. *Everglades Wildflowers.* Guilford, Conn.: The Globe Pequot Press. 243 pp.

Hoyer, M. V., D. E. Canfield, Jr., C. A. Horsburgh, and K. Brown. 1996. *Florida Freshwater Plants: A Handbook of Common Aquatic Plants in Florida Lakes.* Gainesville: University of Florida, Institute of Food and Agricultural Sciences. 264 pp.

Murphy, T. R., D. L. Colvin, R. Dickens, J. W. Everest, D. Hall, and L. B. McCarty. N.d. *Weeds of Southern Turfgrasses.* Gainesville: Florida Cooperative Extension Service, Institute of Food and Agricultural Sciences, University of Florida. 208 pp.

Nelson, G. 1996. *The Shrubs and Woody Vines of Florida: A Reference and Field Guide.* Sarasota: Pineapple Press. 391 pp.

———. 1994. *The Trees of Florida: A Reference and Field Guide.* Sarasota: Pineapple Press. 338 pp.

Rufino, O. 2001. *A Gardener's Guide to Florida's Native Plants.* Gainesville: University Press of Florida. 345 pp.

Scurlock, J. P. 1987. *Native Trees and Shrubs of the Florida Keys: A Field Guide.* Bethel Park, Penn.: Laurel Press. 220 pp.

Taylor, W. K. 1998. *Florida Wildflowers in Their Natural Communities.* Gainesville: University Press of Florida. 384 pp.

———. 1992. *The Guide to Florida Wildflowers.* Dallas: Taylor Publishing. 320 pp.

Wunderlin, R. P., and B. F. Hansen. 2003. *Guide to the Vascular Plants of Florida.* 2nd ed. Gainesville: University Press of Florida. 787 pp.

Index

Note: Page numbers for illustrations are in italics.

Aaron's Skipper, 147, *215*, 231
Abdomen of caterpillars, 6
Abrus precatorius, 97
Abyssinian Mustard, 75, 76, *258*
Acacia: Pineland, 98, *265*; Sweet, 98, 265
Acacia farnesiana, 98, 265
Acacia pinetorum, 98, 265
Acanthaceae, 105, 106, 110, 112, 237–38
Acanthus family, 105, 106, 110, 112, 237–38
Achalarus lyciades, 127, 128, *195*, 271, 273
Acoelorrhaphe wrightii, 152
Adam's Needle, 159, 160, *221*
Admiral: Red, *15*, 109, *189*
Admirals, 5, 101, 112–15
Aeschynomene americana, 80, *266*
Aeschynomene viscidula, 80, 266
African Wild Sensitive Plant, 78, 79
Agalinis fasciculata, 110, *296*
Agalinis maritima, 110
Agalinis purpurea, 110
Agavaceae, 159, 160, 221
Agave family, 159, 160, 221
Agraulis vanillae, 20, *37*, 102, *183*, 297, 298
Alder: Hazel, 85, *258*
Alfalfa, 77
Alicia, 98, *271*
Alkaloids, 65
Alligatorflag, 157, *226*
Alnus serrulata, 85, *258*
Alvaradoa: Mexican, 82, *299*
Alvaradoa amorphoides, 82, *299*
Alysicarpus vaginalis, 126
Amaranth family, 93, 96, 123, 130, 136, 239–40
Amaranthaceae, 93, 96, 123, 130, 136, 239–40
Amblyscirtes aesculapius, 154, *203*, 228
Amblyscirtes alternata, 155, *205*

Amblyscirtes hegon, 153, *203*
Amblyscirtes reversa, 155, *207*, 228
Amblyscirtes vialis, 154, *205*
American Bluehearts, 110
American Cupscale, 139
American Elm, 107, *308*
American Hogpeanut, 125, 127, *267*
American Holly, 90
American Lady, *15*, 108, *189*
American Snout, *36*, 101, *181*, 261
American Wisteria, 125, 126
Amethyst Hairstreak, 86
Amorpha fruticosa, 77, 125, *266*
Amorpha herbacea, 266
Amorpha herbacea var. *crenulata*, 96
Amphicarpaea bracteata, 125, 127, *267*
Amyris balsamifera, 70, 302
Amyris elemifera, 69, 70, 71, *302*
Anacardiaceae, 84, 94, 95, 240
Anaea andria, 14, *15*, 21, *22*, *39*, 115, *191*, 263
Anaea troglodyta floridalis, 58, 115, *191*, 264
Anartia jatrophae, 13, 111, *185*, 310, 311
Anatomy of caterpillars, 3–8
Anatrytone logan, 25, 146, *207*, 227, 228, 231, 232, 233
Ancyloxypha numitor, 138, *205*, 230, 235
Andropogon species, 119, 140, 141
Andropogon virginicus, 120, 136, 137, 146, 157, *227*
Andropogon virginicus var. *glaucus*, 142
Annonaceae, 67, 69, 241–43
Annual Glasswort, 96
Anthanassa frisia, 105, *187*, 237
Anthanassa texana seminole, 14, 104, *187*, 238
Anthocharinae, 76
Anthocharis midea, 76
Ants, 2, 19, 20, 21, 23, 49, 78, 84

Apalachicola Toadflax, 110, 311

Apaturinae, 116–17

Aphid: Woolly Alder, 84, 85, 258; Woolly
    Maple, 84, *236*

Aphrissa statira, 79, *171*, 272

Apiaceae, 67, 71, 243–45

Apios americana, 125, 129, *267*

Apocynaceae, 101, 121, 122, 246–50

Appalachian Brown, 118, *195*, 225

Appias drusilla, 74, *169*, 259, 264

Aquifoliaceae, 84, 90, 250

Arecaceae, 123, 149, 152, 222–23

Areca Palm, 152

Aristolochiaceae, 67, 68, 251–53

Aristolochia elegans, *252*

Aristolochia gigantea, 68, *251*

Aristolochia grandiflora, 68, *251*

Aristolochia hastata, 253

Aristolochia littoralis, 67, 68, *252*

Aristolochia pentandra, 68

Aristolochia ringens, 68, *253*

Aristolochia serpentaria, 67, *253*

Aristolochia tomentosa, 66, 67, 68, 126, *252*

Arogos Skipper, 145, *205*, 233

Arrowroot: Florida, *220*

Arrowroot family, 123, 157, 226

Arugula, 76

Arundinaria gigantea, 117, 138, 146, 148, 154,
    155, *228*

Arundo donax, 138

Asbolis capucinus, 152, *217*, 222, 223

Ascia monuste, 75, *167*, 257, 259, 260

Asclepias curassavica, 50, 121, *246*

Asclepias curtissii, 121, 122

Asclepias humistrata, 121, 122, *246*

Asclepias incarnata, 121, 122, *247*

Asclepias lanceolata, 121, 122

Asclepias longifolia, 121, 122

Asclepias perennis, 121, 122, *247*

Asclepias tomentosa, 121, 122

Asclepias tuberosa, 121, 122

Ash: 61; Carolina, 72, 296; Green, 72, *296*;
    Wafer, *303*; White, 72, 296

Asian Pigeonwings, 126

Asimina angustifolia, 69, *241*

Asimina incana, 69, *241*

Asimina obovata, 69, *242*

Asimina parviflora, 69

Asimina pygmaea, 69, *242*

Asimina reticulata, 69, *243*

Asimina tetramera, 69

Asimina triloba, 69

Aster: 50; Climbing, 256; Eastern Silver, 256;
    Elliott's, 256; Rice Button, *256*; Walter's,
    256

Asteraceae, 74, 83, 93, 100, 104, 106, 108,
    109, 254–56

Aster dumosus, 256

Aster family, 74, 83, 93, 100, 104, 106, 108,
    109, 254–56

Asterocampa celtis, 25, *40*, 116, *191*, 261

Asterocampa clyton, *11*, 12, 17, *18*, 25, 116,
    191, 261

Atala, 17, 85, *171*, 220

Atalopedes campestris, 145, *209*

Ateramnus lucidus, 265

Atlantic Pigeonwings, 126, 128, 269, *271*

Atlantic Sedge, 118

Atlantic White Cedar, 52, 61, 91, *219*

Atlides halesus, 85, *173*, 312

Atrytone arogos, 145, *205*, 233

Atrytonopsis hianna, 152, *215*, 233

Autochton cellus, 127, *197*, 267

Avicenniaceae, 110, 257

Avicennia germinans, 63, 64, 110, *257*

Axonopus fissifolius, 119

Bacopa monnieri, 13, 111, *311*

Bahamian Swallowtail, 20, 70, *165*, 302, 303,
    305

Balloonvine: *306*; Small-fruited, 87

Balsam Torchwood, 70, 302

Bamboo: Common, 138; Golden, 138

Bambusa vulgaris, 138

Bandana-of-the-Everglades, 157, *223*

Banded Hairstreak, 87, *175*, 287, 290

Banded-Skipper: Golden, 127, *197*, 267

Baptisia alba, 133, 134, *268*

Baracoa Skipper, 141, *211*

Barbados Cherry, 130

Barbados Cherry family, 130, 292

Barnyardgrass: 138; Rough, 138

Barred Yellow, 80, *167*, 266, 284, 285

Bartram's Scrub-Hairstreak, 58, 93, *179*, 264

Basilarchia archippus, 10, *11*, 113, *183*, 305

Basilarchia arthemis astyanax, 21, *22*, *38*, 112,

183, 263, 301, 305

Bastard Indigobush, 77, 125, *266*

Bataceae, 76, 96, 257

Batis maritima, 63, 76, 96, *257*

Battus philenor, 5, 17, 67, *163*, 252, 253

Battus polydamas, 5, 14, *18*, 68, *163*, 251, 252, 253

Bay: Red, 73, *290*; Silk, 73, 290; Swamp, 61, 73, 290

Bayberry: Southern, 95, *295*

Bayberry family, 84, 95, 295

Bay Cedar, 93, 94, *306*

Bay Cedar family, 84, 93, 94, 306

Bayleaf Capertree, 74, 76, *259*

Beach False Foxglove, 110, *296*

Beaked Panicum, 138

Beaksedge: Narrowfruit Horned, 118, 151, *225*; Millet, 151, 225

Bean: Garden, 93, 126

Bearded Skeletongrass, 137, 156

Beech family, 84, 88, 89, 92, 95, 123, 131, 132, 287–89

Beggarticks, *254*

Beggarweed: Florida, *274*

Behavior of caterpillars, 12–14, 17–23

Bermudagrass, 139, 140, *229*

Berry's Skipper, 151, *209*

Betulaceae, 85, 113, 258

Bidens alba, 66, 83, *254*

Bigflower Pawpaw, 69, *242*

Biology of caterpillars, 8–12

Birch family, 85, 113, 258

Birdbill Woodoats, 228

Birthwort family, 67, 68, 251–53

Biscayne Pricklyash, 304

Bishopsweed: Mock, 71, *245*

Bitterbush family, 82, 299

Bitterbush: Florida, 82, *299*

Bittercress: Bulbous, 76, *259*; Pennsylvania, 76

Blackbead: Catclaw, 79; Florida Keys, 79, 97, *281*

Blackberry, 66

Black Cherry, 72, 87, 113, *301*

Black Locust, 125, *281*

Black Mangrove, 63, 64, 110, *257*

Black Mangrove family, 110, 257

Black Medick, 77, *279*

Black Mustard, *258*

Blacksenna: Piedmont, 110, 297; Yaupon, 110, *297*

Black Swallowtail, 1, 17, *19*, *20*, *27*, 71, *163*, 243, 244, 245, 304

Black Willow, 113, 305

Bladder Mallow, 93

Bladderpod, 133, *284*

Blechum pyramidatum, 112, *237*

Blue: Cassius, *33*, 84, 96, *181*, 275, 278, 281, 286, 300; Ceraunus, 84, 98, *181*, 268, 270, 271, 276, 286; Miami, 97, *179*, 268, 306; Nickerbean, 58, 84, 97, *179*, 265, 268

Bluehearts: American, 110

Blue Porterweed, 111, *310*

Blues, 4, 21, 47, 84, 96–100

Bluestem: 119, 140, 141; Broomsedge, 120, 136, 137, 146, 157, *227*; Chalky, 142

Bluestem grass, 119, 140, 141

Boehmeria cylindrica, 109, *308*

Bog Hemp, *308*

Boxthorn, 70

Brassicaceae, 74, 75, 76, 258–60

Brassica juncea, 75, 76, 258

Brassica nigra, 75, 76, *258*

Brassica oleracea, 66, 75

Brassica rapa, 66, 75

Brazilian Pepper, 50, 94, 95, *240*

Brazilian Satintail, 138, 147

Brazilian Skipper, 7, *16*, *44*, 157, *217*, 223, 226

Brephidium isophthalma, 96, *181*, 240, 257

Bristlegrass: Coral, 138

Bristly Greenbrier, 84, *236*

Brittle Thatch Palm, 152

Broad-winged Skipper, 148, *215*, 235

Broken-Dash: Northern, 144, *213*; Southern, *16*, 143, *213*

Broomrape family, 110, 296–97

Broomsedge Bluestem, 120, 136, 137, 146, 157, *227*

Brown: Appalachian, 118, *195*, 225

Browne's Blechum, 112, *237*

Brush-footed butterflies, 4, 5, 7, 14, 18, 101–22

Buchnera americana, 110

Buckeye: Common, 13, 109, *185*, 238, 296, 297, 311; Mangrove, 63, 110, *185*, 257; Tropical, 111, *185*, 310

Buckthorn family, 84, 93, 123, 132, 300
Buckwheat family, 84, 93
Buddlejaceae, 100
Bulbous Bittercress, 76, *259*
Burning Nettle, 109, 309
Bursera simarubra, 114, *260*
Burseriaceae, 114, 260
Bushbean: Wild, 93, 126
Butterflybush family, 100
Butterfly gardening, 50
Butterfly Pea: Pineland, 126, 129; Spurred, 126, 129, *269*, 271
Butterflyweed, 121, 122
Buttonwood, 64, 93
Byrsonima lucida, 130, *292*
Byssus Skipper, 146, *207*, 228, 232, 235

Cabbage, 66, 75
Cabbage Palm, 57, 62, 152, *222*
Cabbage White, 75, *167*, 258, 260
Caesalpinia bonduc, 97, *268*
Cakile lanceolata, 76
Calephelis virginiensis, *34*, 100, *181*, 254
Calico Flower, *252*
Callirhoe papaver, 134
Callophrys gryneus, 91
Callophrys henrici, 90
Callophrys hesseli, 91
Callophrys irus, 89
Callophrys niphon, 90
Calotropis gigantea, 121, *248*
Calpodes ethlius, 7, *16*, 44, 157, *217*, 223, 226
Caltrop family, 74, 80, 312
Calycopis cecrops, *32*, 95, *173*, 240, 295
Camphortree, 73
Canada Toadflax, 13, 110, *311*
Candlestick Plant, 78, 79, *282*
Canna, 50; Garden, 157; Yellow, *223*
Cannaceae, 123, 157, 223
Canna family, 123, 157, 223
Canna flaccida, 157, *223*
Canna indica, 157
Canna x generalis, 157
Cannibalism, 14
Cape Leadwort, 97, *300*
Caper: Limber, *259*
Capertree: Bayleaf, 74, 76, *259*
Capeweed, *310*

Capparis flexuosa, 74, 76, *259*
Capsella bursa-pastoris, 75
Cardamine bulbosa, 76, *259*
Cardamine pensylvanica, 76
Cardenolides, 65
Cardiospermum corindum, 87, 93, 97, *306*
Cardiospermum halicacabum, 87
Cardiospermum microcarpum, 87
Carex atlantica, 118
Carex glaucescens, 150, *224*
Carex lupuliformis, 151, *224*
Carex species, 151, 152
Carex verrucosa, 150
Carnivorous plants, 56, 64
Carolina Ash, 72, 296
Carolina Indigo, 98, 133, *276*
Carolina Satyr, 119, *193*, 234
Carolina Wild Petunia, 112
Carolina Willow, 113, *305*
Carpetgrass: Common, 119
Carpetweed, *310*
Carpetweed family, 74, 83
Carphephorus odoratissimus, 100
Carrot family, 67, 71, 243–45
Carya alba, 88, *290*
Carya floridana, 88, 290
Carya glabra, 88, *290*
Cashew family, 84, 94, 95, 240
Cassia alata, 282
Cassia bahamensis, 282
Cassia fasciculata, 270
Cassia fistula, 79
Cassia nictitans, 270
Cassia obtusifolia, 283
Cassia occidentalis, 283
Cassius Blue, *33*, 84, 96, *181*, 275, 278, 281, 286, 300
Catclaw Blackbead, 79
Cat Greenbrier, 84, 236
Ceanothus americanus, 93, 132, *300*
Cedar: Atlantic White, 52, 61, 91, *219*; Bay, 93, 94, *306*; Red, 91, *219*
Cedar family, 84, 91, 219
Celastrina ladon, 99, *179*
Celastrina neglecta, 99, *179*, 262
Celtidaceae, 84, 93, 101, 107, 116, 117, 261
Celtis laevigata, 101, 107, 116, 117, *261*
Celtis occidentalis, 116, 117, 261

Centipedegrass, 142
Centrosema arenicola, 126, 129
Centrosema virginianum, 126, 129, *269*, 271
Ceraunus Blue, 84, 98, *181*, 268, 270, 271, 276, 286
Cercis canadensis, 90, *269*
Cercyonis pegala, 120, *193*, 227
Chalky Bluestem, 142
Chamaecrista fasciculata, 78, 81, 92, 98, *270*
Chamaecrista nictitans, 78, 81, 98, *270*
Chamaecyparis thyoides, 52, 61, 91, *219*
Chapmannia floridana, 98, *271*
Chapman's Oak, 131, 132
Chapman's Wild Sensitive Plant, 78, 79, *282*
Charaxinae, 115–16
Chasmanthium latifolium, 155, 228
Chasmanthium laxum, 118, 138, 147, 148, *228*
Chasmanthium nitidum, 228
Chasmanthium ornithorhynchum, 228
Checkered-Skipper: Common, 134, *203*, 293; Tropical, 135, *203*, 293; White, *16*, 134, *201*, 293
Checkered White, *29*, 46, 74, *167*, 260
Checkerspot: Silvery, 17, 104, *187*
Checklist of Florida butterflies, 313–18
Cheesytoes, 80, *285*
Chenopodium album, 136, 239
Cherry: 20; Barbados, 130; Black, 72, 87, 113, *301*
Chickweed: Indian, 83
Chinese Wisteria, 125
Chitin, 3
Chlorostrymon maesites, 86
Chlorostrymon simaethis, 86, *177*, 306
Chlosyne nycteis, 17, 104, *187*
Chrysalidocarpus lutescens, 152
Chrysalis, 26
Cicuta maculata, 71, *243*
Cinnamomum camphora, 73
Cirsium horridulum, 100, 109, *254*
Citrus arantium, 70, 303
Citrus aurantifolia, 69, 71, 303
Citrus family, 67, 69, 70, 71, 302–5
Citrus limon, 69, 303
Citrus reticulata, 69, *303*
Citrus sinensis, 69, 303
Citrus x paradisi, 70, 303

Cladium jamaicense, 150, *225*
Climbing Aster, 256
Climbing Hempvine, 100
Clitoria mariana, 126, 128, 269, *271*
Clitoria ternata, 126
Clouded Skipper, *16*, 137, *203*, 228, 231, 232, 234, 235
Cloudless Sulphur, 13, *14*, *30*, 78, *171*, 270, 282, 283
Cloudywing: Confused, 129, *197*; Northern, 128, *195*, 285; Southern, 128, *195*, 271, 277
Clover: 99; White, 77, *286*
Clustered Sedge, 150, *224*
Coastalplain Willow, *305*
Coastal Searocket, 76
Coast Cockspur, 138
Coccothrinax argentata, 152
Coconut Palm, 152, *222*
Cocos nucifera, 152, *222*
Cofaqui Giant-Skipper, *16*, 45, 160, *217*, 221
Coffeeweed, 78, 82, *283*
Cogongrass, 50, 136, 138, 146, 147, 156, 157
Coinvine, 80, 92, *272*
Coliadinae, 77–83
Colias cesonia, 77
Colias eurytheme, 77, *169*, 279, 286
Collecting caterpillars, 46
Coloration, 17
Combretaceae, 93
Combretum family, 93
Comma: Eastern, *15*, 25, 107, *189*
Common Bamboo, 138
Common Buckeye, 13, 109, *185*, 238, 296, 297, 311
Common Carpetgrass, 119
Common Checkered-Skipper, 134, *203*, 293
Common Fanpetals, 93, 94, 134, 135, *293*
Common Hoptree, 69, *303*
Common Pawpaw, 69
Common Plantain, 110
Common Pricklyash, 304
Common Roadside-Skipper, 154, *205*
Common Sootywing, 135, *201*, 239
Common Sweetleaf, 88, *307*
Common Wireweed, *293*
Common Wood-Nymph, 120, *193*, 227
Cone-bearing plants, 219–20
Confused Cloudywing, 129, *197*

Conocarpus erectus, 64, 93
Coontie, 85, *220*
Copaeodes minimus, 139, *213*, 229
Coral Bristlegrass, 138
Coral Dropseed, 158, 234
Coral Hairstreak, 87, *173*
Cordgrass: Saltmarsh, 158, 233; Smooth, *233*
Cork Elm, *307*
Corkystem Passionflower, 102, 103, *298*
Corn, 138
Cornaceae, 99
Cornus florida, 99
Cottonweed, 93
Cottonwoods, 113
Cowbane: Water, 71, *244*
Cowpea: Hairypod, 93, 97, 126, 127, *286*
Crabgrass: Southern, 137, 143
Crabwood, 114, *265*
Crataegus marshallii, 89
Creeping Ticktrefoil, 93, 126, 127, 128, *273*
Crescent: Cuban, 105, *187*, 237; Pearl, 14, 25, 35, 106, *187*, 256; Phaon, 17, 105, *187*, 310; 'Seminole' Texan, 14, 104, *187*, 238
Crossline Skipper, 142, *211*, 227
Crotalaria spectabilis, 126
Croton: 101; Healing, *263*; Pineland, 94, 115, *264*; Silver, 116, *263*; Wild, 264; Woolly, 116
Croton argyranthemus, 116, *263*
Croton capitatus, 116
Croton linearis, 94, 115, *264*
Ctenium aromaticum, 64, 145
Cuban Crescent, 105, *187*, 237
Cuban Jute, 134, 135, *293*
Cupressaceae, 84, 91, 219
Cupscale: American, 139
Curcuma zedoaria, 157
Curtiss' Milkweed, 121, 122
Custard-Apple family, 67, 69, 241–43
Cutgrass: Giant, *235*; Southern, 139, 159, *230*
Cuticle, 3, 8
Cyanogenic glycosides, 65
Cyllopsis gemma, 118, *195*, 228
Cymaenes tripunctus, 137, *203*, 235
Cynanchum angustifolium, 122, *248*
Cynanchum scoparium, 248
Cynanchum species, 122
Cynodon dactylon, 139, 140, *229*

Cyperaceae, 118, 119, 150, 151, 152, 224–26
Cypress, 61

Daggerwing: Ruddy, 114, *191*, 294, 295
Dahoon, 90, *250*
Dainty Sulphur, 83, *167*, 254
Dalbergia ecastaphyllum, 80, 92, *272*
Dalea feayi, 77, *272*
Dalea pinnata, 77, *273*
Dallisgrass, 138
Danainae, 121–22
Danaus eresimus, 122, *193*, 246, 248, 249, 250
Danaus gilippus, 42, 121, *193*, 246, 247, 248, 249, 250
Danaus plexippus, 17, 65, 121, *191*, 246, 247, 248, 249, 250
Danglepod, 98, 133, 284
Date Palm, 152
Daucus carota, 1, 71
Deerberry, 113, *263*
Deeringothamnus pulchellus, 69
Deeringothamnus rugelii, 69
Deertongue Witchgrass, 138
Defense, 17–21, 23
Delaware Skipper, 25, 146, *207*, 227, 228, 231, 232, 233
Desmodium floridanum, 126
Desmodium incanum, 93, 126, 127, 128, *273*
Desmodium paniculatum, 93, 126
Desmodium strictum, 128
Desmodium tenuifolium, 126
Desmodium tortuosum, 125, 126, 127, *274*
Desmodium triflorum, 127
Desmodium viridiflorum, 126, 128, 129
Diapause, 10
Dichanthelium aciculare, 142, *229*
Dichanthelium clandestinum, 138
Dicliptera sexangularis, 105, *237*
Dicotyledons, 237–312
Dictyosperma album, 152
Digitaria ciliaris, 137, 143
Dina Yellow, 82, 169, 299
Dingy Purplewing, *15*, 17, 113, *185*, 260
Dion Skipper, 150, *209*, 224, 226
Distichlis spicata, 158, *230*
Diversity of butterflies, 1, 51
Dixie Ticktrefoil, 125, 126, 127, *274*
Dogbane family, 101, 121, 122, 246–50

Dogface: Southern, 77, *169*, 266, 272, 273, 286
Dogwood: Flowering, 99; Jamaican, *280*
Dogwood family, 99
Dorantes Longtail, 126, *197*, 273, 274
Dotted Skipper, 140, *211*
Downy Milkpea, 93, 97, 126, 133, *275*
Dropseed: Coral, 158, 234; Seashore, 158, *234*
Dryas iulia, 102, *183*, 298
Drypetes diversifolia, 74, *264*
Drypetes lateriflora, 74, *264*
Dukes' Skipper, 151, *209*, 224, 225
Dun Skipper, 151, *209*
Dusky Roadside-Skipper, 155, *205*
Duskywing: 12; Florida, 58, *199*, 292; Horace's, 131, *199*, 287, 288, 289; Juvenal's, 131, *199*, 287; Mottled, 132, *199*, 300; Sleepy, *12*, *16*, 130, *199*, 287, 288; Wild Indigo, 133, *201*, *268*; Zarucco, 133, *199*, 274, 275, 284
Dusted Skipper, 152, *215*, 233
Dutchman's-Pipe: Elegant, 67, 68, *252*; Gaping, 68, *253*; Giant, 68, *251*; Largeflower, 68, *251*; Marsh's, 68; Woolly, 66, 67, 68, 126, *252*
Dwarf Pawpaw, 69, *242*
Dyschoriste humistrata, 110, *238*
Dyschoriste oblongifolia, 110, *238*

Earleaf Greenbrier, 84, 236
Eastern Comma, *15*, 25, 107, *189*
Eastern Gamagrass, 137, 138, 147, *235*
Eastern Milkpea, 93, 126, 129, 133
Eastern Pine Elfin, 90, *175*, 220
Eastern Pygmy-Blue, 96, *181*, 240, 257
Eastern Redbud, 90, *269*
Eastern Silver Aster, 256
Eastern Tailed-Blue, 84, 98, *181*
Eastern Tiger Swallowtail, 10, 21, 71, *163*, 291, 292, 296, 301
Echinochloa crusgalli, 138
Echinochloa muricata, 138
Echinochloa walteri, 138
Ecology of butterflies, 2, 8–12
'Edwards' Spring Azure, 99, *179*
Egg laying, 20, 25, 47, 66
Egyptian Paspalidium, 138
Electrostrymon angelia, 94, *173*, 240, 280

Elegant Dutchman's-Pipe, 67, 68, *252*
Elephantgrass, 138
Eleusine indica, 143
Elfin: Eastern Pine, 90, *175*, 220; Frosted, 89, *175*, 278; Henry's, 84, 90, *177*, 250, 269
Elliott's Aster, 256
Elliott's Milkpea, 126, 129, 133, *274*
Elm: 107, 108; American, 107, *308*; Cork, *307*; Winged, 107, *307*
Elm family, 107, 307–8
Emperor: Hackberry, 25, *40*, 116, *191*, 261; Tawny, *11*, 12, 17, *18*, 25, 116, *191*, 261
Emperors, 14, 101, 116–17
English Plantain, 110
Enodia portlandia, *41*, 117, *195*, 228
Epargyreus clarus, *15*, 17, 18, 20, 124, *197*, 266, 267, 274, 275, 281
Epargyreus zestos, 124, *197*, 275
Ephryiades brunneus, 58, *199*, 292
Epidermis, 3
Eremochloa ophiuroides, 142
Erianthus giganteus, 232
Ericaceae, 84, 89, 100, 113, 262–63
Eruca vesicaria, 76
Eryngium cuneifolium, 71
Eryngo: Wedgeleaf, 71
Erynnis baptisiae, 133, *201*, 268
Erynnis brizo, *12*, *16*, 130, *199*, 287, 288
Erynnis horatius, 131, *199*, 287, 288, 289
Erynnis juvenalis, 131, *199*, 287, 288
Erynnis martialis, 132, *199*, 300
Erynnis zarucco, 133, *199*, 274, 275, 276, 284
Eufala Skipper, 156, *207*, 233
Eumaeus atala, 17, 85, *171*, 220
Eunica monima, *15*, 17, 113, *185*, 260
Eunica tatila, 21, *22*, 114, *185*, 265
Euphorbiaceae, 74, 94, 114, 115, 116, 263–65
Euphyes arpa, *16*, 26, 149, *207*, 223
Euphyes berryi, 151, *209*
Euphyes dion, 150, *209*, 224, 226
Euphyes dukesi, 151, *209*, 224, 225
Euphyes pilatka, 59, 149, *207*, 225
Euphyes vestris, 151, *209*
Euptoieta claudia, 103, *183*
Eurema daira, 80, *167*, 266, 284, 285
Eurema dina, 82, *169*, 299
Eurema lisa, 81, *167*, 280
Eurema nicippe, 5, 82, *169*, 282, 283

Eurema nise, 81, *169*, 278

Eurytides marcellus, 14, *20*, 68, *163*, 241, 242, 243

Eustachys petraea, 156

Everes comyntas, 84, 98, *181*

Everglades Palm, 152

Everlasting: Narrowleaf Purple, 108, *255*; Pennsylvania, 108, *255*; Spoonleaf Purple, 108; Sweet, 108, *256*

Exoskeleton, 3

Fabaceae, 74, 77, 78, 79, 80, 81, 82, 86, 90, 92, 95, 96, 97, 98, 99, 109, 123, 124, 125, 126, 127, 128, 129, 133, 134, 265–86

Fagaceae, 84, 88, 89, 92, 95, 123, 131, 132, 287–89

Fakahatcheegrass, *235*

Falcate Orangetip, 76, *165*, 259

Fall Panicgrass, 138

False face patterns, 17

False Foxglove: Beach, 110, *296*; Purple, 110; Saltmarsh, 110

False Hop Sedge, 151, *224*

False Indigobush, *266*

False Mallow, 135

False Nettle, 109, *308*

False Pawpaw: Pretty, 69; Rugel's, 69

False Tamarind, 79, 81, 97, *278*

Fanpetals: Common, 93, 94, 134, 135, *293*

Feay's Palafox, 93

Feay's Prairieclover, 77, *272*

Feniseca tarquinius, 4, 25, *31*, 84, *171*, 236, 258

Fennel: Sweet, 50, 71, *244*

Ferns, 62

Fewflower Milkweed, 121, 122

Ficus aurea, 115, *294*

Ficus citrifolia, 115, *295*

Fiery Skipper, 139, *209*, 229, 234

Fig: Golden, *294*; Short-leaved, *295*; Strangler, *165*, *294*

Finding caterpillars, 46–47

Fingergrass: Pinewoods, 156

Fireflag, *226*

Fishpoison Tree: Florida, 94, 95, 125, *280*

Fixsenia favonius, 89, *173*

Flatwoods, 55

Flax: Florida Yellow, 104

Flax family, 104

Flies, 48, 49

Florida Arrowroot, *220*

Florida Beggarweed, *274*

Florida Bitterbush, 82, *299*

Florida Duskywing, 58, *199*, 292

Florida Fishpoison Tree, 94, 95, 125, *280*

Florida Hammock Milkpea, 96, 97, 124, 126, *275*

Florida Hoarypea, 129, *285*

Florida Keys Blackbead, 79, 97, *281*

Florida Leafwing, 58, 115, *191*, 264

Florida Milkvine, 122, *249*

Florida Paspalum, 138

Florida Pellitory, 109, *309*

Florida Purplewing, 21, *22*, 114, *185*, 265

Florida Royal Palm, 152

Florida Silver Palm, 152

Florida Thatch Palm, 152

Florida Ticktrefoil, 126

Florida White, 74, 169, 259, 264

Florida Yellow Flax, 104

Flowering Dogwood, 99

Foeniculum vulgare, 50, 71, *244*

Fogfruit: Turkey Tangle, 50, 106, 110, 111, *310*

Foldwing: Sixangle, 105, *237*

Fountaingrass, 138

Fourleaf Vetch, 81

Fourpetal Pawpaw, 69

Fowl Managrass, 153

Fraxinus americana, 72, *296*

Fraxinus caroliniana, 72, *296*

Fraxinus pennsylvanica, 72, *296*

Fritillary: Gulf, 20, *37*, 102, *183*, 297, 298; Variegated, 103, *183*

Froelichia floridana, 93

Frosted Elfin, 89, *175*, 278

Fulvous Hairstreak, 94, *173*, 240, 280

Fungus, 2

Galactia elliottii, 126, 129, 133, *274*

Galactia regularis, 93, 126, 129, 133

Galactia striata, 96, 97, 124, 126, *275*

Galactia volubilis, 93, 97, 126, 133, *275*

Gallberry, 55

Gamagrass: Eastern, 137, 138, 147, *235*

Gamochaeta falcata, 108, *255*

Gamochaeta pensylvanica, 108, *255*
Gamochaeta purpurea, 108
Gaping Dutchman's-Pipe, 68, *253*
Garden Bean, 83, 126
Garden Canna, 157
Garden Radish, 75, 126
Gemmed Satyr, 118, *195*, 228
Georgia Satyr, 119, *193*
Giant Cutgrass, *235*
Giant Dutchman's-Pipe, 68, *251*
Giant Milkweed, 121, *248*
Giant Reed, 138
Giant-Skipper: Cofaqui, *16*, *45*, 160, *217*, 221; Yucca, *16*, 159, *217*, 221
Giant-Skippers, 25, 159–60
Giant Swallowtail, 17, *19*, 20, *21*, 69, *165*, 302, 303, 304, 305
Ginger family, 123, 157
Glands, 18–21, 22, 25, 26, 159, 160
Glasswort: Annual, 96; Perennial, 96, *240*; Virginia, *240*
Glassworts, 63, 96
Glassywing: Little, 144, *215*
Glossy Shower, 78, 79
Glucosinolates, 65
Glyceria striata, 153
Glycine, 126
Gnaphalium falcatum, 255
Gnaphalium obtusifolium, 256
Gnaphalium pensylvanicum, 255
Goatweed Leafwing, 14, *15*, 21, *22*, *39*, 115, *191*, 263
Golden Bamboo, 138
Golden Banded-Skipper, 127, *197*, 267
Golden Fig, *294*
Golden Shower, 79
Goosegrass: Indian, 143
Granny-Bush, *264*
Grapefruit, 70, 303
Grasses, 101, 123
Grass family, 117, 118, 119, 120, 136, 137, 138, 139, 140, 141, 142, 143, 144, 145, 146, 147, 148, 149, 153, 154, 155, 156, 157, 158, 159, 227–35
Grass-Skippers, 136–59
Gray Hairstreak, 84, 92, *177*, 270, 272, 273, 277, 286, 293, 300, 306
Gray Ministreak, 95, *173*, 277

Gray Nicker, 97, *268*
Great Purple Hairstreak, 85, *173*, 312
Great Southern White, 75, *167*, 257, 259, 260
Green Ash, 72, *296*
Greenbrier: Bristly, 84, *236*; Cat, 84, 236; Earleaf, 84, 236; Saw, 84, 236
Green Shrimp Plant, *237*
Gregarious caterpillars, 14
Groundnut, 125, 129, *267*
Growth, 25
Guajacum sanctum, 80, *312*
Guiana Plum, 74, *264*
Guineagrass, 137, 138, *231*
Gulf Coast Swallowwort, 122, *248*
Gulf Fritillary, 20, *37*, 102, *183*, 297, 298
Gumbo-Limbo, 114, *260*
Gumbo-Limbo family, 114, 260
Gymnanthes lucida, 114, *265*
Gymnopogon ambiguus, 137, 156
Gymnosperms, 219–20

Habitat, 46, 50–64
Hackberry, 50, 101, 116, 117, 261
Hackberry Emperor, 25, *40*, 116, *191*, 261
Hackberry family, 84, 93, 101, 107, 116, 117, 261
Hairstreak: Amethyst, 86; Banded, 87, *175*, 287, 290; Coral, 87, *173*; Fulvous, 94, *173*, 240, 280; Gray, 84, 92, *177*, 270, 272, 273, 277, 286, 293, 300, 306; Great Purple, 85, *173*, 312; Hessel's, 91, *175*, 219; Juniper, 91, *175*, 219; King's, 88, *175*, 307; Oak, 89, *173*; Red-banded, *32*, 95, *173*, 240, 295; Silver-banded, 86, *177*, 306; Striped, 88, *177*, 262; White M, 84, 92, *177*, 287, 289
Hairstreaks, 4, 5, 10, 21, 25, 47, 84, 85–95, 223
Hairy Indigo, 81, 98
Hairy Lespedeza, 128, 129, *277*
Hairypod Cowpea, 93, 97, 126, 127, *286*
Hammock, 57, 59, 62
Hammock Skipper, 125, *199*, 280
Harkenclenus titus, 87, *173*
Harvester, 4, 25, *31*, 84, *171*, 236, 258
Hawthorn: Parsley, 89
Hayhurst's Scallopwing, 129, *201*, 239
Hazel Alder, 85, *258*
Heads of caterpillars, 4

Healing Croton, *263*
Heartleaf Nettle, 109, *309*
Heartseed, 87, 93, 97, *306*
Heath family, 84, 89, 100, 113, 262–63
Helianthus divaricatus, 104
Helianthus strumosus, 104
Heliconian: Julia, 102, *183*, 298; Zebra, 103, *183*, 297, 298
Heliconians, 101, 102–4
Heliconiinae, 102–4
Heliconius charitonius, *183*, 297, 298
Heliotrope, 50
Hemiargus ammon, 58, 84, 97, *179*, 265, 268
Hemiargus ceraunus, 84, 98, *181*, 268, 270, 271, 276, 286
Hemiargus thomasi, 97, *179*, 268, 306
Hemp: Indian, *293*
Hempvine: Climbing, 100
Henry's Elfin, 84, 90, *177*, 250, 269
Heraclides andraemon, 20, 70, *165*, 302, 303, 305
Heraclides aristodemus, 20, 70, *165*, 302
Heraclides cresphontes, 17, 19, 20, *21*, 69, *165*, 302, 303, 304, 305
Herb-of-Grace, 13, 111, *311*
Hercules-club, 69, *304*
Herissantia crispa, 93
Hermeuptychia sosybius, 119, *193*, 234
Hesperia attalus, 140, *211*
Hesperia meskei, 59, 140, *211*
Hesperiidae, 123–60
Hesperiinae, 136–59
Hessel's Hairstreak, 91, *175*, 219
Heteropogon melanocarpus, 138
Hibernaculum, 10, 11
Hibernation, 10
Hickory: Mockernut, 88, 290; Pignut, 88, *290*; Scrub, 88, 290
Hoary Edge, 127, *195*, 271, 273
Hoarypea: Florida, 129, *285*
Hogpeanut: American, 125, 127, *267*
Holly: American, 90
Holly family, 84, 90, 250
Holywood Lignumvitae, 80, *312*
Hoptree: Common, 69, *303*
Horace's Duskywing, 131, *199*, 287, 288, 289
Horse Sugar, *307*
Host plants, 65, 219–312

Hurricane Palm, 152
Hylephila phyleus, 139, *209*, 229, 234

Identifying caterpillars, 23–25
Ilex cassine, 90, *250*
Ilex opaca, 90
Imperata braziliensis, 138, 147
Imperata cylindrica, 50, 136, 138, 146, 147, 156, 157
Incense Passionflower, 297
Incisalia henrici, 84, 90, *177*, 250, 269
Incisalia irus, 89, *175*, 278
Incisalia niphon, 90, *175*, 220
India Mustard, 75, 76, 258
Indian Chickweed, 83
Indian Goosegrass, 143
Indiangrass: Lopsided, 136, 145, 146, 153, 156, 157, *233*
Indian Hemp, *293*
Indian Shot, 157
Indian Woodoats, 155, 228
Indigo: Carolina, 98, 133, *276*; Hairy, 81, 98; Trailing, 98, 133, *276*
Indigobush: Bastard, 77, 125, *266*; False, *266*; Lusterspike, 266
Indigofera caroliniana, 98, 133, *276*
Indigofera hirsuta, 81, 98
Indigofera spicata, 98, 133, *276*
Invasive plants, 50
Iresine diffusa, 130, *239*

Jamaican Dogwood, *280*
Jamaica Swamp Sawgrass, 150, *225*
Johnsongrass, 138
Jointvetch: Sticky, 80, 266
Jointweed: Tall, 93
Juba's Bush, 130, *239*
Juglandaceae, 84, 88, 290
Julia Heliconian, 102, *183*, 298
Juniper Hairstreak, 91, *175*, 219
Juniperus silicicola, 219
Juniperus virginiana, 91, *219*
Junonia coenia, 13, 109, *185*, 238, 296, 297, 311
Junonia evarete, 63, 110, *185*, 257
Junonia genoveva, 111, *185*, 310
Justicia ovata, 105, 106, *238*
Jute: Cuban, 134, 135, *293*
Juvenal's Duskywing, 131, *199*, 287

Karum Tree, 95, 125
Key Lime, 69, 71, 303
Key to butterfly caterpillars, 23–24
King's Hairstreak, 88, *175*, 307
Kricogonia lyside, 80, *165*, 312
Kudzu, 125, 126, 127

Lace-winged Roadside-Skipper, 154, *203*, 228
Lady: American, *15*, 108, *189*; Painted, 108, *189*
Lamb'squarters, 136, *239*
Lantana, 50
Laportea species, 107
Largeflower Dutchman's-Pipe, 68, *251*
Large Orange Sulphur, 79, *171*, 278, 281
Latexplant, 122, *249*
Lauraceae, 67, 73, 290–91
Laurel family, 67, 73, 290–91
Laurel Oak, 92, 132, *287*
Lead Plant: Miami, 96
Leadtree: White, 95, *277*
Leadwort: 50; Cape, 97, *300*
Leadwort family, 97, 300
Leafless Swallowwort, 248
Leafwing: Florida, 58, 115, *191*, 264; Goat-weed, 14, *15*, 21, *22*, *39*, 115, *191*, 263
Leafwings, 101, 115–16
Least Skipper, 138, *205*, 230, 235
Least Snoutbean, 126
Leersia hexandra, 139, 159, *230*
Legumes, 65
Lemon, 69, 303
Lenticles, 5
Lepidium virginicum, 46, 75, 76, *260*
Lepidoptera, 1
Leptotes cassius, *33*, 84, 96, *181*, 275, 278, 281, 286, 300
Lerema accius, *16*, 137, *203*, 228, 231, 232, 234, 235
Lerodea eufala, 156, *207*, 233
Lespedeza: 129; Hairy, 128, 129, *277*
Lespedeza hirta, 128, 129, *277*
Lespedeza species, 129
Leucaena leucocephala, 95, *277*
Libytheana carinenta, *36*, 101, *181*, 261
Life cycles of butterflies, 25–45
Lignumvitae: Holywood, 80, *312*
Limber Caper, *259*

Lime: Key, 69, 71, 303
Limenitidinae, 112–15
Limenitis archippus, 113
Limenitis arthemis astyanax, 112
Lime Pricklyash, *305*
Linaceae, 104
Linaria canadensis, 13, 110, *311*
Linaria floridana, 110, 311
Lindera benzoin, 73
Linum floridanum, 104
Liriodendron tulipifera, 72, *291*
Litsea aestivalis, 73
Little Glassywing, 144, *215*
Little Metalmark, *34*, 100, *181*, 254
Little Wood-Satyr, 120, *193*
Little Yellow, 81, *167*, 280
Loblolly Bay, 61
Loblolly Pine, 56, 91
Locust: Black, 125, *281*
Locustberry: Long Key, 130, *292*
Long Key Locustberry, 130, *292*
Longleaf Milkweed, 121, 122
Longleaf Pine, 54, 56
Longtail: Dorantes, 126, *197*, 273, 274
Long-tailed Skipper, 5, *15*, 17, 25, *26*, *43*, 66, 125, *197*, 269, 271, 273, 274, 275, 286
Looseflower Waterwillow, 105, 106, *238*
Lopsided Indiangrass, 136, 145, 146, 153, 156, 157, *233*
Love-In-A-Puff, 87
Lupine: Sky-Blue, 93; Sundial, 90, *278*
Lupinus diffusus, 93
Lupinus perennis, 90, *278*
Lusterspike Indigobush, 266
Lycaenidae, 84–100
Lyside Sulphur, 80, *165*, 312
Lysiloma latisiliquum, 79, 81, 97, *278*

Macroptilium lathyroides, 93, 126
Magnoliaceae, 72, 291–92
Magnolia family, 67, 72, 291–92
Magnolia virginiana, 61, 72, *292*
Maidencane, 138, 146, 148, *231*
Malachite, 112, *187*, 237
Mallow: Bladder, 93; False, 135
Mallow family, 84, 93, 109, 123, 134, 135, 293–94

Mallow Scrub-Hairstreak, 84, 94, *177*, 293, 294, 306
Malpighiaceae, 130, 292
Malpighia emarginata, 130
Malvaceae, 84, 93, 94, 109, 123, 134, 135, 293–94
Malvastrum corchorifolium, 135
Managrass: Fowl, 153
Mangifera indica, 95
Mango, 95
Mangrove: 63, 64; Black, 63, 64, 110, *257*; Red, 63, 64, 123, *301*
Mangrove Buckeye, 63, 110, *185*, 257
Mangrove Skipper, 123, *199*, 301
Manila Palm, 152
Marantaceae, 123, 157, 226
Marpesia petreus, 114, *191*, 294, 295
Marshes, 62, 63
Marsh's Dutchman's-Pipe, 68
Martial Scrub-Hairstreak, 93, *179*, 261, 268, 306
Maryland Wild Sensitive Plant, 78
Matchheads, *310*
Matelea floridana, 122, *249*
Maypop, *297*
Medicago lupulina, 77, *279*
Medicago sativa, 77
Medick: Black, 77, *279*
Megathyminae, 159–60
Megathymus cofaqui, 16, 45, 160, *217*, 221
Megathymus yuccae, 16, 159, *217*, 221
Megisto cymela, 120, *193*
Melilotus alba, 77, *279*
Meske's Skipper, 59, 140, *211*
Metalmark: Little, *34*, 100, *181*, 254
Metalmarks, 100
Metamorphosis, 25–45
Mexican Alvaradoa, 82, *299*
Miami Blue, 97, *179*, 268, 306
Miami Lead Plant, 96
Mikania scandens, 100
Miletinae, 84
Milkpea: Downy, 93, 97, 126, 133, *275*; Eastern, 93, 126, 129, 133; Elliott's, 126, 129, 133, *274*; Florida Hammock, 96, 97, 124, 126, *275*
Milkvine: Florida, 122, *249*

Milkweed: 65, 101, 121, 122; Curtiss,' 121, 122; Fewflower, 121, 122; Giant, 121, *248*; Longleaf, 121, 122; Pinewoods, 121, 122, *246*; Pink Swamp, 121, 122, *247*; Sandhill, *246*; Scarlet, 50, 121, *246*; Velvetleaf, 121, 122; White, 121, 122, *247*
Milkweed butterflies, 5, 101, 121–22
Millet Beaksedge, 151, 225
Mimosa strigillosa, 81, *280*
Mimosa Yellow, 81, *169*, 278
Ministreak: Gray, 95, *173*, 277
Ministrymon azia, 95, *173*, 277
Mistletoe: Oak, 86, *312*
Mistletoe family, 84, 86, 312
Mitoura grynea, 91, *175*, 219
Mitoura hesseli, 91, *175*, 219
Mock Bishopsweed, 71, *245*
Mockernut Hickory, 88, 290
Molluginaceae, 74, 83
Mollugo verticillata, 83
Molting, 8–9, 25
Monarch, 17, 65, 121, *191*, 246, 247, 248, 249, 250
Moneywort: White, 126
Monk Skipper, 152, *217*, 222, 223
Monocotyledons, 221–36
Moraceae, 115, 294–95
Morrenia odorata, 122, *249*
Moths, 2, 19, 26, 123, 223
Mottled Duskywing, 132, *199*, 300
Mourning Cloak, 107, *189*
Mouth parts of caterpillars, 4
Mulberry family, 115, 294–95
Mustard: Abyssinian, 75, 76, *258*; Black, *258*; India, 75, 76, 258
Mustard family, 74, 75, 76, 258–60
Myricaceae, 84, 95, 295
Myrica cerifera, 95, 295
Myrica cerifera var. *pumila*, 295
Myrtle: Wax, *295*
Myrtle Oak, 131, 132, *288*

Narrowfruit Horned Beaksedge, 118, 151, *225*
Narrowleaf Purple Everlasting, 108, *255*
Nastra lherminier, 136, *205*, 227, 233
Nastra neamathla, 136, *205*, 227
Nasturtium, 76

Nasturtium family, 76
Nathalis iole, 83, *167*, 254
Neamathla Skipper, 136, *205*, 227
Nectar glands, 20, 78
Needleleaf Witchgrass, 142, *229*
Neonympha areolata, 119, *193*
Neoprociphilus aceris, 84, *236*
Neptunia pubescens, 98
Nests, 10, 14, 15, 16, 17
Netted Pawpaw, 69, *243*
Nettle: 107, 109; Burning, 109, 309;
    Heartleaf, 109, *309*; Stinging, 109
Nettle family, 107, 109, 308–9
Nettletree, 93, *261*
New Jersey Tea, 93, 132, *300*
Nicker: Gray, 97, *268*
Nickerbean Blue, 58, 84, 97, *179*, 265, 268
Northern Broken-Dash, 144, *213*
Northern Cloudywing, 128, *195*, 285
Northern Spicebush, 73
Nymphalidae, 101–22
Nymphalinae, 104–12
Nymphalis antiopa, 107, *189*

Oak: 48, 55, 65, 95; Chapman's, 131, 132;
    Laurel, 92, 132, *287*; Myrtle, 131, 132, *288*;
    Post, 92, *289*; Sand Live, 89, 92, 132, 289;
    Scrub, 131, 132; Southern Red, 131; Tur-
    key, 54, 88, 131, 132, *287*; Virginia Live, 92,
    132, *289*; Water, 92, 132, *288*
Oak Hairstreak, 89, *173*
Oak Mistletoe, 86, *312*
Oblongleaf Twinflower, 110, *238*
Obscure Skipper, 158, *213*, 230, 234
Ocola Skipper, 158, *213*, 230
Oleaceae, 67, 72, 296
Oligoria maculata, 156, *217*, 227, 233
Olive family, 67, 72, 296
Oplismenus hirtellus, 119
Orange: Sour, 70, 303; Sweet, 69, 303; Tri-
    foliate, 70
Orange-barred Sulphur, 13, 78, *171*, 282
Orange Sulphur, 77, *169*, 279, 286
Orangetip: Falcate, 76, *165*, 259
Orangetips, 74, 76
Orchids, 56, 64
Organs of caterpillars, 7, 8

Ornamentation of caterpillars, 5
Orobanchaceae, 110, 296–97
Osmeterium, 20, 21, 67
Overwintering, 10, 12, 13
Oxydendrum arboreum, 100, *262*
Oxypolis filiformis, 71, *244*
Oysterwood, *265*

Painted Lady, 108, *189*
Palafox: Feay's, 93
Palafoxia feayi, 93
Palamedes Swallowtail, *21*, 26, 66, 72, *163*,
    290
Palatka Skipper, 59, 149, *207*, 225
Paleleaf Woodland Sunflower, 104
Palm: Areca, 152; Brittle Thatch, 152; Cab-
    bage, 57, 62, 152, *222*; Coconut, 152, *222*;
    Date, 152; Everglades, 152; Florida Royal,
    152; Florida Silver, 152; Florida Thatch,
    152; Hurricane, 152; Manila, 152
Palmetto: Saw, 55, 149, 152, *223*; Scrub, 149,
    152
Palmetto Skipper, *16*, 26, 149, *207*, 223
Palm family, 123, 149, 152, 222–23
Palms, 58
Panicgrass: Fall, 138
Panicledleaf Ticktrefoil, 93, 126
Panicum: Beaked, 138; Redtop, 138, 146, *232*;
    Savannah, 138
Panicum aciculare, 229
Panicum anceps, 138
Panicum dichotomiflorum, 138
Panicum hemitomon, 138, 146, 148, *231*
Panicum maximum, 137, 138, *231*
Panicum repens, 159
Panicum rigidulum, 138, 146, *232*
Panoquina ocola, 158, *213*, 230
Panoquina panoquin, 157, *213*, 230, 233, 234
Panoquina panoquinoides, 158, *213*, 230, 234
Papilio andraemon, 70
Papilio aristodemus, 70
Papilio cresphontes, 69
Papilio glaucus, 71
Papilionidae, 67–73
Papilio palamedes, 72
Papilio polyxenes, 1, 17, *19*, *20*, *27*, 71, *165*,
    243, 244, 245, 304

Papilio troilus, 73
Paragrass, 137, 138
Paramidea midea, 76, *165*, *259*
Paraprociphilus tesselatus, *258*
Parasites, 48
Parasitoids, 48
Parietaria floridana, 109, *309*
Parrhasius m-album, 84, 92, *177*, 287, 289
Parsley, 71
Parsley Hawthorn, 89
Partridge Pea, 78, 81, 92, 98, *270*
Paspalidium: Egyptian, 138
Paspalidium geminatum, 138
Paspalum: Florida, 138; Thin, 137, 138; Water, 138
Paspalum dilatatum, 138
Paspalum floridanum, 138
Paspalum repens, 138
Paspalum setaceum, 137, 138
Paspalum urvillei, 156
Passifloraceae, 102, 103, 104, 297–98
Passiflora incarnata, 102, 103, 104, *297*
Passiflora 'Incense,' 297
Passiflora lutea, 102, 103, *298*
Passiflora multiflora, 103
Passiflora suberosa, 102, 103, *298*
Passionflower: 20, 50, 66; Corkystem, 102, 103, *298*; Incense, 297; Purple, 102, 103, 104, *297*; Whiteflower, 103; Yellow, 102, 103, *298*
Passionflower butterflies, 66, 102–4
Passionflower family, 102, 103, 104, 297–98
Pawpaw: Bigflower, 69, *242*; Common, 69; Dwarf, 69, *242*; Fourpetal, 69; Netted, 69, *243*; Slimleaf, 69, *241*; Smallflower, 69; Woolly, 69, *241*
Pea: Partridge, 78, 81, 92, 98, *270*; Rosary, 97; Sensitive, 78, 81, 98, *270*
Peacock: White, 13, 111, *185*, 310, 311
Pea family, 74, 77, 78, 79, 80, 81, 82, 90, 92, 95, 96, 97, 98, 99, 109, 123, 124, 125, 126, 127, 128, 129, 133, 134, 265–86
Pearl Crescent, 14, 25, *35*, 106, *187*, 256
Pearly-eye: Southern, *41*, 117, *195*, 228
Pellitory: Florida, 109, *309*
Pencilflower: Sidebeak, 80, *284*
Pennisetum purpureum, 138
Pennisetum setaceum, 138

Pennsylvania Bittercress, 76
Pennsylvania Everlasting, 108, *255*
Pennsylvania Smartweed, 93
Pentas, 50
Pepper: Brazilian, 50, 94, 95, *240*
Pepper and Salt Skipper, 153, *203*
Pepperweed: Virginia, 46, 75, 76, *260*
Perennial Glasswort, 96, *240*
Persea borbonia, 73, *290*
Persea borbonia var. *humilis*, 73, *290*
Persea palustris, 61, 73, *290*
Petroselinum crispum, 71
Phanopyrum gymnocarpon, 138
Phaon Crescent, 17, 105, *187*, 310
Phaseolus vulgaris, 93, 126
Pheromones, 21
Phocides pigmalion, 123, *199*, 301
Phoebis agarithe, 79, *171*, 278, 281
Phoebis philea, 13, 78, *171*, 232
Phoebis sennae, 13, *14*, *30*, 78, *171*, 270, 282, 283
Phoebis statira, 79
Phoenix dactylifera, 152
Pholisora catullus, 135, *201*, 239
Phoradendron leucarpum, 86, *312*
Phyciodes frisia, 105
Phyciodes phaon, 17, 105, *187*, 310
Phyciodes texana seminole, 104
Phyciodes tharos, *14*, 25, *35*, 106, *187*, 256
Phyla nodiflora, 50, 106, 110, 111, *310*
Phyllostachys aurea, 138
Picramniaceae, 82, 299
Picramnia pentandra, 82, *299*
Piedmont Blacksenna, 110, 297
Pieridae, 74–83
Pierinae, 74–76
Pieris rapae, 75, *167*, 258, 260
Pigeonwings: Asian, 126; Atlantic, 126, 128, 269, *271*
Pignut Hickory, 88, *290*
Pinaceae, 84, 91, 220
Pine: 54, 55, 56, 57, 58; Loblolly, 56, 91; Longleaf, 54, 56; Sand, 46, 91, *220*; Slash, 54
Pine Barren Ticktrefoil, 128
Pine family, 84, 91, 220
Pineland Acacia, 98, *265*
Pineland Butterfly Pea, 126, 129

Pineland Croton, 94, 115, *264*
Pinewoods Fingergrass, 156
Pinewoods Milkweed, 121, 122, *246*
Pink Swamp Milkweed, 121, 122, *247*
Pinus clausa, 46, 91, *220*
Pinus palustris, 54, 56
Pinus taeda, 56, 91
Pipevine, 50, 67, 68
Pipevine Swallowtail, 5, 17, 67, *163*, 252, 253
Piriqueta cistoides, 102
Piscidia piscipula, 94, 95, 125, *280*
Pitcher plant seeps, 64
Pithecellobium keyense, 79, 97, *281*
Pithecellobium unguis-cati, 79
Pitted Stripeseed, 102
Plantaginaceae, 110
Plantago lanceolata, 110
Plantago major, 110
Plantago virginica, 110
Plantain: Common, 110; English, 110; Virginia, 110
Plantain family, 110
Plants: one seed leaf, 221–36; two seed leaves, 237–312
Plumbaginaceae, 97, 300
Plumbago auriculata, 97, *300*
Plumegrass: Silver, 147, 155; Sugarcane, 138, 147, *232*
Plum: Wild, 87
Poaceae, 117, 118, 119, 120, 136, 137, 138, 139, 140, 141, 142, 143, 144, 145, 146, 147, 148, 149, 153, 154, 155, 156, 157, 158, 159, 227–35
Poanes aaroni, 147, *215*, 231
Poanes viator, 148, *215*, 235
Poanes yehl, 148, *215*, 228
Poanes zabulon, 9, 147, *215*, 228
Poison Hemlock, 65
Poisons, 17, 48, 65, 66, 71
Polites baracoa, 141, *211*
Polites origenes, 142, *211*, 227
Polites themistocles, 141, *211*, 229
Polites vibex, 143, *211*, 234
Polydamas Swallowtail, 5, 14, *18*, 68, *163*, 251, 252, 253
Polygonaceae, 84, 93
Polygonella gracilis, 93
Polygonia comma, 15, 25, 107, *189*

Polygonia interrogationis, 106, *189*, 261, 307, 308
Polygonum pensylvanicum, 93
Polygonus leo, 125, *199*, 280
Polyommatinae, 96–100
Pompeius verna, 144, *215*
Poncirus trifoliata, 70
Pond Pine, 56
Pondspice, 73
Pongamia pinnata, 95, 125
Pontia protodice, 29, 46, 74, *167*, 260
Poplar: Yellow, *291*
Poppymallow: Woodland, 134
Populus species, 113
Porterweed: 50; Blue, 111, *310*
Post Oak, 92, *289*
Powderpuff, 81, *280*
Prairieclover: Feay's, 77, *272*
Prairies, 58, 60
Predation, 17, 49
Pretty False Pawpaw, 69
Pricklyash: Biscayne, 304; Common, 304; Lime, *305*
Privet Wild Sensitive Plant, 78
Problema byssus, 146, *207*, 228, 232, 235
Prociphilus tesselatus, 84, 85, *258*
Prunus serotina, 72, 87, 113, *301*
Prunus species, 87
Pseudognaphalium obtusifolium, 108, *256*
Ptelea trifoliata, 69, *303*
Pterourus glaucus, 10, 21, 71, *163*, 291, 292, 296, 301
Pterourus palamedes, 21, 26, 66, 72, *163*, 290
Pterourus troilus, 10, *15*, 26, *28*, 66, 73, *165*, 290, 291
Ptilimnium capillaceum, 71, *245*
Pueraria montana, 125, 126, 127
Purple: Red-spotted, 21, *22*, *38*, 112, *183*, 263, 305
Purple False Foxglove, 110
Purple Passionflower, 102, 103, 104, *297*
Purple Thistle, *254*
Purplewing: Dingy, *15*, 17, 113, *185*, 260; Florida, 21, *22*, 114, *185*, 265
Pygmy-Blue: Eastern, 96, *181*, 240, 257
Pyrginae, 123–36
Pyrgus albescens, 16, 134, *201*, 293

Pyrgus communis, 134, *203*, 293
Pyrgus oileus, 135, *203*, 293

Queen, *42*, 121, *193*, 246, 247, 248, 249, 250
Queen Anne's Lace, 1, 71
Quercus chapmanii, 131, 132
Quercus falcata, 131
Quercus geminata, 89, 92, 132, 289
Quercus inopina, 131, 132
Quercus laevis, 54, 88, 131, 132, *287*
Quercus laurifolia, 92, 132, *287*
Quercus myrtifolia, 131, 132, *288*
Quercus nigra, 92, 132, *288*
Quercus stellata, 92, *289*
Quercus virginiana, 92, 132, *289*
Question Mark, 106, *189*, 261, 307, 308

Radish: Garden, 75, 126; Wild, 75, 258
Raphanus raphanistrum, 75, 258
Raphanus sativus, 75, 126
Rattlebox: 126, 133, 284; Showy, 126
Rearing caterpillars, 47, 48
Red Admiral, *15*, 109, *189*
Red-banded Hairstreak, *32*, 95, *173*, 240, 295
Red Bay, 73, *290*
Redbud: Eastern, 90, *269*
Red Cedar, 91, *219*
Red Mangrove, 63, 64, 123, *301*
Red Mangrove family, 123, 301
Red Maple, 61
Red-spotted Purple, 21, *22*, *38*, 112, *183*, 263, 305
Redtop: Tall, 138
Redtop Panicum, 138, 146, *232*
Reed: Giant, 138
Reversed Roadside-Skipper, 155, *207*, 228
Rhamnaceae, 84, 93, 123, 132, 300
Rhizophoraceae, 123, 301
Rhizophora mangle, 63, 64, 123, *301*
Rhynchosia minima, 126
Rhynchospora inundata, 118, 151, *225*
Rhynchospora miliacea, 151, 225
Rice Button Aster, 106, *256*
Riodinidae, 100
River Oats, 228
Roadside-Skipper: Common, 154, *205*;
    Dusky, 155, *205*; Lace-winged, 154, *203*,
    228; Reversed, 155, *207*, 228

Robinia pseudoacacia, 125, *281*
Rocklands, 58
Rosaceae, 67, 72, 87, 89, 113, 301
Rosary Pea, 97
Rose family, 67, 72, 87, 89, 113, 301
Rough Barnyardgrass, 138
Roughfruit Scaleseed, 71, *245*
Roystonea regia, 152
Ruddy Daggerwing, 114, *191*, 294, 295
Rue, 70, *304*
Ruellia caroliniensis, 112
Rugel's False Pawpaw, 69
Rutaceae, 67, 69, 70, 71, 302–5
Ruta graveolens, 70, *304*
Sabal etonia, 149, 152
Sabal palmetto, 57, 62, 152, *222*
Saccharum alopecuroides, 147, 155
Saccharum giganteum, 138, 147, *232*
Saccharum officinarum, 138
Sacciolepis striata, 139
Sachem, 145, *209*
Salicaceae, 108, 113, 305
Salicornia bigelovii, 96
Salicornia perennis, *240*
Salix babylonica, 113, 305
Salix caroliniana, 113, *305*
Salix nigra, 113, 305
Salix species, 108
Saltgrass, 158, *230*
Saltmarsh Cordgrass, 158, *233*
Saltmarsh False Foxglove, 110
Salt Marsh Skipper, 157, *213*, 230, 233, 234
Saltwort, 63, 76, 96, *257*
Saltwort family, 74, 96, 257
Sandhill Milkweed, *246*
Sandhills, 54
Sand Live Oak, 89, 92, 132, 289
Sand Pine, 46, 91, *220*
Sapindaceae, 84, 87, 93, 97, 306
Sarcocornia perennis, 96, *240*
Sarcostemma clausum, 122, *250*
Sassafras, 73, *291*
Sassafras albidum, 73, *291*
Satintail: Brazilian, 138, 147
Satyr: Carolina, 119, *193*, 234; Gemmed, 118,
    195, 228; Georgia, 119, *193*
Satyrinae, 117–20
Satyrium calanus, 87, *175*, 287, 290

Satyrium favonius, 89
Satyrium kingi, 88, *175*, 307
Satyrium liparops, 88, *177*, 262
Satyrium titus, 87
Satyrodes appalachia, 118, *195*, 225
Satyrs, 101, 117–20
Savanna, 56
Savannah Panicum, 138
Sawgrass: Jamaica Swamp, 150, *225*
Saw Greenbrier, 84, 236
Saw Palmetto, 55, 149, 152, *223*
Scaleseed: Roughfruit, 71, *245*
Scallopwing: Hayhurst's, 129, *201*, 239
Scarlet Milkweed, 50, 121, *246*
Schaus' Swallowtail, 20, 70, *165*, 302
Schinus terebinthifolius, 50, 94, 95, *240*
Scirpus cyperinus, 150, *226*
Sclerites, 3
Sclerotization, 3
Scrub forests, 55
Scrub-Hairstreak: Bartram's, 58, 93, *179*, 264;
    Mallow, 84, 94, *177*, 293, 294, 306; Martial,
    93, *179*, 261, 268, 306
Scrub Hickory, 88, 290
Scrub Oak, 131, 132
Scrub Palmetto, 149, 152
Searocket: Coastal, 76
Seashore Dropseed, 158, *234*
Sea Torchwood, 69, 70, 71, *302*
Secondary compounds, 65
Sedge: 101, 123; Atlantic, 118; Clustered,
    150, *224*; False Hop, 151, *224*; Warty,
    150
Sedge family, 118, 119, 150, 151, 152, 224–26
Segmentation, 3
'Seminole' Texan Crescent, 14, 104, *187*, 238
Senna, 13, 20, 48, 50
Senna alata, 78, 79, *282*
Senna didymobotrya, 78, 79
Senna ligustrina, 78
Senna marilandica, 78
Senna mexicana var. *chapmanii*, 78, 79, *282*
Senna obtusifolia, 78, 82, *283*
Senna occidentalis, 78, 82, *283*
Senna pendula, 50, 78, 79, 82, 282
Senna surattensis, 78, 79
Sensitive Pea, 78, 81, 98, *270*
Septicweed, 78, 82, *283*

Serenoa repens, 55, 149, 152, *223*
Sesbania herbacea, 98, 133, 284
Sesbania punicea, 126, 133, 284
Sesbania vesicaria, 133, *284*
Setae, 4
Setaria macrosperma, 138
Severinia buxifolia, 70
Seymeria cassioides, 110, *297*
Seymeria pectinata, 110, 297
Shelters, 10, 14, 15, 16, 17
Shepherd's Purse, 75
Shiny Woodoats, 228
Short-leaved Fig, *295*
Showy Rattlebox, 66, 126
Shrimp Plant: Green, *237*
Shyleaf, 80, *266*
Sicklepod, *283*
Sida acuta, 93, 94, 134, 135, *293*
Sida rhombifolia, 134, 135, *293*
Sidebeak Pencilflower, 80, *284*
Signalgrass: Tropical, 119, 156
Silk, 10
Silk Bay, 73, 290
Silver-banded Hairstreak, 86, *177*, 306
Silver Croton, 116, *263*
Silver Plumegrass, 147, 155
Silver-spotted Skipper, *15*, 17, 18, 20, 124,
    197, 266, 267, 274, 275, 281
Silvery Checkerspot, 17, 104, *187*
Siproeta stelenes, 112, *187*, 237
Sixangle Foldwing, 105, *237*
Skeletongrass: Bearded, 137, 156
Skipper: Aaron's, 147, *215*, 231; Arogos, 145,
    205, 233; Baracoa, 141, *211*; Berry's, 151,
    209; Brazilian, 7, *16*, *44*, 157, *217*, 223, 226;
    Broad-winged, 148, *215*, 235; Byssus, 146,
    207, 228, 232, 235; Clouded, *16*, 137, *203*,
    228, 231, 232, 234, 235; Crossline, 142,
    211, 227; Delaware, 25, 146, *207*, 227, 228,
    231, 232, 233; Dion, 150, *209*, 224, 226;
    Dotted, 140, *211*; Dukes,' 151, *209*, 224,
    225; Dun, 151, *209*; Dusted, 152, *215*, 233;
    Eufala, 156, *207*, 233; Fiery, 139, *209*, 229,
    234; Hammock, 125, *199*, 280; Least, 138,
    205, 230, 235; Long-tailed, 5, *15*, 17, 25,
    26, *43*, 66, 125, *197*, 269, 271, 273, 274,
    275, 286; Mangrove, 123, *199*, 301;
    Meske's, 59, 140, *211*; Monk, 152, *217*,

Skipper—*continued*
222, 223; Neamathla, 136, *205*, 227; Obscure, 158, *213*, 230, 234; Ocola, 158, *213*, 230; Palatka, 59, 149, *207*, 225; Palmetto, *16*, 26, 149, *207*, 223; Salt Marsh, 157, *213*, 230, 233, 234; Silver-spotted, *15*, 17, 18, 20, 124, *197*, 266, 267, 274, 275, 281; Swarthy, 136, *205*, 227, 233; Tawny-edged, 141, *211*, 229; Three-spotted, 137, *203*, 235; Twin-spot, 156, *217*, 227, 233; Yehl, 148, *215*, 228; Zabulon, *9*, 147, *215*, 228; Zestos, 124, *197*, 275

Skipperling: Southern, 139, *213*, 229

Skippers, 4, 5, 7, 14, 17, 18, 25, 26, 123–60

Sky-Blue Lupine, 93

Slash Pine, 54

Sleepy Duskywing, *12*, *16*, 130, *199*, 287, 288

Sleepy Morning, 94, *294*

Sleepy Orange, 5, 82, *169*, 282, 283

Slender Woodoats, 118, 138, 147, 148, *228*

Slimleaf Pawpaw, 69, *241*

Slimleaf Ticktrefoil, 126

Smallflower Pawpaw, 69

Small-fruited Balloonvine, 87

Smartweed: Pennsylvania, 93

Smilacaceae, 84, 236

Smilax auriculata, 84, 236

Smilax bona-nox, 84, 236

Smilax family, 84, 236

Smilax glauca, 84, 236

Smilax tamnoides, 84, *236*

Smooth Cordgrass, *233*

Snakeroot: Virginia, 67, *253*

Snout: American, *36*, 101, *181*, 261

Snoutbean: Least, 126

Soapberry family, 84, 87, 93, 97, 306

Soldier, 122, *193*, 246, 248, 249, 250

Sootywing: Common, 135, *201*, 239

Sorghastrum secundum, 136, 145, 146, 153, 156, 157, *233*

Sorghum halepense, 138

Sour Orange, 70, 303

Sourwood, 100, *262*

Southern Bayberry, 95, *295*

Southern Broken-Dash, *16*, 143, *213*

Southern Cloudywing, 128, *195*, 271, 277

Southern Crabgrass, 137, 143

Southern Cutgrass, 139, 159, *230*

Southern Dogface, 77, *169*, 266, 272, 273, 286

Southern Pearly-eye, *41*, 117, *195*, 228

Southern Red Oak, 131

Southern Skipperling, 139, *213*, 229

Southern Wild Rice, 138, 139, 149, *235*

Soybean, 126

Spanish Bayonet, 159, 160, *221*

Spanish Needles, 66, 83, *254*

Sparkleberry, 89, *262*

Spartina alterniflora, 158, *233*

Speedwell family, 110, 111, 311

Spermolepis divaricata, 71, *245*

Spicebush: Northern, 73

Spicebush Swallowtail, 10, *15*, 26, *28*, 66, 73, *165*, 290, 291

Spoonleaf Purple Everlasting, 108

Sporobolus domingensis, 158, 234

Sporobolus virginicus, 158, *234*

Spotted Water Hemlock, 71, *243*

Spread-winged Skippers, 123–36

Spring Azure: 'Edwards,' 99, *179*; 'Summer,' 99, *179*, 262

Spruce Pine, 57

Spurge family, 74, 94, 114, 115, 116, 263–65

Spurred Butterfly Pea, 126, 129, *269*, 271

St. Augustinegrass, 119, 138, 140, 143, *234*

St. John's-wort, 64

Stachytarpheta jamaicensis, 111, *310*

Staphylus hayhurstii, 129, *201*, 239

Statira Sulphur, 79, *171*, 272

Stenotaphrum secundatum, 119, 138, 140, 143, *234*

Sticky Jointvetch, 80, 266

Stinging Nettle, 109

Strangler Fig, 115, *294*

Striped Hairstreak, 88, *177*, 262

Stripeseed: Pitted, 102

Strymon acis, 58, 93, *179*, 264

Strymon columella, 94

Strymon istapa, 84, 94, *177*, 293, 294, 306

Strymon martialis, 93, *179*, 261, 268, 306

Strymon melinus, 84, 92, *177*, 270, 272, 273, 277, 286, 293, 300, 306

Stylosanthes biflora, 80, *284*

Stylosanthes hamata, 80, *285*

Sugarberry, 101, 107, 116, 117, *261*

Sugarcane, 138

Sugarcane Plumegrass, 138, 147, *232*

Sulphur: Cloudless, 13, *14*, *30*, 78, *171*, 270, 282, 283; Dainty, 83, *167*, 254; Large Orange, 79, *171*, 278, 281; Lyside, 80, *165*, 312; Orange, 77, *169*, 279, 286; Orange-barred, 13, 78, *171*, 282; Statira, 79, *171*, 272

Sulphurs, 5, 17, 74–83

Summer Farewell, 77, *273*

'Summer' Spring Azure, 99, *179*, 262

Sundial Lupine, 90, *278*

Sunflower: Paleleaf Woodland, 104; Woodland, 104

Surianaceae, 84, 93, 94, 306

Suriana maritima, 93, 94, *306*

Swallowtail: Bahamian, 20, 70, *165*, 302, 303, 305; Black, 1, 17, *19*, *20*, *27*, 71, *163*, 243, 244, 245, 304; Eastern Tiger, 10, 21, 71, *163*, 291, 292, 296, 301; Giant, 17, *19*, 20, *21*, 69, *165*, 302, 303, 304, 305; Palamedes, *21*, 26, 66, 72, *163*, 290; Pipevine, 5, 17, 67, *163*, 252, 253; Polydamas, 5, 14, *18*, 68, *163*, 251, 252, 253; Schaus', 20, 70, *165*, 302; Spicebush, 10, *15*, 26, *28*, 66, 73, *165*, 290, 291; Zebra, 14, *20*, 68, *163*, 241, 242, 243

Swallowtails, 6, 10, 14, 17, 67–73

Swallowwort: 122; Gulf Coast, 122, *248*; Leafless, 248

Swamp Bay, 61, 73, 290

Swamps, 60, 63

Swamp Twinflower, 110, 238

Swarthy Skipper, 136, *205*, 227, 233

Sweet Acacia, 98, 265

Sweetbay, 61, 72, *292*

Sweetclover: White, 77, *279*

Sweet Everlasting, 108, *256*

Sweet Fennel, 50, 71, *244*

Sweetleaf: Common, 88, *307*

Sweetleaf family, 84, 88, 307

Sweet Orange, 69, 303

Sweet Tanglehead, 138

Switchcane, 117, 138, 146, 148, 154, 155, *228*

Symphyotrichum carolinianum, 256

Symphyotrichum concolor, 256

Symphyotrichum dumosum, 106, *256*

Symphyotrichum elliottii, 256

Symphyotrichum walteri, 256

Symplocaceae, 84, 88, 307

Symplocos tinctoria, 88, *307*

Tailed-Blue: Eastern, 84, 98, *181*

Tall Jointweed, 93

Tall Redtop, 138

Tamarind: False, 79, 81, 97, *278*

Tangerine, 69, *303*

Tanglehead: Sweet, 138

Tannins, 65

Tawny-edged Skipper, 141, *211*, 229

Tawny Emperor, *11*, 12, 17, *18*, 25, 116, *191*, 261

Tephrosia florida, 129, *285*

Terpenoids, 65

Thalia geniculata, 157, *226*

Theclinae, 85–95

Thin Paspalum, 137, 138

Thistle: Purple, *254*; Yellow, 100, 109, *254*

Thorax, 5

Thorybes bathyllus, 128, *195*, 271, 277

Thorybes confusis, 129, *197*

Thorybes pylades, 128, *195*, 285

Threeflower Ticktrefoil, 127

Three-spotted Skipper, 137, *203*, 235

Thrinax morrisii, 152

Thrinax radiata, 152

Ticktrefoil: Creeping, 93, 126, 127, 128, *273*; Dixie, 125, 126, 127, *274*; Florida, 126; Panicledleaf, 93, 126; Pine Barren, 128; Slimleaf, 126; Threeflower, 127; Velvetleaf, 126, 128, 129

Toadflax: Apalachicola, 110, 311; Canada, 13, 110, *311*

Toothachegrass, 64, 145

Toothache Tree, *304*

Torchwood: Balsam, 70, 302; Sea, 69, 70, 71, *302*

Torpedograss, 159

Trailing Indigo, 98, 133, *276*

Trema micranthum, 93, *261*

Tridens flavus, 138

Trifoliate Orange, 70

Trifolium repens, 77, *286*

Tripsacum dactyloides, 137, 138, 147, *235*

Tropaeolaceae, 76

Tropaeolum majus, 76

Tropical Buckeye, 111, *185*, 310

Tropical Checkered-Skipper, 135, *203*, 293

Tropical Puff, 98

Tropical Signalgrass, 119, 156

Tuliptree, 72, *291*
Tupelo, 61
Turkey Oak, 54, 88, 131, 132, *287*
Turkey Tangle Fogfruit, 50, 106, 110, 111, *310*
Turneraceae, 102
Turnera family, 102
Turnip, 66, 75
Twinevine: White, 122, *250*
Twinflower: Oblongleaf, 110, *238*; Swamp, 110, 238
Twin-spot Skipper, 156, *217*, 227, 233

Ulmaceae, 107, 307–8
Ulmus alata, 107, *307*
Ulmus americana, 107, *308*
Ulmus species, 107, 108
Upland habitats, 53
Urbanus dorantes, 126, *197*, 273, 274
Urbanus proteus, 5, *15*, 17, 25, *26*, *43*, 66, 125, *197*, 269, 271, 273, 274, 275, 286
Urochloa distachya, 119, 156
Urochloa mutica, 137, 138
Urticaceae, 107, 109, 308–9
Urtica chamaedryoides, 109, *309*
Urtica dioica, 109
Urtica species, 107, 109
Urtica urens, 109, 309

Vaccinium arboreum, 89, *262*
Vaccinium stamineum, 113, *263*
Valamuerto, 50, 78, 79, 82, 282
Vanillaleaf, 100
Vanessa atalanta, *15*, 109, *189*, 308, 309
Vanessa cardui, 108, *189*
Vanessa virginiensis, *15*, 108, *189*, 255, 256
Variegated Fritillary, 103, *183*
Vaseygrass, 156
Veitchia merrillii, 152
Velvetleaf Milkweed, 121, 122
Velvetleaf Ticktrefoil, 126, 128, 129
Verbenaceae, 106, 111, 310
Veronicaceae, 110, 111, 311
Vervain family, 106, 111, 310
Vetch: Fourleaf, 81
Viceroy, 10, *11*, 113, *183*, 305
Vicia acutifolia, 81

Vigna luteola, 93, 97, 126, 127, *286*
Violaceae, 104
Viola species, 104
Violet family, 104
Violets, 104
Virginia Glasswort, *240*
Virginia Live Oak, 92, 132, *289*
Virginia Pepperweed, 46, 75, 76, *260*
Virginia Plantain, 110
Virginia Snakeroot, 67, *253*
Viscaceae, 84, 86, 312

Wafer Ash, *303*
Wallengrenia egeremet, 144, *213*
Wallengrenia otho, 16, 143, *213*
Walnut family, 84, 88, 290
Walter's Aster, 256
Waltheria indica, 94, *294*
Warty Sedge, 150
Wasps, 48, 49, 50
Water Cowbane, 71, *244*
Water Hemlock: Spotted, 71, *243*
Waterhyssop, *311*
Water Oak, 92, 132, *288*
Water Paspalum, 138
Waterwillow: Looseflower, 105, 106, *238*
Wax, 3, 25, 26, 123, 149, 159, 160, 236
Wax Myrtle, *295*
Wedgeleaf Eryngo, 71
Weeping Willow, 113, 305
Whirlabout, 143, *211*, 234
White: Cabbage, 75, *167*, 258, 260; Checkered, *29*, 46, 74, *167*, 260; Florida, 74, *169*, 259, 264; Great Southern, 75, *167*, 257, 259, 260
White Ash, 72, 296
White Cedar: Atlantic, 52, 61, 91, *219*
White Checkered-Skipper, *16*, 134, *201*, 293
White Clover, 77, *286*
Whiteflower Passionflower, 103
White Leadtree, 95, *277*
White Mangrove, 64
White M Hairstreak, 84, 92, *177*, 287, 289
White Moneywort, 126
White Peacock, 13, 111, *185*, 310, 311
Whites, 10, 74–76
White Swamp Milkweed, 121, 122, *247*

White Sweetclover, 77, *279*
White Twinevine, 122, *250*
White Wild Indigo, 133, 134, *268*
Whitewood, 74, 264
Wild Banyan Tree, 115, *295*
Wild Bushbean, 93, 126
Wild Croton, *264*
Wild Indigo: White, 133, 134, *268*
Wild Indigo Duskywing, 133, *201*, 268
Wild Lime, 50, 69, 70, 71, *305*
Wild Petunia: Carolina, 112
Wild Plum, 87
Wild Radish, 75, 258
Wild Rice: 149, Southern, 138, 139, 149, *235*
Wild Sensitive Plant: African, 78, 79;
    Chapman's, 78, 79, *282*; Maryland, 78;
    Privet, 78
Willow family, 108, 113, 305
Willows, 108
Winged Elm, 107, *307*
Wiregrass, 54
Wireweed: Common, *293*
Wisteria: American, 125, 126; Chinese, 125
Wisteria frutescens, 125, 126
Wisteria sinensis, 125
Witchgrass: Deertongue, 138; Needleleaf,
    142, *229*
Woodland Poppymallow, 134
Woodland Sunflower, 104
Wood-Nymph: Common, 120, *193*, 227
Wood-Nymphs, 101, 117–20
Woodoats: Birdbill, 228; Indian, 155, 228;
    Shiny, 228; Slender, 118, 138, 147, 148, *228*
Wood-Satyr: Little, 120, *193*
Woodsgrass, 119
Woolgrass, 150, *226*
Woolly Alder Aphid, 84, 85, *258*
Woolly aphids, 84
Woolly Croton, 116
Woolly Dutchman's-Pipe, 66, 67, 68, 126, *252*

Woolly Maple Aphid, 84, *236*
Woolly Pawpaw, 69, *241*

Yaupon Blacksenna, 110, *297*
Yehl Skipper, 148, *215*, 228
Yellow: Barred, 80, *167*, 266, 284, 285; Dina,
    82, *169*, 299; Little, 81, *167*, 280; Mimosa,
    81, *169*, 278
Yellow Canna, *223*
Yellow Passionflower, 102, 103, *298*
Yellow Poplar, *291*
Yellow Thistle, 100, 109, *254*
Yellowwood, 304
Yucca aloifolia, 159, 160, *221*
Yucca filamentosa, 159, 160, *221*
Yucca flaccida, 221
Yucca Giant-Skipper, *16*, 159, *217*, 221
Yuccas, 123

Zabulon Skipper, *9*, 147, *215*, 228
Zamiaceae, 84, 85, 220
Zamia family, 84, 85, 220
Zamia pumila, 85, *220*
Zanthoxylum americanum, 304
Zanthoxylum clava-herculis, 69, *304*
Zanthoxylum coriaceum, 304
Zanthoxylum fagara, 50, 69, 70, 71, *305*
Zanthoxylum flavum, 304
Zarucco Duskywing, 133, *199*, 274, 275, 284
Zea mays, 138
Zebra Heliconian, 103, *183*, 297, 298
Zebra Swallowtail, 14, *20*, 68, *163*, 241, 242,
    243
Zedoary, 157
Zerene cesonia, 77, *169*, 266, 272, 273, 286
Zestos Skipper, 124, *197*, 275
Zingiberaceae, 123, 157
Zizania aquatica, 149
Zizaniopsis miliacea, 138, 139, 149, *235*
Zygophyllaceae, 74, 80, 312

Marc C. Minno is an insect ecologist and works as a senior regulatory scientist for the St. Johns River Water Management District. He has written or coauthored many scientific and popular articles on butterflies and moths as well as *Florissant Butterflies: A Guide to the Fossil and Present-Day Species of Central Colorado* (1992), *Butterflies of the Florida Keys* (1993), *Florida Butterfly Gardening* (1999), and *Butterflies Through Binoculars: Florida* (2001).

Jerry F. Butler is professor emeritus of entomology at the University of Florida. As a medical and veterinary entomologist with the Department of Entomology and Nematology, his research has focused on vertebrate host/arthropod interactions, attractants, repellents, and forensic entomology. He has authored more than 100 scientific publications, secured nearly 80 patents, and won a number of awards for excellence in teaching. He enjoys photographing butterflies and other insects.

Donald W. Hall is professor of entomology at the University of Florida. He served on the faculty of the University of Massachusetts, Amherst, from 1970 to 1975 before returning to the University of Florida. He has authored numerous scientific publications on insect pathology, medical entomology and educational technology. He has a wide range of interests including general insect natural history, butterflies, and Florida native plants.

Related-interest titles from University Press of Florida

A Field Guide and Identification Manual for Florida and Eastern U.S. Tiger Beetles
Paul M. Choate, Jr.

Florida Butterfly Gardening: A Complete Guide to Attracting, Identifying, and Enjoying Butterflies of the Lower South
Marc C. Minno and Maria Minno

Florida's Fragile Wildlife: Conservation and Management
Don A. Wood

Florida's Snakes: A Guide to Their Identification and Habits
R. D. Bartlett and Patricia Bartlett

Florida Wildflowers in Their Natural Communities
Walter Kingsley Taylor

Gardening with Carnivores: Sarracenia Pitcher Plants in Cultivation and in the Wild
Nick Romanowski

Grasshoppers of Florida
John L. Capinera et al.

Guide to the Vascular Plants of Florida, second edition
Richard P. Wunderlin and Bruce Hansen

Landscaping for Florida's Wildlife: Re-creating Native Ecosystems in Your Yard
Joe Schaefer and George Tanner

The Liguus Tree Snails of South Florida
Henry T. Close

Your Florida Garden, 5th edition, abridged
John V. Watkins and Herbert S. Wolfe

Your Florida Guide to Butterfly Gardening: A Guide to the Deep South
Jaret C. Daniels

For more information on these and other books, visit our website at www.upf.com.